Robert O Lee

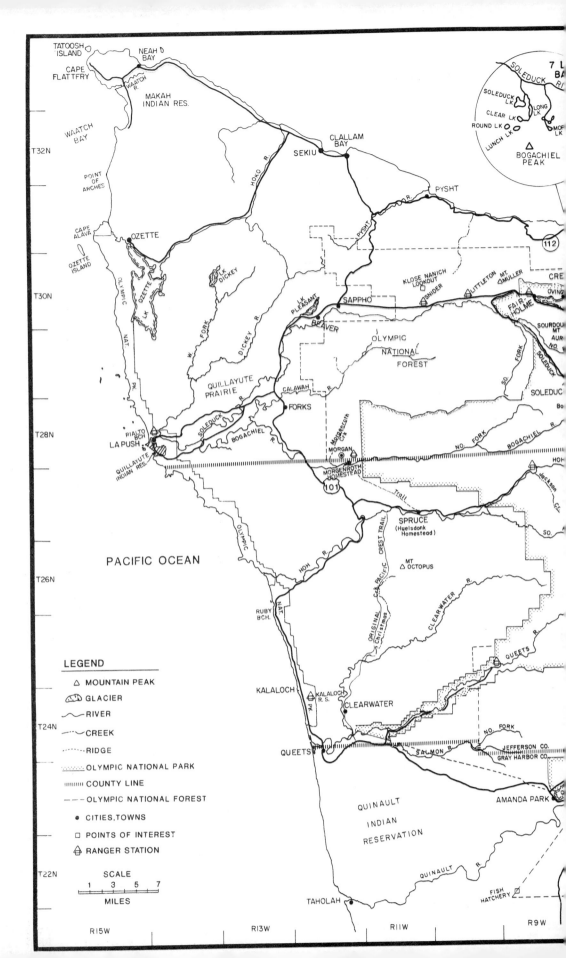

OLYMPIC NATIONAL PARK

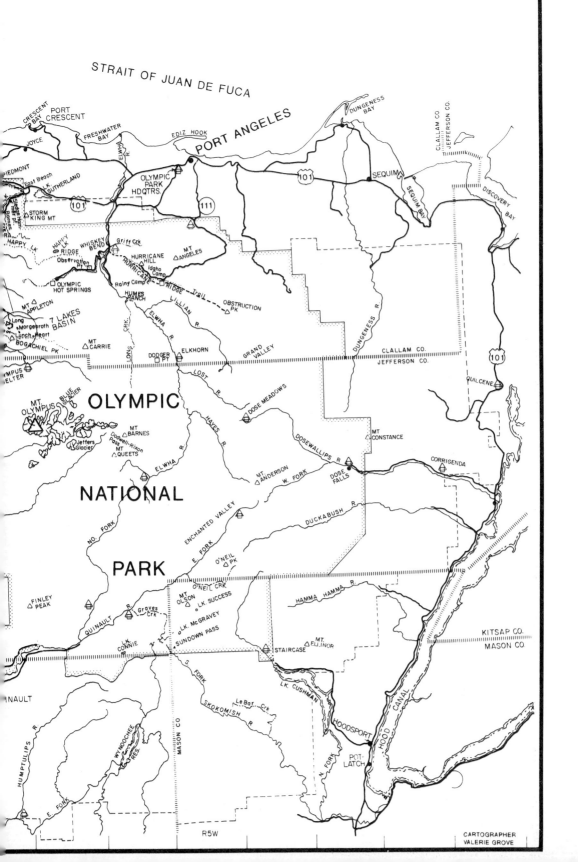

STRAIT OF JUAN DE FUCA

Footprints in the Olympics

Chris Morgenroth
1871-1939

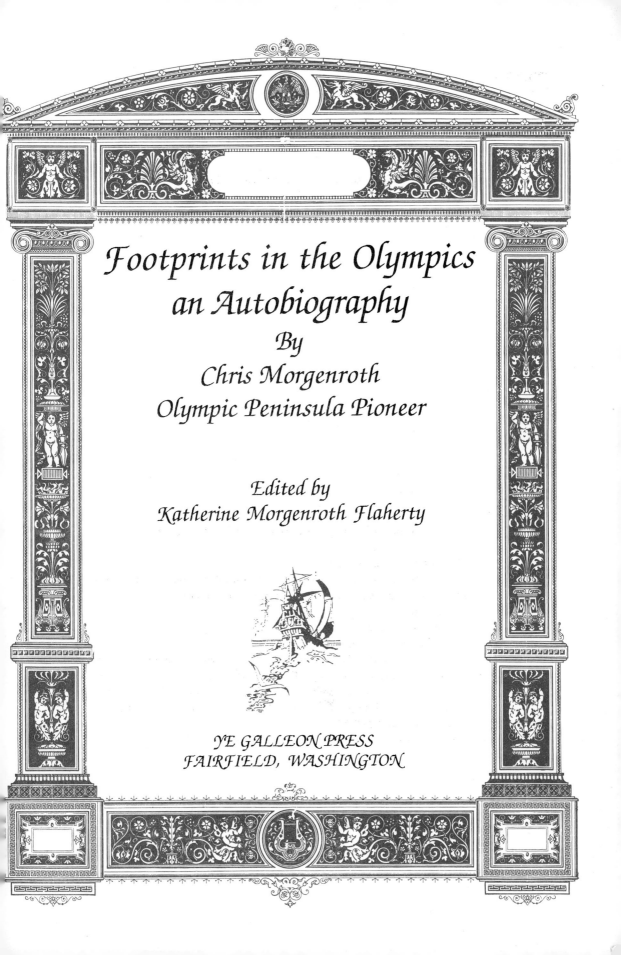

Footprints in the Olympics
an Autobiography
By
Chris Morgenroth
Olympic Peninsula Pioneer

Edited by
Katherine Morgenroth Flaherty

YE GALLEON PRESS
FAIRFIELD, WASHINGTON

FRONT COVER PICTURE:
Trail below Bogachiel Peak leading southeast down into the Hoh Valley. Mt. Olympus in distance.

Unless otherwise indicated, all pictures are from Chris Morgenroth files.

Library of Congress Cataloging-in-Publication Data

Morgenroth, Chris, 1871-1939.
    Footprints in the Olympics : an autobiography / by Chris Morgenroth : edited by Katherine Morgenroth Flaherty.
    p. cm.
    Includes index.
    ISBN 0-87770-497-X
    1. Morgenroth, Chris, 1872-1939. 2. Olympic National Forest (Wash.) — History. 3. Olympic Peninsula (Wash.) — History. 4. Forest rangers — Washington (State) — Biography. 5. United States. Forest service — Officials and employees — Biography. I. Flaherty, Katherine Morgenroth. II. Title.
SD129.M59A3   1991   634.9'092-dc20   [B]   91-17116

Contents

FORWARD

THIS BOOK WAS WRITTEN IN MOST PART BY
CHRIS MORGENROTH WHO SHARED HIS
EXPERIENCES AND LOVE OF NATURE
WITH HIS FELLOW MAN.

HE LOVED PEOPLE AND DEVOTED
HIS LIFE TO THE SERVICE OF THIS,
HIS ADOPTED COUNTRY.

HE WAS A MAN WHOSE EARLY PIONEERING
LIFE FOSTERED A VISION OF PRESERVING
THE GREAT OLYMPIC WONDERLAND.

ACKNOWLEDGEMENTS

To my son John Flaherty and daughter Kathie Flaherty Green,
grandson and granddaughter of Chris,
go an immeasureable amount of credit for their encouragement
and many hours of assistance in the preparation
of this manuscript for publication.

Katherine M. Flaherty

EDITORS PREFACE

My Mother, bless her soul, was a "saver" and this book was born from her forsight to save things she considered worthy mementos to a persons accomplishments. After her death in 1958 I came across three scrapbooks she had made about my Dad, several boxes of clippings, correspondence and old diaries plus hundreds of old Kodak pictures he had taken, some dating back to the early 1900's. All of this material was relative to his career in the Forest Service and the ten years that followed.

Sifting through all of this material it seemed it would fill some of the voids in the manuscript that he had written. So the struggle began to fill in the blank spots of which there were many and still are.

I feel fortunate to have had the parents I had. They gave me a lot of stability and direction for my life. For instance, when I was a teen-ager, my Dad said more than once, "I don't care what you do just finish what you start out to do."

So here I am after eight years of sifting, sorting and rewriting what those old treasure boxes held. I have finished the project and feel it was worth the effort. I hope it will add in some way to the enlightment of the place and time frame in which my Dad devoted his life.

Katherine M. Flaherty

Mercer Island, Washington
April, 1991

INTRODUCTION

This book begins when I am fourteen years of age in Germany and follows step by step the hardships I endured in my struggle to exist after leaving my homeland. From the minute I jumped off the gangplank of the German ship <u>Elbe</u> in Hoboken, New Jersey, and started running for freedom, I never knew what lay before me or what companionship I might be thrown into. A step in any direction could have changed my life. Looking back at this period of three years on the East Coast, I realize that it was the helping hands extended to me that kept me on the right track and contributed to my maturity and well being.

Never once did I abandon my early objective of pioneering in the New World and I did succeed in finding America's last great frontier on the west side of the Olympic Peninsula. After homesteading and doing my share of pioneering I became a U.S. Forest Service officer in a period of the earliest history of the Forest Reserve.

Much credit for safeguarding the resources of the Olympic Mountains is due to the U.S. Forest Service and I am proud to have been a part of the stewardship and development of the Olympic National Forest.

The short stories in this book are some of the highlights and adventures of my life from the fifty years that I tramped and came to know and love these wondrous Olympic Mountains.

The Indian legends were related to me first hand from the older members of the Hoh and Quileyute Indian Tribes.

-Chris Morgenroth

THE PIONEER: I SING THE PIONEER

By Arthur Guiterman

Long years ago I blazed a trail
Through lovely woods unknown 'till then
And marked with cairns of splintered shale
A mountain way for other men;

For other men who came and came
They trod the path more plain to see,
They gave my trail another's name
And no one speaks or knows of me.

The trail runs high the trail runs low
Where wildflowers dance or columbine
The scars are healed that long ago
My ax cut deep on birch and pine.

Another's name my trail may bear
But still I keep in waste and wood,
My joy because the trail is there,
My peace because the trail is good.

Part I

Preface: Story of Early Life, 1886-1890

When Hilarius and Margaret Morgenroth, Chris' mother and father were young marrieds around 1866, Prince Otto Von Bismarck had just become Prime Minister and Secretary of Foreign Affairs of Prussia. Bismarck was determined to unite the German people in one empire during the period of 1863 to 1873 and was in the process of realizing this dream. He said the problems of his time could be solved by "blood and iron", and he meant that only war and force could bring the rivaling German states together. Three wars were fought during these ten years. He went on to become the first Chancellor of the German Empire and became known as the "Iron Chancellor".

Thuringen was a pastoral, peace-loving province with forests and mountains. Chris' father was a God-fearing, morally sound Christian man who hated war or violence. He was content to live a simple life as a farmer and sheep herder but wanted the best for his children. Both parents wished their six children to be independent and successful in whatever they chose to do. By 1880, talk at home often centered on Bismarck's goal for a strong militaristic nation and how the three eldest boys, Hermann, Julius and Christian would all face enforced military conscription within the next few years. This left many German youths in a state of uneasiness and misgiving, and many left to seek their personal freedom elsewhere, mostly in America.

While growing up Chris had read many books on Africa, America and Australia. His wanderlust developed early when he talked to his school chums about far away places and adventure. By the time he was fourteen in 1886, the limited livelihood in the rural community was having its effect on his wanting to leave home. Julius had joined the navy and Hermann would be eligible to join the military the following year.

By September of that year Chris had landed in New York Harbor and for the next three years he experienced a new life full of adventure and narrow escapes.

After testing a dozen different jobs in the city for a year and a half, he answered an advertisement and was hired as a caretaker at a summer home on Lake Hopatcong in upper New Jersey. Here he settled down for a year. His employer was R.L. Edwards, president of the Bank of the State of New York. One summer day during a storm, Chris rescued the banker's daughter after a sailing accident on the lake and was rewarded for his deed in bravery by being given a job as porter at the State Safe Deposit Vault in New York City. This paid well and Chris paid off all he owed his mother and Hermann. Six months later in March of 1890 he had ac-

1

cumulated $1000 and decided he was ready to move West.

Placed at intervals during this period on the East Coast are excerpts from letters from his family and teenage chums. Hermann, the older brother, wrote Chris the most often, always wanting to help financially and encouraging Chris to make a success so the rest of the family could come to America.

Steamship *Elbe*

Chapter 1

"Leaving Home"

I was born in Eisfeld, Thuringen, Germany on July 15, 1871, the third of six children. My parents owned and operated an inn and had a small farm of about thirty acres near the city of Eisfeld.

In April of 1886, at the age of fourteen, I left school to work with my elder brother Hermann. He was chief clerk in a large winter resort hotel in Meran, a city in Tyrol. His plan was that I also learn the hotel business. On the way to Meran, I visited many historical places.

When I arrived at the hotel, my brother instructed me in the usual duties of a bellhop. The salary amounted to very little, but he put me to work with another bellhop who was well versed in the tip-extortion game. Under his tutelage, I soon became an expert in supplementing my small income.

While in Meran, I read many books about frontier life in Africa and America. I had the wanderlust, with a desire to join the pioneers, and penetrate into the unknown wilds of any country.

Herman left in May for London, England where he had accepted a position in a hotel. The hotel where I worked closed in August so I left Meran for home, going by way of Italy, Switzerland and France. I thoroughly enjoyed this trip as I got to see many cities, their people and costumes and much beautiful scenery. Along the way I collected a variety of daggers and stilettos, thinking I would need them for barter or self-protection against Hottentots or Indians.

When I got home, I discovered that one of my stilettos was broken, so I took it to a knifesmith in Eisfeld. It so happened that the knifesmith was a friend of my father. One day my father met the smith who gave him the stiletto to bring home to me. My father was a peace-loving man, and had never seen such a savage looking knife. He searched my trunk, and upon finding the rest of the murderous collection, took all of the knives away from me. We fought bitterly over their possession, but my father would not return them.

Brooding over the loss of the knives and my shattered ambitions, I decided to run away. In a boyish fit of temper I planned to go to Africa to hunt lions, elephants and wild men.

Although I had very little money left from my summer earnings, I packed my trunk and smuggled it to the depot. When I told my mother of my plans she cried a lot and was terribly upset, but she knew my father was very angry and would make life miserable for me at home. She loaned me three-hundred marks ($75) until I could get work elsewhere, but made me promise not to go to Africa.

I left that night on a train to Dresden and from there to Bremerhaven. Most of my money had gone for railroad fares, so I had to find cheap lodging to conserve what little I had left. I wrote a letter to Hermann in London, asking for his help and advice.

He wrote me and advised that I stay where I was as he was returning to enlist in the Army in a few weeks. I found a job sweeping and cleaning up in a grocery store for a couple hours each morning. In the afternoons I hung around the docks getting a line on steamers and their destinations. I was still determined to go to Africa.

On the docks, I met another young fellow about two years older who wanted to go with me. We became friends and made up our minds to stick together. One afternoon we located a steamer that was departing for some African port. We got a bottle of water and some lunch and waited our chance to sneak on.

We watched a crew of men loading coal through a chute in the side of the ship. When we thought no one was looking, we climbed up in the bunkers , jumped down the chute, and landed very hard on a great pile of coal below deck. The place was very dark, but after our eyes became accustomed to it, we could see cracks of light which we figured were around a door where the coal was probably taken out. However large iron doors barred our escape.

We lay a long time in this hot black chamber. Sometime during the night, the coal chute was removed and the opening covered. We now were scared for we thought we were locked in without water.

Finally we heard bolts sliding and a small door opened. Two men carrying lanterns came in and found us. They made us follow them out into the boiler room and climb a ladder onto the main deck, where an officer escorted us down the gang plank. It was daylight and we went to our lodging for a much needed cleanup. Thus ended our first try for passage to Africa.

We tried to get on many other ships by offering to do any kind of work, but were always met with the same response--- too young, no parents' consent, or no passports.

It was now late August and as the days went by I began anticipating my brother's arrival. I made it a point to be on hand whenever a steamer from England came in. Finally one afternoon, Hermann walked down the gangplank. He was with another young man and did not recognize me, so I did not make myself known until after they entered a restaurant.

He was quite surprised, but disappointed at my somewhat shabby attire. He made some explanation to his companion, then invited me to dine with them. Believe me, I appreciated that meal, as it was the first good one I'd had for weeks!

After talking matters over he gave me one hundred marks, a lot of advice and an understanding that I must not go to Africa but to America, preferably to the United States.

After that, I tried to get on ships bound for America but was refused for the same reasons as before. . .

The steamship Elbe, a crack passenger ship of the North German Lloyd Line was due to sail for New York City. I was on the dock one morning when a scuffle broke out and I learned the coal-passer crew was going on strike. I was at the right place at the right time, and with a lot of other young fellows, we were hired. We had no passports or seamen's papers, so the German authorities made the captain of the Elbe guarantee to bring us back.

I was now a coal passer in the lower hold of the ship. We worked in shifts of four hours on and four hours off, passing coal from the bunkers to the furnaces of the great vessel. It was the hottest place I had ever been in and I came near to caving in several times. Many of the boys fainted and had to be taken up on deck or to the ship's hospital to be revived.

As near as I can remember, we were about eight days crossing from Bremerhaven to New York. During this time, we talked among ourselves about running away if the chance came. I did not see shore until we were in New York Harbor, where I received a big thrill when we passed Bedlow Island and I saw the Statue of Liberty. (Footnote) We slowly steamed up the North river past New York, to the city of Hoboken, where the Elbe docked.

After the passengers disembarked we coal passers received orders to carry the firing tools to a blacksmith shop on the wharf. I knew this would be the only chance to make a break, and I was prepared for it. I had on two suits of underwear, two shirts and two pairs of trousers, but had purposely not worn a hat or coat. I also had all of my money, some of it I had exchanged for American coin.

Excitement ran high among us--- we were going to make a try at gaining our liberty! We lined up, and each received a load of tools. Under guard of a petty officer, we were marched down the pier to a nearby blacksmith shop where we deposited the tools. While our guard was talking to the smith, we started on a run down the street. Our guard shouted at us to come back, but we kept running, dodging through traffic. None of us returned.

There were sixteen of us who ran away, six became separated, but ten of us reached a ferry boat quite a distance from our starting point. I was the only one in the bunch with money, so I purchased tickets and we all went on board. We were greatly relieved when the ferry pulled away

5

from the shore and later landed somewhere on the waterfront of New York City.

By now the excitement and fear had worn away and hunger had set in. We hunted for a cheap restaurant and again, I had to pay the bill. I told two of my best acquaintances that for the sake of safety and to conserve my money, we would have to cut loose from the rest. By midnight we had lost them. We found a large pile of baled cotton where we three concealed ourselves and fell asleep. This was the end of my first day in America.

In the morning we followed the waterfront , and fortunately, did not meet any of our former companions. When night came, I had one dollar left. It was then that I decided to break away from the other two and go it alone. We three returned to the cotton bales for the night, but it was cold, so we prowled around to keep warm. Shortly before daylight I ditched my companions and started down a street looking for shelter. I found a wagon with a cover over the seat, climbed to the seat, curled up and went to sleep.

When I awoke, the street was alive with men and teams. I left my "hotel room" and mixed with the crowd. At first I felt a little guilty for leaving my friends, but as time went on I found myself returning to those friendly cotton bales in search of my companions, but they were not there. I was now in a strange country without family or a friend to turn to, no money, not even a coat on my back, and unable to speak the language. Soon I was crying. Why did I ever buy those terrible Italian knives?

(Footnote) The Statue of Liberty was in place and was about to be dedicated in September, 1886.

Chapter 2

"On My Own In The Melting Pot Of The U.S.A."

When daylight came, I again took up my wanderings. I made my way from the waterfront into town. I was crying part of the time from sheer homesickness, and the realization of the seriousness of my plight. I was standing on a street corner near a building, when a large yellow, covered delivery wagon drove up. A man jumped from the seat, went to the back of the wagon and passed me carrying a large piece of ice with a pair of tongs. He turned and saw me crying, looked at me and then went into the building. On his return to the wagon, he looked at me again, climbed to his seat and looked at me a third time. He said something which I did not understand, then beckoned me to come to him. I climbed up next to him and we started up the street.

He was shouting, "Ice, ice, Knickerbocker ice!" and was watching the windows for someone to give him a order. Neither of us could understand the other. He was Irish and I was German. He kept saying over and over to me, "Holler, 'Ice'. . . 'Knickerbocker Ice' I finally got the idea that he wanted me to broadcast his wares, so began shouting at the top of my lungs, "Holler ice, holler ice, holler ice!" The Irishman began laughing and stopped the team. Some people stopped and began to laugh, and more people stopped to see what was causing the commotion. Soon there was a traffic jam. I suspected that something was wrong, and stopped my yelling.

Carrying the ice became my duty and when we tied up in front of a saloon, I was sent in to fill the ice box while the driver argued with some men while he had a drink of whiskey. The bartender, who spoke German, gave me a large glass of beer and told me to eat all I wanted of the free lunch, as it was to be my dinner. He also acted as an interpreter between me and the iceman whose name he said was Pat. I was to receive room and board and fifty cents a day, and would also receive a coat which would be paid for out of my salary.

By nightfall, Pat had disposed of the entire load of ice. We drove across town to the east side and halted in a narrow filthy alley-way. He unhitched the horses and together we led them to a small stable. Pat took me to a lean-to shanty which was his home and introduced me to "Mrs. Pat".

There were only two rooms, a kitchen and a bedroom. Both of them were very small and roughly furnished. I sat on a box (part of the furnishings) while Mrs. Pat prepared supper. They talked, but I did not know what they were saying. Pat taught me some English by showing me objects and pictures. Presently he picked up a lamp, Mrs. Pat got a blanket, and we all went out to the stable. Here, they made my bed from baled hay, the blanket, and two rubber horse covers. This was the best room and bed that I had slept in since landing in the good old U.S.A.

Early next morning after breakfast, we hitched up the horses, and drove to a dock where many other wagons were also getting Knickerbocker ice to peddle. Some people here could speak both German and English and in this way I picked up a lot of information. I was told that Pat would never pay me anything, that he was just using me to do his heavy work.

During the next five days as I delivered ice, I saw so much misery and poverty that I began to doubt the stories of abundance I had read and heard about before leaving home. Pat had not paid me, and when I asked him several times for a coat, he put me off saying, "tomorrow".

On the sixth day, he told me to deliver ice to a nearby tailor. When I came out of the shop, a policeman who spoke German called me over and asked me how I was getting along with Pat. I told him my troubles, and he also advised me to leave Pat, saying he was no good. While Pat was in a saloon a bartender from another saloon asked me to fill his ice box. He paid me one dollar. I figured this dollar, with the fifty cents I had received from the tailor, was about what Pat owed me. Putting the money in my pocket, I abandoned the ice wagon and the first job I had in America.

After walking many blocks, I came to Hester Street, the Hebrew Quarter of New York City. Many of the shops opened out onto the sidewalk and everyone wanted to sell me clothing. The merchants grabbed at me, pulling on my clothes and nearly tearing them off. I finally bought a thin coat for fifty cents. I felt all dressed up, but had no place to go.

I wandered around and found the waterfront again. I longed for open country, so boarded a ferry and landed in Jersey City. There were many railroad tracks and that night I slept in a box-car for the first time.

Next morning I started following the tracks, hoping they would lead me out to the Great West. Tramping all day over endless marshes and across several rivers I came to another city, Newark. I began to wonder where the great frontier of my story books was.

I was dead tired and had not tasted food since noon of the day before. I fell asleep on a park bench but was awakened by a policeman who took me to the police station where some of the men could understand me. They were interested in my story, shared their lunch with me and gave me a place to sleep. I left the station in the morning with an invitation to come back if I didn't find work. I got work that day chopping up boxes for kindling wood in a grocery store owned by a German. He listened to my story, then told me that his mother and sister ran a farm and he thought they could use me. He was expecting his sister to come in from the country that evening with some farm produce and milk. She arrived about dark and I helped unload some cans of milk and apples. She took a supply of groceries and started on the return trip, 10 miles out of Newark, with me in tow. We arrived late at her home, and I was made welcome.

In the morning my duties began. This girl, about twenty-five years of age, was to be my boss. She milked five cows while I cleaned the barn, fed hay to the cows, and carried milk to the house. After breakfast I set to work picking up windfall apples in the orchard and sawing and piling wood in the wood shed.

That evening the girl showed me how to milk a cow while balancing myself on a one-legged stool. When my bucket was partly full she said, "You finish milking this cow while I milk another one." As soon as I was on my own, the cow objected and swiped her hind leg forward sweeping the deck clean. . . stool , milk and I went rolling on the floor. My instructor was not pleased with this performance. Each time I attempted to milk, the same thing happened, and each time I would receive a tongue lashing from the girl. So ended my first milking lesson.

One afternoon just before leaving on her usual trip to town, the girl told me to move a six month old calf to a new grazing place. It was tethered at the end of a long chain, and as I pulled up the stake, the calf became playful and started running. I stumbled, fell, and lost my hold on the chain. The calf was now free to go as fast and as far as it wanted to. There was a small quarter acre vineyard which must have looked like a race track to "Bossy" and she tore between the rows full length and back again. The chain and stake got tangled in the grape vines and bunches of grapes were torn down. Looking at this catastrophe I became scared for I did not want to face another tongue lashing. Again I decided to run away. I went to my room, put on all of my clothes, and took an old rusty revolver that I had found. I thought I might need it later for self-protection against Indians and wild animals in the West. The revolver contained one shell.

I headed for the nearest woods and wandered in them all afternoon. Towards evening, I emerged in open country near a small village. Some boys were playing ball in a school yard, so I went over and sat on the fence to watch. They asked me to play with them, but when they found that I couldn't speak English, they became more interested in me than in their game .

One of the boys took a liking to me and invited me home to his parents who were part Negro. They took me in, fed me, gave me a bed, and in the morning started me on the right road back to Newark, where I sought the friendly police station for my night's lodging.

The next morning they directed me to an employment office, where I paid my last dollar for a job. It was on a farm again about four miles out in the country, and I got there about noon in good spirits. The farmer questioned me about my milking and plowing abilities. I honestly could not give myself a good recommendation. I was not hired but was given my dinner, some more "good advice", and shown the road back to Newark.

While tramping back to town, I saw three huge wagons loading furniture from a large house near the road. These wagons belonged to Alex Martin of Newark, who was doing all of the delivering for Hahn Brothers Department Store, at that time the largest store in Newark. I asked one of the men, who turned out to be Mr. Martin, if I could work with them and he said I could help move a piano. We finished loading the furniture then drove to town where I helped unload the furniture into storage.

Mr. Martin hired me at $3 a week plus my room and board. My work consisted of keeping the stable clean, feeding and bedding eighteen horses every day, and keeping the harnesses washed and oiled. Occasionally I would help deliver furniture. This was the best job I'd had so far and I decided to keep it for the winter.

I wrote my mother a letter giving her my address. I had written other letters home but could not give them an address where they could reach me. I brought her up to date on my adventures but did not want to worry her with the hardships I had been through. In January of 1887 I received a most welcome letter from my mother. I was now 15 and a half years old.

Letter: From Mother to Chris, January 1887

"Dear Christian

You wrote that nobody cares about you. You know that I care for you, and we have taken care of you. It is not my fault that you are so far away. But we think you are better off than we are. We still have to work so hard as you know from former times. We want you all to learn something so you will have it better than we, and until we do that we will be old, for Ernst is only eight years old. We are well and feel quite happy. Father is still a shepherd.

Be efficient and good, then all will turn out well. Be thrifty for you are better off with no debts. And don't miss your military 'time', for you have to position yourself so that you can go wherever you want in life.

Please write us what kind of work you are doing. We all are sending you heartfelt greetings.

Greeting you,
Your mother."

In February Mr. Martin told me he would have to let me go. He wished me luck and told me if I ever needed a letter of recommedation he would be glad to oblige.

Christian Morgenroth, Graduation Derby High School 1889. New York City (18 yrs.)

11

Chapter 3

"Captain Denbeigh"

I had saved some money working for Mr. Martin that winter and decided to move to a boarding house near the Passaic River and look for other work. Some men who lived at the same boarding house, worked nearby on Canal Street at Balback and Sons Gold and Silver Refinery. They said there would probably be openings coming up, and I should stand in line at the gate with others in the morning. I was taken on and set to work helping load a smelting furnace. The pay was $1.50 per day and this was big money then. After ten days of work, I became very sick with lead colic. I was taken to a hospital and put in a ward maintained by the company. After I recovered I took my place in the call line again one morning.

While standing in line a man in a sailor's uniform came along and called me to one side. He introduced himself as Captain Denbeigh, owner of the coastal schooner E.C. Hay. After questioning me at length I agreed to go to work for him on the schooner. The crew would be Captain Denbeigh, his son, Will, an experienced sailor named Jack, and myself. I picked up my possessions at the boarding house and went with the Captain to his home where I met his wife, daughter and son, Will.

The next day Will took me to the schooner which was loaded with great building stones, some weighing several tons. These were to be delivered to 159th Street in New York City. We sailed the next morning from Newark to the New York Harbor. During the two day voyage, I helped with cooking, learned how to hoist sails, and did other odd jobs. I felt like a real sailor.

In New York Captain Denbeigh left Will in charge. It was too late in the day to start unloading so Jack, Will and I spent the evening in town. We returned around eleven p.m. to find that river pirates had broken into the cabin and taken our clothes, blankets, and all of our provisions. Will had to do some shopping next morning before we could even have breakfast.

It took two days to unload these enormous stones. By then Captain Denbeigh had returned, and we sailed back to Newark for another load.

We set a trap for the pirates every night by placing a dishpan full of tin utensils on the edge of the stairway. It was connected by a cord to the cabin door which separated the main deck from the deck below. If anyone opened the door, the pan would be upset and sound the alarm.

One night I thought I heard noises on deck so I decided to investigate. Remembering the trap, I carefully stepped around the pan of utensils as I went up the stairs. I knew I didn't dare open the regular cabin door, so I opened a small sliding door and looked around. No one was on deck, so I closed the sliding door but forgot and stepped on the string, and all the utensils went clattering down the stairs. Will and Jack jumped out of their bunks yelling "pirates!", and started beating on me. I shouted for them to stop but I took quite a beating before my yelling halted their attack. They lit a lamp, I explained everything, and we all felt pretty silly. We fixed the snare and turned in for the night, knowing we had an effective alarm.

On one return trip to Newark, we were to take a cargo of baled cotton to Clark's Cotton Mills. The captain and Will had gone home, leaving Jack and myself in charge of the schooner. We were berthed at one of the many piers on the North River, waiting our turn to receive bales from an ocean liner that was discharging its cargo on to lighters.

During the night, fire broke out in the hold of the big liner and spread rapidly through the cotton. Tugs finally got the burning liner out into the middle of the river, but in spite of efforts of the fire boats, the dock and many vessels loaded with cotton were now burning. Jack went in search of a tug to pull us away from the pier and burning ships around us. With a bailing bucket I was trying to extinguish blazes that had started on our deck and in the sails. Things looked hopeless. The heat was getting unbearable and I was ready to go overboard, when a tug came backing in among the burning lighters. Jack was at the stern with a hawser. The heat was so intense that I could hear the glass in the wheelhouse of the tug cracking. As soon as the tug touched our bow, Jack jumped across and together we made fast to the tug. He scrambed to the wheel and shouted at me to cut all lines to the pier. The pilot of the tug wasted no time and was already moving out. Our boat was still on fire in several places so I continued to throw water from the bucket. I noticed the jib sail blazing fiercely so I climbed out on the bow-sprit, lifted the bucket to throw the water and fell into the river. Struggling, I grabbed for the bow chain. Luckily, Jack saw me go in and rushed to my aid and I was able with his help to regain the deck. We got the fire out while the tug towed us over to the Jersey side of the river where we anchored.

We looked back on a sea of fire. The large steamer was burning in mid stream, a number of lighters and other cotton-laden boats were afire, and the entire dock was ablaze. We were the only ship in the harbor to get out safely. Our sails were badly damaged and one side of our hull was scorched and blistered, also my hands and face, but Jack and I were happy we had saved the schooner and I felt lucky to be alive.

The next afternoon after much searching, Captain Denbeigh found us and his schooner. We were towed to Newark for repainting and new sails.

I had saved most of my earnings which now amounted to nearly $75. I wrote a letter to my mother enclosing $25 of the money she had loaned me but I did not tell her that I was about to set out on another trip, this time to see the South.

I purchased a ticket to Philadelphia, stayed there several days, then went by boat to Baltimore. Here I met a Welsh coal miner, who was on his way to Alabama to work in the coal mines. We became acquainted after staying together several days in Baltimore. The boat fare to Richmond, Virginia was too expensive, so we decided to try beating our way by freight trains and walking. This was all right with me for I was willing to try anything once.

We left Richmond on foot, walked about five miles to a freight yard, picked a train going south, and concealed ourselves in a box car. The train travelled many miles before leaving us on a siding in a small town. From here on, we rode flat cars, and in and on top of box cars. Sometimes we stole the rides, but other times we had consent by helping load wood for the wood-burning locomotive.

Once we stopped to earn some money by removing pitch from pine trees for the manufacture of resin. We took to the rails again finally arriving in Atlanta, Georgia where we stayed a few days.

While walking the tracks toward Birmingham, we noticed some strange looking grey birds that were running among the brush. We started throwing rocks and succeeded in killing one. We picked up the bird and had just resumed our journey when a colored man climbed up the railroad embankment carrying a shot-gun about five or six feet long and shouted for us to stop. We ran as fast as our legs would carry us until out of reach of his gun. The bird was still ours so we cut off its head and continued on down the tracks. I later learned this was a domestic chicken called a guinea fowl and probably belonged to the man with the gun. That evening we stopped by a sluggish little stream and made a fire with old railroad ties and I received my first lesson in outdoor cooking.

My companion made a small incision through the breast of the bird, and without removing the feather or innards he rolled the bird in clay to form a ball, then buried it in the hot coals. The ball of clay was taken from the ashes an hour or so later and left to cool. When the clay was cracked, the feathers and skin came off along with the clay. Upon opening the chicken we found the intestines had shrunk to a small hard ball and were easily removed. The meat was white and tender and even without salt it made a very good meal. I made use of this technique many times in my later experiences as a pioneer. I discovered that it worked with fish as well as fowl, although fish must first be wrapped in leaves or

14

grass.

We slept beside a stream and took to the rails the next day. At a way station we hopped onto what we thought was an empty blind baggage car on a passenger train. Everything was going along fine until the end door opened and we were discovered. We were taken to the main baggage car where the conductor questioned us and told us that if we arrived in Birmingham as tramps we would be taken by the police and put on a chain gang. We said we had no money and that we weren't professional tramps. Since we were fairly well dressed he believed us and took us to a passenger coach and advised us to get off with the other passengers. While riding into Birmingham first class we washed and cleaned up. We took some money out of our shoes and on leaving the train, offered it to the conductor for his kindness. He refused, but said he wished us luck in our endeavor.

Next day we took a train to a small town about fifteen miles south of Birmingham as paid passengers. We settled ourselves in a boarding house and went straight away to the office of the mining company. My friend did all the talking and secured work for both of us, but we were to be in different mine shafts. I had never been underground before and did not know what to expect. As I rode in a small bucket car on rails down a long incline I became very nervous. All day I shovelled coal into little bucket cars.

I worked eight days then told my friend I did not like the South or working below ground. The wages were $1 per day so I assigned my $8 to my friend and said goodbye. After purchasing a ticket to Chattanooga, Tennessee, I had only $10 left.

From Chattanooga I decided to tramp it back to Newark, New Jersey. I now had some knowledge of locating trains and their destinations, and soon found a box car labeled " Cincinnati, Ohio". Its side doors were sealed, but a little end door was unlocked, so I crawled in. The car was loaded with watermelons. I dug a hole among the melons and sat down and waited. Early in the evening, my box car was attached to a train and we pulled out. Watermelons made up my diet for the next two days and nights.

Through the grating in the side door I could see the country-side. After crossing a large river signs began to appear advertising Cincinnati goods and I knew it was time for me to get out. I tried the little end door but it had been sealed, so I placed my feet against the door and my back against the great pile of watermelons and gave a strong push. The door gave way and I was free.

I continued on for days hiking and hopping trains through Pittsburgh, Harrisburg, and Lancaster. When I got to Philadelphia I began to feel sick and weak. I crossed the river to Camden and in the freight yards found a train bound for Newark. I pulled myself onto a flat car nearest the engine and fell asleep. I was awakened by the switchman shouting and kicking me in the back. He was yelling and pushing me off the car but I was too sick to be interested. The engineer who had heard the commotion came over and I told him I was sick and had to get to Newark. They put me back on the flat car and the engineer told me he would see that I got there. At Newark he helped me off the train and wished me good luck. Somehow I found my way to the river and Captain Denbeigh's schooner. I did not have the strength to climb on board, so I lay down on the dock and passed out. Will Denbeigh found me and sent me by ambulance to Sister's Hospital on High Street. The nuns told me later that I was raving and wandering all over the ward and that I had to be strapped down and packed in ice.

I do not know how long I lay there unconscious but when I opened my eyes a sheet had been drawn over my face and I could see candles burning at the head of my bed. My mind was clear but my body seemed paralyzed. It suddenly occurred to me everyone thought I was dead! I tried to make some sign of life and got one finger to move. I worked hard to get the circulation started. Breathing was difficult and I decided I had to do something drastic and fast. Taking a painful deep breath I lunged onto my side. The man in the next bed saw me move and hollered. Two nuns came running, but screamed and fled. An orderly came on the run and checked my temperature and pulse then yelled instructions to the nurses and orderlies. They told me the fever had burned itself out leaving me weak and paralyzed.

Meanwhile the poor fellow in the next bed who had sounded the alarm, was carried out of the ward. I learned afterwards that the shock had been too much for his heart and it was he they buried instead of me. I was told I had contracted an extremely severe case of typhoid fever from bad water, extreme heat and my watermelon diet for two days. Once more I had cheated death and felt lucky to be alive.

During my stay in the hospital, Captain Denbeigh and his family came often to see me, bringing fruit, which was promptly taken away.

After six weeks, I recovered sufficiently to leave the hospital and Captain Denbeigh took me back to the schooner. I was nursed back to health with good food, lots of rest and my wonderful caring friends, the Denbeighs.

I had written to Hermann and told him of my close encounter with death but I did not want to worry my mother. A short time later I received an answer from Hermann.

16

LETTER: From Hermann to Chris , January 22, 1888, Metz, Germany

"Dear Brother,

Have had your very kind letter last night and I was very glad to hear you are still alive. I am very glad you are well again after being in the hospital for six weeks. I wish you would come back to Germany as soon as possible, as the sooner you serve your three years for soldier, the sooner you can go back to America. Afterwards we shall go together to Australia or India. Again I think it would be better to live in America.

The parents have been very upset about your silence. They thought you were dead. Father was asking in every letter he wrote to me about you. Mutter wrote me that he was very sorry for what happened.

I am in the Officer's Casino as head waiter. Julius is going into the Marines. How long will you stay in your present place? A Happy New Year. Good Night.

Your true brother, Hermann
7th Company, 4 Rgt., Metz"

I remained on the schooner until spring but I knew this was not the life for me, so I began to read the newspaper ads. An attorney in Newark wanted a young man to take care of his summer home and to assist his family while he and his wife made a trip to England. I wanted to be out of doors, so I answered the ad. After a personal interview I was hired for the position. In mid-April I said goodby to the Denbeighs and moved with the Knights to their summer home on Lake Hopatcong, New Jersey.

Chapter 4

"Lake Hopatcong, New Jersey"

The Knight's summer home was quite large and situated on ten acres by the lake. The acreage also included a big yard, a barn, an ice house and a chicken house with forty Plymouth Rock chickens. I was to take care of all this plus exercising a trotting horse and a large bird dog. The family included Mr. and Mrs. Knight, their two children and Mrs. Knight's mother. A Bohemian girl as cook, a nurse girl (about eighteen years old), and I completed the group.

About a week after the Knights left in May, the mother-in-law informed me that some of the chickens were missing. She suspected skunks and told me I must set traps for them. I had never seen or heard of skunks, but was willing to try my hand at trapping. She procured a dozen small steel traps and explained that the skunks burrowed underground near the chestnut trees.

I found many holes in the ground by the chestnut trees, which were close to the chicken coop. I set the traps and captured five large chickens on the first day. Their legs were broken, so I killed and buried them. Then I moved the traps further away from the chicken yard. The next day I had to dispose of two more chickens. The mother-in-law told me that I must get the skunk before it got any more chickens. My traps were now some distance from the hen house and I got no more chickens for a while.

Then one morning I went to the trap line and found a chicken in the first trap. After disposing of it in the usual way, I inspected the other traps. By one of the holes I had captured a beautiful creature about the size of a cat. I did not want to kill this pretty animal, so I went to the barn and fixed up a box for a cage, got a long pole, and returned. The animal was still sitting in front of his home with one foot in the trap. With the pole, I picked up the trap and its anchor and carried the animal back to the barn. I put the trap on the ground not far from the dog house and while opening the cage, the dog barked and made a charge at my little black and white furry friend. Immediately the air became polluted with a sickening odor and my beautiful animal was running down the trail dragging the trap with the dog following, dragging his dog house behind him.

I stopped the dog, and recaptured my animal by fastening the trap chain to the long pole. Then I brought the dog and his house back to their place by the barn where the odor was terrible.

I decided to go to the house and tell the mother-in-law about my capture, but she "sensed" my coming and yelled for me not to come inside.

She handed me a revolver and box of shells and instructed me to kill the skunk and bury it along with all my clothes. After that I was to burn straw in every place where I'd had trouble with him.

So this was a skunk! And now I would have to kill it. I approached the poor little fellow, who looked so innocent sitting there, and steeled myself for murder. It took over thirty shots before I could kill the skunk and this gave him lots of time to liven up the atmosphere. I buried the skunk with my clothing and burned a lot of straw. Then I took a bath in the lake and put on a complete change of clothing. Finally, I went around and pulled up all my traps. So ended my first experience as a trapper, the result was the loss of eight chickens, a skunk, one suit of clothes, and almost a full day of hard work.

I then cleaned the revolver, reloaded it and returned to the house. The nurse and the cook were in the kitchen so I handed the gun to the nursemaid, muzzle end toward myself. I ˜ a careless manner, she took the gun by its handle. "Look out, it's loaded!", I said. But she jerked it out of my hand and the gun exploded. I was in the pantryway near a shelf of canned raspberries. The bullet broke several of these jars, and red juice began running onto the floor. The nurse girl gave a wild scream thinking she had shot me and proceeded to faint. The cook started screaming, thinking I had shot the girl. I had just picked up the gun when the mother-in-law, hearing the shot and screams, came running in. The cook was crying hysterically that I had killed the nurse. The mother-in-law took the gun from me and started accusing me of murder, for there on the floor lay the girl in a pool of red raspberry juice.

I tried to explain it was not blood, but I could not convince them until the nurse girl started to get up saying, "Chris, I did not mean to shoot you!" It wasn't easy to explain to her that I was all right until I showed her the broken jars.

Meanwhile I felt a warm but wet sensation within my left trouser leg and discovered real blood coming through my clothing. I had been shot after all. The bullet had cut the skin on the inside of my leg above the knee before breaking the three jars of raspberries. The mother got bandages, carbolic solution, and salve, and sent me to the bathroom to dress my wound. It healed in a few days and everything was again quiet on Lake Hopatcong. Once more I felt lucky to be alive. Several days later a shoemaker heard about me trapping the skunk and came to dig it up. He skinned it for the fur and rendered out the fat to sell as a cold cure remedy.

Mr. and Mrs. Knight came home from England at the end of summer and everyone got ready to move to the city for the winter.

I had, however, secured another position across the lake on the estate of Mr. R.L. Edwards, who was a bank president in New York City. Another man named Ed, and I were to take care of his horses and summer home during the coming winter. I had turned seventeen that summer. Among the letters from my school chums and family I received another letter from my mother who was still concerned about my military service.

LETTER: From Mother to Chris, Summer, 1888

"Dear Christian,

We got all of your letters that you had written to us and to your brothers and sister. They were very happy. We would have written sooner but Hermann always tells us your address.

We sent in a petition for your military service, to defer you another year, which also has been granted. So you won't get into trouble. Your name is in the main register. The mustering took place, but they did not read out your name. Now you can do as you please. You can join the service this year or next year. Have you already been to the mustering at the German Consul?

Karoline no longer likes it at all in the 'Deutsches Haus'.
She is a good worker and people praise her, but she says Mr. Kunert pulled her hair and she is blamed for someone else's mistakes. She has to stay there for another three months to get paid, otherwise she would leave. Hermann will be out of the military soon and he could take care of her. After that she will have to go to a big hotel. But she wants to go to America, and there you have it.

Julius was on a 14 day leave and visited us twice. We have had bad weather and cannot plant much at all. Father is still quite well and does a lot of work as he used to, as you know. He even still dances when things are going good. He still is playing cards. But he is no longer a sheepherder. Herr Walter has sold all his sheep. Father does not like to write and does not have time. Mathilde is better again.

Greetings to you,
From your mother."

Ed and I went to work in October for Mr. Edwards. We built a new road, filled the ice house, and did numerous other odd jobs. Mr. Edwards came to the lake several times during the winter to direct our work.

That winter and spring I continued to receive more letters at Lake Hopatcong from my family and my chums.

LETTER: From Mathilde (sister), January 6, 1889

"Dear Brother

I did not get much from the Holy Christchild. I got a box of writing paper and a small chest with drawers. Ernst got a coloring box for Christmas and a picture-book and a harmonica from Herr Walter. Dear brother, please don't hold it against me, I cannot yet write too well, as I was home from school for two years because of my illness. We all send our regards.

Greeting you,
Your sister Mathilde."

LETTER: From Ernst (brother) January 25, 1889

"Dear Christian,

We have received your photograph and enjoyed it very much. We had it framed real nicely. We have always had only rain and wind and no snow yet. Mathilde is sick again.

You don't have to come back to Germany if you don't want to. When I get out of school I, too, plan to visit you. When your military draft time is over you can come for a visit here and you can take me along to America.

A big stable is being built now and large horse raising is being done. The sheep will all be sold and no new ones will be bought. I am 9 years old and Mathilde is 12. Mathilde's illness is not bad.

Greeting you,
Your brother Ernst."

LETTER: From Armin Gleichmann (school chum) to Chris, January, 1889

"Dear Friend,

I received your letters of April 18, 1887 and December 13, 1888 and I answered you, but my letters came back. After Easter I want to start 'wandering'. Maybe I will get close to where you are. The goal of my trip is Coburg and from there to the Elbe River, along the Elbe to Hamburg and to Bremen or Kiel where Julius is as a "Marine".

I bought myself a Longkoster rifle which cost 90 M. I also built myself a museum. It is in a garden and there are old and new things in it as follows: stuffed birds and animals, old and new rifles, pistols, swords, daggers and knives, portraits and I would like one of yourself. Bugs and butterflies, old and new gold coins, various animal and bird quivers, deer, stag and geese. There are also living animals in the garden, like hares, foxes, ring-doves, turkeys, squirrels and various small birds. I also have a waterfall in it. Over the holidays I stuffed a mountaincock, a sparrow and a bullfinch.

Please write what kind of work you are doing and how much you make a week.

21

I also have and collect stamps, shells, and various stones and rocks.
Greetings to you,
Your friend, A. Gleichmann"

LETTER: From Armin Gleichmann, May 24, 1889

"Dear Friend,

I told my parents at Easter that I planned on leaving on a trip after the holidays and they were happy then. But when I wanted to leave that certain day they refused me for my father had read your letter a few days before and found out that I wanted to go to America. I long to be over there. When I walk in the woods, and along the river and look at the trees and the river bank and don't see a single animal then I cannot stay from longing, I would like to flee over there right now to where there are still many birds and animals that nobody bothers about, Now I cannot come.

You have watched me skinning squirrels, can't you send me some whole skins? (here he goes into detail on skinning the squirrel and how to stuff the skin and draw around it.)
With Greeting,
Armin Gleichmann"

Early in June the Edwards family moved up from Brooklyn to spend the summer at Lake Hopatcong. Besides Mr. and Mrs. Edwards there were five grown children. It was my job every morning to drive Mr. Edwards to the railway station about five miles away and come after him each evening with a fast trotting horse.

One day I was near the lake, running a steam pump which was filling the large water tank on the hill. I was watching a sailboat coming down the lake under full sail. Suddenly, a squall struck the boat, upsetting it. I raced to the boat house, got a small boat and began rowing to the rescue.

Three young people were clinging to the overturned sail boat. One was Mr. Edward's daughter, the other two were brother and sister who were staying at the hotel across the lake. The lake was very rough, and I had some difficulty getting the girls into the small row boat. There was not enough room to take the boy without risking another spill, so I told him to hang on to the sailboat and I would come back for him. He resented this very much and began swearing at me and promising bodily harm if he ever got ashore. I left him clinging to the boat while I landed the girls at the boathouse, where the family gathered. I rowed as fast as I could to the upset sail boat and helped the young lad climb into the boat. I guess he'd had time to cool off a bit, for he neither spoke nor offered fight after landing. I made a final trip to the shipwreck with Ed, and together we towed the capsized sailboat to a sheltered sandy beach. After all this rescue work, I was late getting to the station. Mr. Edwards was impatiently waiting and immediately began heaping much abuse upon me, calling me lazy and giving me no opportunity to explain. There was only one thing for me to do, so I kept still. In the quietness of the drive home, I pondered what I would do.

When we reached the stable I took care of the horse, then went to my room and packed my belongings. I asked Ed to row me across the lake to a farm house where I knew the people. We were carrying my baggage to the boat house, when Mr. Edwards came rushing after us. He had heard about the accident and took my arm and fairly dragged me back to the house, shaking my hand and apologizing, even shedding tears because he was so grateful for rescuing his daughter . He would have no part of my going away, so I stayed. That summer I turned eighteen.

LETTER: From Hermann to Chris, September 2,1889

"Dear Brother,

I got your letter with the money and was very glad to get it for I have not any proper shirt or clothes. I got 83 marks for the twenty dollars you sent to me and I hope I can send it back soon.

I will finish my three years in the military on the September 29. I shall go home for a few days to see the parents, then go to the south of France for a short time. I have a place at Wiesbaden as head waiter and I hope to make good money there for I am determined to go to America next year.

It is right that you write an English letter to me for it is very good for you to learn writing English. It had some faults in it but it does not matter for you will learn it by and by. I fear you don't understand my letter in English, but I will learn it again when I come to you.

You can stay there until you are American Citizen then you can come back to Germany for a month only. I will write you what place I will be in Wiesbaden. Write soon again to the parents and to me.

Yours truly
Your brother Hermann"

In the fall the Edwards family moved back to Brooklyn and Ed and I were left alone for another winter. About two weeks after the family had gone, I received a telegram saying to be ready the following Saturday to go with Mr. Edwards to New York City.

When I returned to the city with Mr. Edwards I learned he was president of the Bank of the State of New York at the corner of Williams Street and Exchange Place. I was given employment in the bank and spent a few days in his home until I found living quarters elsewhere. I began my position in October of 1889 as the outside gatekeeper of the huge vault. Later I was promoted to porter where my duties were to help patrons carrry their safety boxes to and from the private rooms. Sometimes I was asked to help cut coupons and in this way I made many friends.

LETTER: From Hilarius (Chris's father) to Hermann, December, 1889

"Dear Hermann

We received your letter and also one from Christian the same day, that made us very happy. When we opened Christian's letter there were $15 enclosed, which we certainly can use. We can now pay off some old debts. We all wish to thank you very much for the big presents. When you write to your Christian please tell him that we did not thank him in the letter we wrote to him.

It seems to me that this is a strict rulership, the entire Bockstadt is being rebuilt, everybody has horses, and pheasants in the woods. He leased the entire hunt.

I want to close
Hilarius Morgenroth"

LETTER: From Ferdinand Schilling (school chum) December, 1889

"Dear Buddy,

The following have to go into the military: Ottomar Mueller, Infantry Regiment 95; Karl Schulmeister, Infantry Regiment 32; Albin Truckenbrodt, Infantry Regiment 32; Karl Gottwalt and I have been placed back which I don't like for I had rather become a soldier with my buddies.

We are all in "full freshness" and are well. Ottomar is 1.75 meters tall, without mustache. Albin is 1.75 meters without mustache, Karl Schulmeister is 1.65 meters without mustache, a stout, strong man. Karl Gottwalt is 1.72 meters without mustache, and I am 1.63 meters with full beard and mustache.

My parents and brothers and sisters also send their regards.

Your friend and buddy,
Ferdinand Schilling"

LETTER: From Armin Gleichmann to Chris, February 7, 1890

"Dear Friend,

I was very happy when I got your photograph. I had just bought an album in which I keep photographs. I have a good customer again for stuffing animals. He is the new estate owner of Von Bockstadt. In 14 days I preserved 3 pheasants, a big vulture, and a squirrel. I got 17 Marks for the 5 pieces. I will have to conserve everything that is being shot. Hans is the regional ranger, he does nothing all day but run around with a rifle.

I also learned how to ride and made myself a saddle. Tomorrow I will ride to Hildburghausen and get my new Mauser Rifle.
> Greeting you, your friend
> Armin Gleichmann"

That winter on Mr. Edward's urging, I finished the eighth grade at night school. My diploma was hard-earned, and I still keep it as a much prized possession.

I was earning good money and at Christmas received many generous gifts from the bank and vault patrons. I had saved nearly $1000 and had paid back all the money my mother and brother had advanced me, and was getting along nicely in my new position. However, I was still dissatisfied and restless. I wrote Hermann that I would soon be going "out west" and wrote both parents also of my intentions of leaving New York City.

LETTER: From Hermann, March 16, 1890 Hotel & Badhaus Zum, Spiegel, Wiesbaden

"Dear Brother,

I was surprised about all the news and about the picture. Mainly I have to tell you that you look marvelous and I am no longer worried that you are going among the wild people. I don't want to say anything about your new undertaking, for I would have done the same thing in your place, but I only beg one thing of you and that is don't forget the parents, and don't let them wait too long for a letter, for mother really worries. I have written a consoling letter so they won't worry so much. The two of us don't want to let them down.

I will follow your advice and save as much as I can, so that I can come. I looked at the map, and it looks very good to me, of course it takes courage and a desire, that you have. If you have a few days sometime, get on your horse and carry a letter to the nearest post office and write us how it will be for us to write to you.

Dear brother, now you are almost there, where we have always dreamed of going even when we still were in school, in the gold fields. Julius will probably be surprised when he hears of it. I would just love to come there right away, if only it weren't for the parents. For I don't care when or where I die.

Have you already equipped yourself properly with arms, clothing, and tools for your new home, or will you buy things only when you get to Helena, Montana. Are the horses very expensive?

Can't you tell me what you are going to do there, maybe be a gold digger? But that is not supposed to be good anymore. You probably will not get employed at any banks. Are you planning on not writing for years? Now I am anxious to know what the parents will say about all this. I write long letters. Mathilde is very sick again. Father had to pick her up at school, she will probably not live that much longer. Ernst is fine. What do you want him to be? Shall I bring him along to America? It is not very far to San Francisco for you anymore now, things are supposed to be very good there. I would like to have a photograph of you sitting on the horse. This is the longest letter I have ever written.

So many young men in Bockstadt prefer to not go beyond their own dung hill. I prefer to be a waiter away from home than to have stayed at home and become a shoemaker or a tailor. You too, have probably not regretted, for at least WE know what it means to be "in the world". I hope you will be satisfied and happy. I hope you will have good luck and I wish all good things for you. Remember me sometimes and think of home. Don't forget the parents.

Thus I remain your brother
Hermann"

Herman Morgenroth (brother) 1888, 22 years old. German Army

PART II

Preface: Homesteading and Pioneering, 1890-1892

Little was known about the Olympic mountain ranges and the forested jungle regions surrounding them prior to 1885. The name Olympic is a derivation of the word Olympus which is the name of the dominant mountain of this group of jagged snow-capped ranges.

In 1885 Lieutenant Joseph P. O'Neil of the U.S. Infantry stationed at Fort Townsend set out to explore the upper Dungeness Valley. On reaching the top of a high ridge, he surveyed the horizon to the south and west. What he saw was a sea of mountains that he hoped some day to explore.

In October 1889, S.C. Gilman and his father C.S. Gilman, ex-Lieutenant Governor of Minnesota were poled in canoes by Indian guides up the Quinault River as far as possible where the two men alone on foot continued to within a short distance of Mt. Constance. They climbed a few peaks, saw Mt. Olympus, then retraced their steps down the Quinault River and proceeded by canoe to Pysht on the Straits of Juan de Fuca. Here they crossed overland on the western side of the Olympic Peninsula on existing settler trails and ocean beaches to finally reach the Quinault River some fourteen miles above its mouth. "The Olympic Country", an article written by young Gilman was published in the National Geographic Magazine in April 1896, six and a half years after their sojourn into the Olympics.

The Press Exploring Expedition took place from December 1889 to May 1890. This maiden trip from north to south across the Olympics was via the Elwha River Valley, across the Queets Divide and down the Quinault River Valley toward Aberdeen. Six hardy and rugged men pitted their physical strength for six months against all manner of hardships including bitter cold and deep snows. The expedition proved to be more of an adventure and a conquest through survival.

In July of 1890 just after the Press Party had completed the sojourn through the Olympics, Lieutenant O'Neil led a party of sixteen men to the headwater of the North Fork of the Skokomish River. He sent his men off on side trips to explore the Dosewallips, Duckabush, Satsop and Wynoochee Rivers. With a few men he crossed into the valley of the Quinault River and proceeded down to Hoquiam at Grays Harbor. Part of the party headed for Mt. Olympus but there is some doubt that any of the peaks of the great mountain were conquered.

Of the three expeditions, only the one made by the Gilmans reveals detailed description of the mountain topography and scenery. All three

27

Theodore Rixon – R. O. Lee worked for him for 3 summers ('36–37–1938) as a chainman surveying timber + road right of ways around Sekiu, Pysht and Clallam Bay

expeditions concluded there was no great fertile central valley as settlers had hoped, just mountains and more mountains. Except for the publicity given the Press Expedition at the time, the knowledge gained by these expeditions, for some unknown reason was buried in the files of the government and the news media. Most people never knew they had taken place. Prior to the Dodwell-Rixon Exploration and Survey of the Reserve in 1898 and 1899, more detailed knowledge about the interior mountains and valleys came firsthand from trappers, hunters, prospectors and some curious settlers, who ventured to explore what lay beyond their homesteads.

Chris had heard about this last great wilderness while still on the east coast. Before making up his mind to come west he had applied for a place on an expedition to the Yucatan with the Academy of Natural Sciences. He had also made inquiries about an expedition to the interior of Alaska that was seeking "able bodied men". He probably decided on the west coast since he would see archaic Indian ruins, mountains and also be able to claim free land and be part of a new settlement.

After reaching Seattle he met Gus who became a partner in homesteading on the Bogachiel River. They stuck together helping each other build their cabins, clearing land and planting gardens. Gus does not figure in the explorations. It is assumed he abandoned his claim within the first year.

After settling in on his claim, Chris makes his first exploration trip into the interior. Starting from his front door, he follows the Bogachiel River some twenty-five miles to its source.

He continues to improve his homestead and help new settlers to locate.

He relates his experiences in blazing and building some eighty miles of trail between Forks and the Queets River which opened up the area for future settlement. This stretch of trail came to be known as the "Pacific Trail". It later was graded into a wagon road that finally, with relocation of a few original survey lines, became part of Highway 101 or the Olympic Loop Highway.

He relates some of the hardships encountered as an early pioneer and pays tribute to his lifelong friends and neighbors the John Huelsdonks.

Chris had all the traits of the true frontiersman: physical strength to endure, combined with inquisitiveness and a will to succeed. He was exuberant, high spirited and restless, which comes with freedom. He was compatible with nature and people.

R. O. Lee spent an afternoon with John at his place on the Hoh in about 1937. He was a strong old man then.

Chapter 5

"Finding The Way To The Bogachiel"

I purchased a ticket over the New York Central and Canadian Pacific Railways and started my journey across the continent to America's last frontier. On the train out of St. Paul, I became friends with a logger who was also going to Puget Sound. We decided to stick together to look for work in the woods.

On April 1,1890, we arrived in Vancouver, B.C. and took a boat to Seattle via Victoria, B.C. From Seattle we travelled by train to Tacoma.

After a few days in Tacoma, we returned to Seattle which was more cosmopolitan. It had been nine months since Seattle's great fire, and major construction was underway. The business part of town which was clustered around Yesler Square and the waterfront, was being rebuilt. There were many tents among the scattered buildings that had survived the fire, as well as a few hastily constructed new buildings.

After a week of looking around, we accepted an offer to work in a logging camp at the head of Port Orchard Bay. We reached the camp on a small boat from Seattle and carried our bed rolls and belongings up a hill to a long, log building called a bunkhouse in which we were assigned straw-filled bunks. We joined about thirty men for a big noon meal in the cookhouse, another long log building.

After this feast I was given a double-bit ax to grind. It was the most vicious tool I had ever seen, and my partner cautioned me not to show ignorance or I might not have a job for long. Then we were taken to where a crew was building a skid road. Two teams of six oxen each with a driver were pulling out logs and stumps. My job was to assist the hook-tender with the chains and fastening the hooks to the stumps. All went well for a few days. One afternoon the teamster had to leave so the foreman said he would show me how to drive the team.

Driving a three-yoke ox team is not a job, it's a profession, and a difficult one at that. The oxen must start slowly, pull together, keep in line and hang tough. The driver must know each ox by name, and how and when to give orders. If the ox does not show immediate action, a long pole with a spike nail in the end, called a goad stick, is used to achieve the necessary results.

I was instructed in team driving for a half hour, then the goad stick was handed to me. The foreman watched my team pull out a few small stumps, then left. I hooked the team on to a large stump and gave the command. The oxen strained but the stump remained firmly in place. I gave the command again but with no results. By now the team was getting nervous, and so was I. On the third pull, I used the stick at the wrong time on the wrong ox. Suddenly the lead ox swerved around and became entangled with the other oxen. Their horns were everywhere, and I was afraid to go near them. Running down to camp, I found the foreman, told him about the mess and that I wanted nothing more to do with team-driving. He insisted I go back, so, reluctantly I followed him up the hill to the jobsite. We found the team wound up into a tight knot. The foreman waded in among them, unhooked some chains, and in a few moments, had them untangled. He teamed them back up and they were hooked to the same stump. Then he shouted some orders and they pulled the stump out on the first try. He gave me a lot more instructions, then left.

Near quitting time I got into trouble again. We were dragging a heavy log when the chain broke and the team became tangled in the brush and fallen timber. Again I ran back to camp, found the foreman, and this time told him I was quitting. He said I couldn't do that, as I would get no pay until the end of the month.

I hastily packed my belongings and was well on my way down the trail to the bay before the crew returned to the bunkhouse. I got a boat back to Seattle and resolved never again to take a job involving any of the bovine family. My experiences in learning to milk a cow, tether a calf, and drive an ox team had been enough.

A few days later in Seattle, I met a young Colorado prospector named Gus. He wanted to go farther west, so we decided to strike out together. From Seattle we went by boat to Port Townsend which looked very prosperous and had two street car lines in operation. From here we took the small missionary steamer Evangel, which stopped in Port Angeles for a few hours and then continued on to Port Crescent. We were told this was a booming town and men were being hired with good pay.

The promoters of this town wanted the county seat so they were hiring men of all ages regardless of citizenship so they could vote as residents. Port Angeles also wanted to be the county seat of the government. Washington had become a state the previous November and the county seat was at Dungeness. After the vote was taken, Port Angeles had won and the building boom at Port Crescent collapsed. Gus and I had been hired to help build the breakwater at Port Crescent, which was to rival the natural breakwater forming the bay at Port Angeles. This project was stopped along with the rest of the town's future so Gus and I decided to see what lay beyond. (Footnote)

We boarded the Evangel again and continued on west to Pysht, another twenty-five miles, where we were put ashore in a rowboat with the mail. With the mail we walked through ankle deep water over the flats a quarter mile to the mainland. The Postmaster, named Crawford, met us and invited us to stay at his place.

Mr. Crawford introduced us to Mr. South and Mr. Ford who had settled on the Forks Prairie farther west where there were about twenty other pioneer families. They told us that the western slopes of the Olympic Mountains were impenetrable and only a few settlers had attempted to venture beyond Forks.

Ford, a Civil War veteran, deemed it his duty to give us a lot of advice about the forty miles of trail between Pysht and Forks. He drew a map and explained that the first sixteen miles of trail to Beaver Lake was over a burned mountain area and that no drinking water was obtainable.

Next morning we made up our packs with food for the three day trek and remembering Ford's advice about the lack of drinking water, we filled six bottles from the Pysht River adding these to our packs which now weighed about seventy-five pounds each. Gus's weighed a little more since he had a bottle of whiskey.

About one mile out along the narrow Pysht river trail, we had to ford the river hip deep and a little farther along, we waded it again. We were surrounded by lush forest and there was no sign yet of the terrible fire that Ford had told us about. Along the way, Gus had patronized the whiskey bottle frequently with the excuse that it lightened his load and conserved his water. By noon we had travelled eight miles and had forded the river fourteen times! We figured this to be a popular joke played on newcomers so ditched the water bottles and continued plodding on, crossing many little mountain streams along the way. When Gus discovered that we had no water shortage, he continued to solicit support from the whiskey bottle claiming it gave him the strength and courage to continue. Towards evening he became very sick and could go no further. I made a bark lean-to near a creek, fixed his bed, covered him with his blankets and proceeded as fast as I could with oncoming darkness, to Beaver Lake. I reached a trapper's cabin where a Mr. Fielsten lived. Another man was staying with him and I told them about Gus. They took a lantern and set out to the rescue. They told me to stay at the cabin and get some sleep.

At daylight they returned with Gus, who felt fairly well by this time. The trappers had finished the whiskey, for which I was thankful. We had coffee and some breakfast and all turned in for a good sleep. Next morning Gus and I continued on the pioneer trail to the western frontier. We spent two nights more camping with isolated settlers before reaching the settlement of Forks.

The Olaf Nelson Ranch became our headquarters. We wanted to explore new country and were told that there were a few settlers on the Bogachiel River south of Forks but that there were no trails and we would

31

have to follow the river. We made up light packs with provisions, blankets and two newly purchased axes and hiked the trail to Selalit, the Indian canoe landing on the Bogachiel River. Here we started following up the Bogachiel River. The undergrowth and brush along the river was like a jungle, making our progress very slow. We saw lots of deer, elk and bear but did not kill any.

On the third day out, we came upon three men who had just staked their claims, so we continued on up river through several broad, park-like bottoms. At one of these, we walked into a great herd of over two-hundred elk. This apparently was a favorite stomping ground as the benchland had been well browsed and there was open grassland near the river. This area seemed very beautiful to me with giant trees, bigger than I had ever imagined, growing all around. One big fir was near eleven feet in diameter and was surrounded by many others almost as large. I decided that this was the place I would stake as my claim. Gus liked this bottom land too and took a claim across the river.

We made camp and next morning laid my foundation logs and posted the description, my name and the date on a tree. Then we forded the river and did the same on Gus's claim. This constituted squatters rights and would protect and hold our claims for six months against jumpers. We did not know for sure in which county we were located. All we knew was that we were on the Bogachiel River somewhere on the western slope of the Olympic Mountains. I was very excited and I know my heart skipped a beat when I saw my name on that tree, for I knew that I was now a part of the U.S.A. It was May,1890, two months shy of my nineteenth birthday.

After securing our claims, we made our way back to Forks. An Indian canoe with a load of provisions from the Dan Pullen Trading Post at LaPush was due to arrive at Selalit. Gus and I returned in the canoe the sixteen miles to LaPush. We purchased about seven hundred pounds of supplies and tools at the Trading Post but immediately met an obstacle. An Indian wanted forty dollars to take our supplies up-river to our homesteads, a distance of about twenty-eight miles. We thought the price too high, so we purchased a canoe including paddles and poles for fifteen dollars and started back to our homesteads paddling our own canoe. We narrowly escaped losing our supplies in the river several times.

We planted potatoes, carrots and turnips on each claim, then helped each other build one-room log cabins. We even made some furniture and boxes for our surplus supplies. We felt we were sitting on top of the world, with good claims and plenty of ambition to help develop a new country.

(Footnote): Shortly after this boom town was abandoned, the Seattle

Logging Company which was promoted by Mr. Michael Earles and financed by Mr. C.F. Clapp of Seattle, started logging operation at Crescent Bay. Like other timber speculators during the 80's and 90's, companies were hiring men to take up Government timberland under the preemption law. Then the company agents would be paid to make final proof and witness. The would-be claimant would be paid $300 to $600 for signing over his claim. This was easy money for a claimant and cheap timber for the timber speculator.

This logging operation was in one of the largest and best stands of Douglas fir and red cedar on the Olympic Peninsula. The town of Port Crescent boasted docks, warehouse, a railroad, hotel and many other buildings. It thrived on the lucrative logging industry for twenty years and when all the timber tributary to this shipping point had been logged, the town was abandoned. The rails were taken up, the wharf wrecked and the buildings burned. A young stand of timber soon grew over the townsite, leaving no trace of this once thriving community. The town of Port Crescent went back to being called Crescent Bay. (Port Crescent is an example of what happened to other communities dependent primarily on logging operations.)   - Ch. Morgenroth

Chapter 6

"Back to Seattle"

We needed to earn some money to improve our homesteads and see us through the winter, so Gus suggested we go back to Seattle. We secured our property and headed out.

When we reached Pysht, we heard that a California outfit was starting a camp at West Clallam where tanning extract would be made from hemlock bark. A boat, the Ferndale, was due to arrive in Pysht with men and equipment for this new project. We were rowed out to the Ferndale, and taken to West Clallam. We hired on felling hemlock trees and peeling off the bark, which we then corded up to dry. George Mare, the owner's son, was in charge of the operation.

After six weeks of work, we got word that wages had been cut twenty percent and the crew went on strike. We were anxious to leave but there was no boat due for several days. We idled the time away washing our clothes and getting our pay checks, which were to be payable at a Port Townsend bank.

Some of the crew including myself, went to the store, where young Mare was also the storekeeper. We took the platform scale down from the counter and proceeded to weigh ourselves. I attempted to lift the scales back to the counter, but the platform pulled loose and the scales dropped to the floor breaking into several pieces. George said, "Chris, that will cost you $15." I replied, "O.K., you can hold it out my check."

I hunted up Gus and told him of my bad luck. He said, " We won't pay it if we can get out of here." There was an Indian smoke house around the point and I volunteered to go and make arrangements for a large sealing canoe to take us to Port Angeles. Two Indians agreed to take ten of us at two dollars apiece. Next morning the canoe landed, and as the men were getting their personal belongings into the canoe, someone suggested we take some lunch with us. We all went to the cook house where the tables were set for dinner and helped ourselves to bread, butter, cold meats, cheese and pie. The cook, a Frenchman, came running after us with a butcher knife. But when we outran him, he turned and ran to the store to tell George. By then we had shoved off, and the two Indians were paddling us out into the bay. George launched a life boat with some other men and started rowing after us shouting for us to come back and settle our damages. He especially wanted me to pay for the scales. We all took to the paddles and soon had outdistanced them.

We stopped at Port Crescent and while on shore some of the boys bought a couple bottles of whiskey. By the time we were half way to Port

Angeles, all were drunk or asleep except 'one Indian, another fellow and myself. We brought the canoe into the bay, landing early Sunday morning near the steamer <u>George E. Starr</u>, which was ready to leave for Seattle, All except the Indians got on board.

Shortly after leaving Port Angeles, the purser came around for our fares. The other fellows paid theirs but Gus and I insisted that our time checks were all we had. The purser refused these, saying he would put us off the boat. He meant it, for when we came close to Port Williams, we were taken ashore in a small boat. A man with a canoe agreed to take us to the head of Washington Harbor, where we followed the trail which took us to Discovery Bay. While having dinner at the mill, we learned that a train carrying railroad officials and passengers from Port Townsend to Quilcene on its maiden run, had passed earlier in the day and would be making the return trip about four o'clock. We walked around the head of the bay to a platform and when the train approached we flagged it down and were taken aboard. The coaches were loaded with passengers and when the conductor asked for our fares, we again tendered our time checks. He returned them with a smile saying, "Boys, anyone who has the nerve to stop the first official train on this newly completed railroad, can ride free to end of the line!" Thus we travelled as guests of the Port Townsend Southern Railroad on its inaugural trip.

Next morning in Port Townsend, Gus and I were at the bank when it opened to cash our checks. We learned later in the day that a telegram had come over the government line from Cape Flattery, advising the bank to hold $15 out of my check. . . the telegram had come too late! That afternoon we boarded a small boat for Seattle.

One of the letters of referral I had with me was from Mr. Day, Manager of the State Bank of New York, where I had worked in the vaults. It was addressed to Mr. F.W.D. Holbrook, Manager of the Seattle, Lake Shore and Eastern Railway Company. We called on Mr. Holbrook and landed jobs on the Lake Washington Belt Line Railway. We were assigned to a construction crew working on a portion of the new line from Renton to Woodinville. About three weeks later, I cut my foot badly so Gus took me to Seattle for treatment. We stayed in town about a week while my foot was healing.

Gus played Faro every night at Clancey's, which was at that time the largest wide-open gambling hall in Seattle. Once I went in to watch him play. He had stacks of money in front of him, mostly $20 gold pieces. He told me it amounted to about $1500. I wanted him to quit but he said, "No, I'm lucky tonight and I will make enough so that we won't have to go back to work. We can go back to our homestead and not have to come out for a while." I left him and went to bed. In the morning, I saw that his bed had not been disturbed. I started looking and found him sitting on a fence post. He was broke, without even the price of breakfast. That night he begged me for money to try his luck again. I gave him $20 and by midnight when I found him, he had a little over $100. I persuaded him to quit and the following night we were on the boat for Pysht. It took five days to reach our homesteads as my foot was not completely healed. We found our cabins and belongings just as we had left them and our little gardens were doing fine.

My Homestead Cabin, Bogachiel River, built 1890

Chapter 7

"Start Of The Pacific Trail"

In the fall of 1890 after returning from Seattle, Gus and I decided a trail should be built from Forks to our settlement on the Bogachiel, a distance of about ten miles. We went down river to seek the co-operation of the three neighbors who agreed that a trail should be built and the sooner the better.

Tools and cooking utensils were taken down the river in our canoe and then to Forks. Groceries and staples were purchased from the LaPush Trading Post, and the Forks settlers, on hearing our plans, were happy to help and donated pork and vegetables. Our base camp was Forks.

Gus and I and one other settler from the Bogachiel started out from Forks to locate and blaze the trail line, keeping a compass direction along the top of a ridge. It took about a week to establish this line. We returned to Forks where we were joined by the other two settlers from the Bogachiel River. Three more men looking for land wanted to join our crew. Six settlers on the Forks Prairie also offered to help. We now had a crew of fourteen, five from the Bogachiel and nine who had never been beyond Forks but were curious about the great unknown wilderness.

Early in January of 1891, two months after starting at Forks, we finished building ten miles of trail through the wilderness jungle to the Bogachiel River. This piece of trail was the first phase of what was later to be called the Pacific Trail.

Everyone was helping to locate new settlers. Some were not satisfied with Forks or the Bogachiel River and wanted to push farther south.

Later in January of 1891 a party of six of us, some looking for new land to settle, left my cabin on the Bogachiel River and struck out in a southerly direction to blaze more trail. The country was flat and densely timbered. Tangled undergrowth and many cedar swamps made progress very slow. For two days we blazed a line along the best going when we came into a wide valley---the valley of the Hoh River. We learned later that we were about eighteen miles above the mouth of the river. Three of our party located on the Hoh and after selecting claims and helping them lay foundations for their homes, we all returned to the Bogachiel and Forks. Another seven miles of the Pacific Trail had been blazed into the western jungle.

Gus and I were not sure in which county our claims were located, so while building trail from Forks to the Bogachiel we decided to petition for

37

for a land survey. Shortly after that we learned that a Mr. Kline from Tacoma had gotten a contract to survey two and one half townships of land in our area. He selected two crews of five men each from the settlers and each crew set to work with a survey engineer. I was a chain man at $40 per month and stayed with the job until it was completed. We learned that the Bogachiel River is partly in Jefferson and partly in Clallam counties and that our homesteads were in Jefferson County. This was disappointing news for those of us whose homesteads were in Jefferson county for that county seat was in Port Townsend, a much farther distance than the Clallam County seat in Port Angeles.

During the following year, 1892, many people found their way to the Bogachiel and Hoh River valleys along the Pacific Trail. Some went up river and some settled toward the mouth of the rivers, but for the time being no one attempted to go any farther south.

Building first trail through Westside of Olympic Jungle Forks to Bogachiel River, 1892

Chapter 8

"Exploring the Headwaters of the Bogachiel River"

I first saw Mt. Olympus and all its surrounding glory in the summer of 1892. My homestead was on the banks of the Bogachiel River and I had a strong urge to follow the river to its source and see the mountains that I had been told lay in the interior.

A neighbor agreed to go along and we estimated the distance to be about twenty-five miles in an easterly direction. We packed our gear and rations accordingly and set out through unknown country.

For many miles we traversed sand bars, canyons, and dense forests of beautiful virgin timber with jungle-like undergrowth. Elk trails were going in and coming out in all directions. Sometimes a trail would follow the river and this made our traveling easy. For three days, at the rate about six miles per day, we followed the river that led us between low hills then higher mountain slopes entirely covered with timber. Douglas fir dominated the south exposure, while hemlock, white fir, a little pine, and cedar dominated the north exposure. The lower valley floor had a liberal stand of Sitka spruce.

On the fourth day we were above the timber, and the vegetation cover gave way to alpine types of scattered trees. By early evening we emerged into a huge park-like basin of open country surrounded by grassy, rock-strewn slopes, some with large snow banks reaching upwards from the basin floor. Here was the headwaters of the south fork of the Bogachiel River.

We sat down near a clump of firs to rest. Slipping off our packs, we stepped forward from the cover of the alpine trees to take a better look. Imagine our surprise and thrill at seeing a huge herd of elk, perhaps close to 200. Most of them were in clusters, lying down on the snow banks while others were feeding or just standing around. We also saw two black bears and two deer. My friend and I sat slowly down and did not move for some time, enjoying this imposing scene. After a while our legs began to cramp so we had to stand up. Our movement was detected by a cow elk and she began to walk slowly toward the forest cover with her calf. Then all the cows with calves began to follow. The bulls sensing alarm, stood at attention looking straight in our direction. A few bulls broke into a run and suddenly the whole herd was stampeding for cover. In less than five minutes the elk had vanished. The only sound was a shrill warning call of a whistling marmot, "watchman of the mountains."

We camped under the shelter of a clump of alpine hemlock, ate supper and rested near the campfire. We talked over the experiences of

39

the day and agreed that our estimate of twenty-five miles to these headwaters was nearly accurate. It was a bright moonlit night and a number of deer were peacefully feeding on the rim of the basin above us. After planning our adventure for the next day, we fell asleep.

Next morning after breakfast we decided to climb the high peak above us. It took two hours to reach the top and what we saw was a superb, breathtaking 360 degree view of the horizon. Looking south not over six miles away, across what had to be the immense Hoh River Valley, was mighty Mount Olympus. To the east was a range of mountain peaks. Still farther to the east and southeast lay a jumble of snow-covered peaks, glaciers and large snow fields. Facing north and directly below us, lay the huge peaceful basin where we had camped the night before. It appeared to be about two miles wide and a thousand to fifteen hundred feet deep. The floor of the basin was covered with loose slide rock from the surrounding high rim. Low hillocks and ridges lay within the basin with scattered clusters of stunted alpine trees on them. This natural amphitheater could easily seat a million spectators. Looking beyond the basin to the northeast were several snow capped peaks, some with glaciers. To the west, some forty miles distant we could see the Pacific Ocean with a tiny ship far out at sea. We turned and faced Mt. Olympus again, this time observing it as a backdrop for the heavily forested Hoh Valley, which lay between us and the mountain. The Hoh River could be seen threading its way through the dense forest like a silver ribbon on its way to the sea.

We stood on this high barren peak a long time, pointing out and locating our surroundings, aware of being, perhaps, the first white men to stand on this spot. I had seen the grandeur of the Swiss and Austrian Alps as a young teenager, but this spectacular sea of mountains with their inspiring beauty filled me with a greater sense of God's awesome power than I had ever had before.

We decided to name this high point where we stood, "Bogachiel Peak". A long snowbank extended down the steep slope into the basin below and seemed to invite a challenge. The sun had softened the surface of the snow, so we sat down and pushed off, sliding on our rear ends, we made good time to the bottom of the basin.

All afternoon we wandered about, exploring and admiring the details of the crater-like basin. Besides the alpine trees there was much heather and an endless variety of flowers, ferns and mosses. We counted seven lakes within the basin. (Footnote 1)

We made camp that night on the shore of a very deep and irregular shaped lake near the north rim of the valley. (Footnote 2) Next morning we climbed the east rim of the basin and found it to be a high divide between the Soleduck and the Hoh Valleys. From that time on, it became know as the "High Divide". This "divide" continued on around the south side of the basin back to Bogachiel Peak where we had been the day before, a jaunt of about three miles. We had seen wild life of all kinds and had counted thirteen alpine lakes within or near-by the basin. Some were connected by waterfalls that had cut deep canyons into the rocky floor. A small band of bull elk, their horns still growing and covered in velvet, grazed in a meadow on the Hoh side of High Divide. These would-be "exalted rulers" seemed to be in executive session, waiting for August or September when regular meetings would be called to settle the business between rival rulers of a herd.

We stood again on the peak, this time noting that Bogachiel Peak with its connecting High Divide, appeared to be the watershed of the Bogachiel, Hoh and Soleduck Rivers. Once more we drank in the spectacular views of the Hoh Valley with Mt. Olympus and its many glaciers as a backdrop, then took the rapid decent on the same snow chute to our base camp in the basin below. Here we spent our final night before returning to our homesteads. We were satisfied that we had solved some of the mysteries of the unknown wilderness. We had traced the Bogachiel to its source as planned, but had not located any farming or grazing land that many of the settlers in the low country had hoped there would be.

The grandeur and beauty I had seen became indelibly etched on my mind and was the beginning of a love affair with the Olympic Mountains that continued the rest of my life.

Footnote 1: The basin which we had explored, we did not name at that time but on a later visit in 1900 by Bill Stewart and myself. We referred to it as the "Basin of the Seven Lakes", and it is known today as "Seven Lakes Basin." About 1924, the Forest Service in co-operation with the county Game Commission, stocked four of these lakes with Brook and Montana Black Trout. In 1936, the National Park Service completed stocking the rest of these lakes with trout. . Chris Morgenroth.
Footnote 2: Probably Lake Morgenroth. . . . Editor

High Divide and Bogachiel Peak

Chapter 9

"Locating Trail, Hoh to Queets"

News had come that a settlement was being established south of the Hoh River. These settlers were coming by boat from Tacoma to the mouth of the Queets River, and from there they traveled inland. It now seemed logical that a trail should be located south of the Hoh River to the Queets River. The settlers on both the Bogachiel and the Hoh asked for help from Jefferson County. Ed Walker, the county engineer, was sent to locate a permanent grade line that would eventually be a wagon road connecting all west side settlements from the Bogachiel to the Queets River. We organized a crew of seven men including Mr. Walker. Jefferson County paid for the provisions, which were brought by canoe up the Bogachiel River from LaPush. This was early December of 1892, and I was now twenty-one years old.

We located a new line between the Bogachiel and Hoh Rivers about one mile west of our original Pacific Trail. At the Hoh, we crossed just above Hell Roaring Creek and struck out for eight miles up Winfield Creek to its head in an unknown jungle.

Our first camp was located back on the Hoh River and since provisions were getting low, two men were sent back to bring up the remainder of our supplies. Cornelius Huelsdonk, a new settler on the Hoh, and I volunteered to explore the country ahead.. We had almost continuous rains and everything was very wet, including our blankets.

Cornelius and I struck south through the jungle and found a creek running northwest, which today is called Nolan Creek. A ridge to the south looked inviting, so we climbed through heavy timber to the top to get a better view. The top of the ridge was still so heavily timbered that we could see nothing, so we felled a few of the smaller trees on the south slope for an opening. This still didn't help, so I climbed a large tree and from the top had a good view to the south and west. Cornelius had pencil and paper, so as I gave him the "lay of the land" and directions with my little pocket compass, he made a crude map of the hills, creeks and valleys. There was no opening or break in the timber as far as I could see. About six miles to the south lay a large valley which we decided was our objective, the Queets. A fair sized creek could be traced from this valley to about a mile west of our position. This information should make our going a little easier.

I came down from my perch and we discussed the map. It was the first map of the vicinity and proved to be a great help in our advance toward the Queets. We continued on eastward along the top of this ridge, observing that there were many short ridges running in every direction from the apex of our ridge. We decided to name this ridge "Mt. Octopus". We descended into a broad level valley and followed a creek which flowed south. This creek had been named Snahapish by the Indians. The timber here was the best quality that I had seen so far. We camped for the night here and named the area Snahapish Valley.

The next day, Cornelius and I headed back hoping to find the main camp. We had been traveling north then guessed we should turn west. It had rained all day and at times the wind blew very hard, but we dared not stop as we had no food and were soaking wet. Just before dark we smelled smoke so we followed it, shouting out for someone to hear us. Our calls were answered and we were guided into camp. Our sense of direction had been near accurate. We were glad to be back and all we wanted was to get warm, dry out and get some food.

The packers had not yet returned with supplies, so we rested all the next day.

The following day was Christmas, and about an inch of wet snow had fallen. I decided to take a short hunting trip alone to where Cornelius and I had struck the foot of Mt. Octopus. I picked up bear tracks going south, and followed them to a creek where I overtook and killed the bear. This was the same creek that I had spotted from the tree on Mt. Octopus and which I thought flowed into the Queets River. I named the creek "Christmas Creek." I took a good load of the bear meat back to camp, and when the packers returned the next day with vegetables, everyone had plenty of Mulligan stew.

Our crew resumed trail locating following down Christmas Creek to its junction with a large river. We did not believe this to be the Queets River as we had been told that the Queets was milky white water from the glaciers on Mt. Olympus. This river was running clear, and was not as large as we had heard the Queets to be. We learned later that it was called the Clearwater River, a tributary of the Queets.

We made camp at the junction where Christmas Creek emptied into the Clearwater. Our provisions were beginning to run out again but we were too deep into unknown country to send anyone back for supplies. A heavy torrential rain began to fall. This melted the snow and we could see the river beginning to rise. We knew we would have to cross quickly or be cut off from our destination. We felled a spruce tree over the river and one of the fellows and I managed to get to an island sandbar, then forded the rest of the way up to our armpits in the swift current. Before the others could follow, the tree was swept downstream, leaving them stranded. They went down river a few hundred yards and felled another tree, which held just long enough for all of them to get across safely. Once

43

we were reunited on the other side of the river, we built a fire, made camp, ate short rations, and then bedded down for a very wet night. We heard a fog horn to the west so we consoled ourselves that we were close to the coast.

By morning the rain had stopped. Everything was soaked and we were weak from lack of food. Our laborious struggle through the heavy undergrowth had slowed our progress and our supplies were exhausted. All we had left was coffee and lard. After drinking the last of the coffee, we pressed on to the south.

We reached a small creek, this one barely three feet wide. There, thrashing its way upstream, we spied a big thirty-six inch long salmon. Like a pack of hungry wolves, we made excited preparation for its capture. One man sat down in the water to dam the stream below the salmon, while another blocked the way above, and the rest of us prepared sharp poles to spear our prey. But when we finally captured the fish, we found it was bruised and worn out from its long spawning journey up this rocky creek. Two of us grabbed the fish and threw it out onto the bank. It was nearly dead and could hardly flap its tail. The flesh was torn, fins half gone, it was covered with leprous spots, and yet to our hungry bunch, it was the finest fish we had ever seen. Our spirits were raised 100 percent. Everyone was for camping right there and enjoying barbecued salmon but we decided to get our bearings before the fog drifted in. From a rise of ground we could see the river, barely a half mile away. Then we saw smoke and heard a rooster crow. I yelled, "Come on boys, throw away that darned fish, there are settlers ahead!" As we neared the river we could hear the chopping of wood. We began whooping and yelling for joy as we charged through the brush to a clearing on the river bank. Here we came face to face with two men on the opposite shore, with rifles aimed and ready to fire, We screamed, "for God's sake, don't shoot!" Within minutes they had us poled across the river in an old canoe.

They said they were the McKinnon family and apologized for the unfriendly welcome. They thought a herd of elk was being chased by a pack of wolves. They needed meat and were ready to shoot and were dumbfounded when seven men came crashing out of the brush!

We explained our survey mission, how we had missed our direction and run out of rations. Mr. McKinnon said this was the Queets River and they had been there only three months. He had just finished his cabin and the day before had brought his family, provisions and a couple dozen chickens to the homestead. He said his wife had fled to the house but would be glad to give us some dinner. One of our men was still carrying the spotted salmon. I told him to get rid of it, that we were going to have fried chicken instead.

44

Our clothes were torn to shreds and two of the men needed overalls. The rest of us made ourselves decent with soap, water, needle and thread. After a while we were introduced to Mrs. McKinnon who was preparing the meal. We sat down on benches around a homemade table. On each tin plate was a potato and a piece of hard tack. In the center of table was a cedar shake which held our "planked" salmon, burned to a crisp and still showing some of its leprous spots around the edges! We were no less thankful than if it had been fried chicken and we did eat heartily.

Next day, Mr. McKinnon took Mr. Walker and me down river in his canoe to a little store which had just gotten started. Mr. Walker gave an order for food and clothing to be paid by Jefferson County, and we poled the canoe back up river to McKinnon's homestead.

After a few days rest, we hired Indians to take us and our supplies up the Clearwater River to Christmas Creek. From there, we finished locating our line down the Clearwater River to its confluence with the Queets. At this time there was not one settler on the Clearwater River, but several found their way along this stream the following spring.

When our survey was completed, we all went to the mouth of the Queets River and began our long foot journey up the beach to the mouth of the Hoh River, a distance of approximately thirty miles. We followed up the Hoh River then cross-country on our blaze line to the Bogachiel and our starting point. We had been gone sixty days and had pierced the last unknown jungle of the western United States, locating and surveying some sixty miles of trail between the Bogachiel and Queets Rivers.

During the next two years, the settlers of the Bogachiel, Hoh and Queets rivers built the trail along this survey line. This trail, together with ones we had built from Forks to the Bogachiel and the Hoh, became known as the Pacific Trail. In time this trail was widened into a wagon road. It was the settlers hope that some day this route would become the main road connecting all of western Jefferson and Clallam Counties.

Thirty-nine years later, in 1931, the Olympic Peninsula Highway was completed around the western part of the Olympic Peninsula. While not built on exactly our original location, its direction and destination was the same. I attended the ribbon-cutting ceremonies of this scenic piece of state highway on August 27, 1931 with Governor Roland H. Hartley presiding. It was attended by a few of the original white settlers, and some members of the coastal Indian tribes. As I wandered through the crowds, I was greatly saddened to find so few pioneers of the 1890's there, and none of that original locating crew except myself. This western portion of the Olympic Highway is a memorial to the early pioneers who settled there and worked so hard building the trails and the wagon roads that opened up the west.

45

Chapter 10

"Rugged Life Of Bogachiel and Hoh Pioneers"

The earliest white settlers who homesteaded along the Bogachiel and Hoh Rivers came between 1889 and 1897. These pioneers were hardy individuals, full of curiosity, a will to conquer adversity and a spirit of co-operation necessary to survive.

They were attracted by free land and a temperate climate. The land could be acquired from the U.S. Government which required a homesteader to live on his land for three years and at the end of that time to have one-eighth of his claim cleared and under cultivation. The temperate climate included a heavy rainfall averaging 90 to 140 inches a year. Just fifty miles to the north at Neah Bay and Cape Flattery, the average annual rainfall is 150 to 188 inches a year. Snowfall in these near sea-level valleys is very wet and rarely stays on the ground more than a few days either being melted by warm rains or Chinook winds.

The rivers that drain the western side of the Olympics traverse the level valley floors for some thirty to forty miles after leaving the mountains on their way to the ocean. Broad gravel bars that form in the middle of the rivers are channelled with small streams. Young alders, willow and cottonwood trees grow on these gravel bars causing great piles of logs to be windrowed during high water every little ways as one proceeds up river. This forces the river to meander from year to year and from one side of its banks to the other. For this reason the early settlers like myself who were located on the fertile river benches, built our cabins well back from the edge of the stream.

Most of the early settlers maintained homes on their claims. Some on the Hoh River made their homes inside large spruce logs, burnt hollow. One of them had a log seventeen feet in diameter and about forty feet long, partitioned off into three compartments. Woodshed in one end, barn, with room for one cow and hay in the other end, and living room in the middle.

The only transportation that the earliest pioneers had was by foot over primitive trails or by poling supplies in an Indian dugout canoe up river from the nearest trading post which in my case was at LaPush on the ocean twenty miles away. Sometimes the heavily loaded canoes would upset with total loss of cargo and even damage to the canoe.

Farming was slow, hard work in this timbered country, where the undergrowth was like a jungle. Only enough garden produce was raised for home consumption. There was no market for our produce as there was no large town near our forest wilderness. Forks was only ten miles distant from my place but those setters raised their own produce and were completely self-sufficient except for the same staples we all depended on from the trading post.

Nearly all of us had a few head of cattle. In the spring and summer they browsed on young underbrush, weeds and grasses along the river bottoms and bench lands. Some of the cattle withstood the winter grazing on the river benches and the lower hills, seeking shelter in the forest during storms. They browsed on black stem and other ferns and dried grasses and unless it was a very severe winter they came out in good shape in the spring. Occasionally a few head of cattle which could be driven out over the trails, could be sold.

Many settlers supplemented the family income by working away from home part of the year. In the late 1890's the logging operation at Port Crescent was a popular place for earning these extra dollars. To reach this destination the settler took a well worn Indian foot trail from Forks to Lake Crescent. Here he hired a canoe to take him to the north end of the lake at Piedmont where he hiked another twelve miles to Port Crescent. The return trip back home was just as long a journey.

My land fronted on the banks of the swift flowing Bogachiel River. There was a natural clearing, circular in shape, extending back toward the forest giants. This clearing carried a thick stand of high grass and had been the favorite stomping ground of a herd of elk in the old days and was one of the reasons I had first been attracted to the place. My first home was a one room cabin which I built well back from the river's edge. By the mid-nineties I had a roomy house, a large barn, a thriving vegetable garden and an orchard with pear and apple trees. The whole area had to be fenced to keep out the deer and elk.

Near the edge of the forest on my land was a Douglas fir tree which was eleven feet in diameter. I later discovered it to be one of the largest of its kind in the Olympic forest. There were others on my land averaging nine feet in diameter and holding their size very well for the first 200 feet. Huge Sitka spruce and western cedar also of considerable size were numerous in the surrounding woods. Spruce are easily identified as their tops seem to break off in the high winds that move inland from the ocean. I recall a cyclone in 1901 that took out a quarter mile of spruce near my place about Christmas time, killing nine head of my cattle. One bull I found had been in the act of jumping over a log as a tree struck, literally cutting him in two. Everywhere on the river banks young spruce trees grow with beautiful plumy blue-green stems still tender and soft to the touch. As these young trees mature this foliage develops into sharp needles. Wherever there is a clearing on the benchland along the rivers you will find huckleberry and salmonberry bushes and large clumps of

47

wild blackberry bushes, eight to ten feet high. Swampy places are filled with patches of devil's club, a large rangy exotic-looking shrub with giant maple-like leaves whose undersides and stems are covered with needle-like thorns.   In the deep shade under the forest cover the ground is carpeted with oxalis, a kind of sorrel having a three-part leaf and violet-like white flowers. Mingling among the ground mosses and oxalis are deer fern whose lower fronds spread out flat on the ground with the central core of fronds extending straight up and ending in curls at the top. Huge sword fern clumps are everywhere. Great quantities of green moss hang from the giant western maples and embrace their trunks like a thick down comforter. A wiry whisker-like gray moss called "old man's beard", hangs from the arching limbs of the vine maples and the struggling young hemlocks. This lush vegetation is due to the heavy rainfall.

On the west side of the Olympic Range along the Bogachiel, Hoh and Queets river valleys, elk were plentiful because they had never been hunted in this area for their teeth and antlers. The Indians killed elk for years before the white man came but only for meat and hides. They never came close to exterminating them for they knew from instinct that perpetuation of the herds was necessary for a balance of nature.

Other wild game available to the settler were deer, bear, grouse, pheasant and quail. Numerous small fur-bearing animals were trapped along the steams and mountain sides. These included marmot, beaver, weasel, squirrel, skunk, raccoon and bobcat. Predatory animals were cougar and timber wolf and were usually tracked by dogs. These animals were a menace to the settler's livestock so the state paid a bounty for their capture. Many early settlers became expert bounty hunters. I was never a trapper or a bounty hunter.

The rivers were full of fish all year round with varieties of stream trout, salmon and steelhead. The Bogachiel, I soon discovered was a superb fishing stream. Unlike the Hoh and Queets Rivers, which were milky glacier-fed streams, the Bogachiel was clear except for being muddied by a heavy rainfall. No stream in the Olympics can compare with it for fishing. I found the best method for catching the great fighting steelhead was to ride a pony out into the middle of the stream and fish downstream from his back. That way I never had to get wet as the pony was far more sure-footed than I. Fastening the fishline to the saddlehorn was an advantage too.

The following account of the Huelsdonk family will give my reader some idea of the spirit of endurance and courage that was necessary to raise a family in this harsh and remote wilderness. This is a success story.

Chapter 11

"The Iron Man of the Hoh"

In 1891, Cornelius Huelsdonk settled two miles west of Lake Crescent on the divide between the Soleduck River and the lake. This was a very heavily timbered area, except for five acres of swamp which he hoped to drain and bring under cultivation.

Cornelius started to dig a deep drainage ditch on the Soleduck side of the ridge which was a slow one-man job. Fortunately Cornelius' brother, John, came from Iowa that summer and together they finished it. The ditch began to do its job and the swampy water poured out, but they found that many unforeseen deep places could not be drained. This was discouraging because it meant that their land could never be farmed.

The Huelsdonk brothers were determined pioneers, they had come from a farm in Iowa and it was farm land they were hunting. They heard that settlers were claiming land farther west in the valleys of the Bogachiel and Hoh. When they learned that these rivers discharged directly into the Pacific, they were excited. A river connection to the ocean meant a means of transportation that would connect them with sea-going vessels. Without second thought, they decided to move on and take a chance of finding suitable locations on river bottom land. Forks was the nearest settlement, thirty miles to the west of their swampy home but there was no trail connecting the two points. The Huelsdonks, however, decided trail or no trail, they were heading west.

Cornelius had a small trunk into which they packed all of their belongings. They set out one morning in a southwesterly direction, rifles in hand and slinging the trunk on a pole between them. It was a back-breaking job, trudging through the dense forest and heavy underbrush. On the second day they came to a small river. This was the north fork of the Calawah River. They followed down its channel and found the traveling considerably easier.

On the fourth day, they saw the first opening in the unbroken forest. Leaving the river they climbed the bench and found an extensive prairie of about two thousand acres. Cabins with smoke coming out of the chimneys, were clustered together. The cabins were surrounded by fields of oats and potatoes. This was the settlement of Forks which had been the most remote settlement of whites in the area until 1890 when Gus and I, and a few others claimed land on the Bogachiel River.

The brothers carried their awkward load to the nearest farm house where they were invited to stay for a few days. It soon was noised about that two new settlers had arrived which meant more land would be

49

cleared, more trails built and more people would be attracted to tame the Olympic wilderness.

When it was learned that the Huelsdonks were looking for bottom land, they were advised to take our new trail to the Bogachiel River.

They left their trunk in Forks, taking axes, rifles, blankets, and provisions and headed south on the new Pacific Trail. When they reached the Bogachiel they learned that seven more miles of trail had been blazed south to the Hoh River. It took all the next day to reach the Hoh River, where the next day they followed the river up stream for about ten miles. Cornelius liked the looks of the extensive bottom land and decided to locate his claim here. The next day they crossed the river in a narrow place on a big log and continued up the south side of the river for about a mile. They came upon more bottom land with vine maples, large spruce trees, good glacial silt soil, and a clear large spring. This furnished all the specification for a future home-site for John, He and Cornelius placed four logs as a cabin foundation and laid claim to this land be tacking a notice on a tree.

They returned to Forks for their trunk and more provisions and tools. These loads were large and heavy and had to be back-packed twenty-five miles to their claims. The first ten miles of this journey from Forks was on trail but the last fifteen miles was through primitive wilderness.

John and Cornelius built their cabins that year, then cleared about one-half acre on John's place for spring planting. John kept on clearing and improving his little farm. He was building trail at the same time down river for the ten miles to connect with the Hoh to Bogachiel Trail. Two other parties settled about six miles below John on the north side of the river, but no one ever settled beyond the Huelsdonks on the south side.

In the summer of 1892 John went back to his old home in Iowa for a few months. While there he married his childhood friend Dora and they started the long journey back to their new home on the Hoh. John hiked and she rode horseback from Pysht to Forks, then together they hiked the twenty-five miles of primitive trail to John's canoe landing on the Hoh. There he ferried his bride to the far side of the river and their new home. Dora had never seen such unbroken forests and jungles. What her thought might have been, it did not matter, for John had worked hard to prepare this wilderness home for her and he was now by her side. They would face together whatever hardships might come.

John grew all kinds of vegetables very successfully. Game was plentiful and the pelts of fur-bearing animals furnished the basis for exchange at the LaPush trading store. He hunted and trapped such animals as bear, wild cat, cougar, wolf, raccoon, mink and martin. This enabled him to buy staples and other supplies which had to poled by canoe twenty miles up the Bogachiel River to Forks then packed over land to the Hoh and again poled ten miles upstream to John's home.

John and Cornelius soon learned from settlers on the lower Hoh that Indians would transport supplies by ocean canoe from the LaPush Trading Post down the coast to the mouth of the Hoh River. Hoh settlers including John, who had their own river canoes, could then pole their supplies to their homesteads upriver. The distance from the mouth of the Hoh to John's place was thirty miles, which was an appreciably shorter trip. The average fall of water was about thirty feet per mile making the journey treacherous, and many canoes upset in the swift current. This happened to the Huelsdonk brothers once while poling an eight-hundred pound load to their homesteads. An accident of this kind was a great financial loss and necessitated leaving home to earn a new grubstake in some far away logging camp like Port Crescent of Clallam Bay.

Soon after Dora arrived on the Hoh, another brother of John's, Henry, came from Iowa and settled nearby on the north side of the river.

In 1893 a baby girl, Lena, was born to John and Dora. At this time Dora was the only woman living on the Hoh and there was no doctor or hospital within a hundred and fifty miles. The only people she had to help in the birth were her husband John, her brother-in-law Henry, who had read up on such matters, and a neighbor who lived fifteen miles down river named Mr. Hamilton. The delivery was successful and in due course of time three other girls were born with father John being the only attending doctor.

By the mid 1890's the Huelsdonks had accumulated some cattle, a few sheep and two horses. Their clearing had grown to about six acres. Soon after John and Cornelius settled on the Hoh, another brother, Henry, came from Iowa and settled nearby on the northside of the river. Eventually John's mother, father and two younger brothers moved out from Iowa, and took another homestead adjoining John's. The clearings were enlarged and for many years wheat and rye were grown, and part of their flour was ground from this at home with a hand mill.

Anyone wishing to cross to the Huelsdonk place had to go to the river and yell at the top of his voice, because John's house was back in the woods, a quarter of a mile from the river. You waited and if he was at home and heard you, he would emerge from the brush, cross the gravel bar to the river, push the canoe out into the swift current and pole across to pick you up. There was only enough room for two passengers and you would be told to sit down as he maneuvered the little craft back into the swirling rapids. The water is white with silt and shows no bottom, even near shore. Your nerves would be tense and you would instinctively grip the sides of the canoe. John would warn you that no good sailor should do this and at the same time assure you he was an expert boatman and had never upset any passengers. On reaching the opposite shore, you would be guided along a trail through the woods to the farm house, where you would meet his good, smiling wife, Dora.

The four Huelsdonk daughters received their grammar and high school education in a little one-room school house on the old homestead. Al four graduated from the University of Washington and all married sons of pioneers of the Olympic Peninsula.

How did John and Dora manage to give these girls a university education? They raised and sold cattle, sheep and turkeys and in the winter John made good money by trapping and hunting cougar and bobcats for bounties. The girls also made money by filling orders from the county game commissioner for baby elk. They would go into the forest and find a newborn calf and when the mother elk was away feeding they would bring the calf home and feed it on cow's milk for about four weeks. When these baby elk were big and strong enough they were driven over the trail like cattle to Forks. About forty young elk were brought out this way and planted in other parts of Washington and Alaska.

Following are a few true incidents describing the rugged character of John Huelsdonk.

In 1891, shortly after John had settled on the Hoh River, I was on my way to Forks from the Bogachiel to get a load of supplies. I met John coming up a steep hill on the trail carrying what appeared to be a very heavy pack which was covered with his coat. We stopped to talk and he suggested we sit down on a log to rest saying his pack was a #7 cast iron stove. I knew this size stove weighed about 110 pounds, so I said, "You must have a heavy load." He replied, "Yes, it is heavy but I don't mind carrying the stove, it is the fifty pound sack of sugar in the oven that keeps shifting around that is giving me the trouble." He carried this load twenty-five miles from Forks to his home on the Hoh.

Another time, he hired out on a survey crew that had a contract with the county to sectionize a township. Survey parties included two packers who each day would travel about two miles ahead of the survey crew. They were responsible for packing all the provisions, setting up camp and cooking the meals. John was hired as a packer at $40 a month and he asked to do the job alone, providing they pay him the wages of two men. The crew boss agreed and John efficiently did the work of two men at double the pay!

When his girls were going through the University, John was hard pressed to meet these extra expenses including his taxes one year. He met a man on the trail who had come from the Upper Clearwater River who said he had seen fresh large cougar tracks in Snahapish Pass, about six miles from the Hoh. They parted and John decided he had to get that cougar.

Next morning at daybreak, he left home with his two trustworthy dogs. Near noon the dogs took a track and followed it.. When the track got warm they started barking and suddenly they came to a halt and barked "treed". When John reached the spot, he shot down the cougar but it was only half grown and could not be the big one the Clearwater man had seen. The other dog was now barking up another tree about one hundred yards away. John went over and shot down another small cougar. He circled hoping to find the old one, but had not gone far when again the dogs barked "treed". John took aim and brought down a third small cougar. He thought this good business, but wanted the big one. While collecting his three cats, the dogs informed him that they had treed the fourth cat. When it was shot down, it also proved to be another small one. He knew the big female was somewhere near and that there would be no more small cats, for a cougar rarely has over four young. While making a wide sweep of the area, the older dog picked up the track and shortly barked treed. It was the big cat this time, and John dispatched him as quickly as he had done the other four.

Five cougars was a considerable skinning job. When John came home late that night he was very tired but rejoicing was great. The $20 bounty for each cat plus the price of five skins would solve the tax and tuition problem in the Huelsdonk household for that year.

Another story concerns a bear hunt by John and a neighbor named Pete Brandeberry. With John's two dogs the men went up river about six miles one morning to see what easy money might be wandering about. The dogs came across the track of a wild cat and treed the animal some distance away. By the time the two men reached the tree and killed the cat, they heard the dogs barking furiously, as if fighting something. The men ran as fast as they could and found the dogs fighting with a large black bear. After shooting the bear they found one dog had a badly lacerated hind leg. They bandaged the dog's leg, skinned the bear and the wild cat and started down river towards home. The wounded dog had to be carried most of the time. About three miles down river the other dog turned up missing. Brandeberry took the pack of skins and the wounded dog and continued on down river while John went back to find the other dog. A short distance up John found the dog barking into the shell of an old rotten log. The roots of a tree had grown over the log forming a large chamber and in this sat a big black bear. John pulled the dog clear of the entrance, stuck his rifle in and fired. All was still, so he decided he had killed the bear. It was getting late, so he and the dog went down river and caught up with Pete. They decided to camp for the night. Next morning they tied up the dogs and taking a hatchet and candle went back up river to the bear. Pete being the smaller of the two men, elected to crawl into the bear's den and pull the bear out. He fastened a rope to the dead bear's head and backed out. The two men pulled with all their strength, but the bear did not budge. Again, Pete crawled into the den, squeezing past the bear in order to push while John pulled, but nothing happened. John passed the hatchet to Pete so he could chop away some roots and make a bigger hole. He also passed the candle so Pete could see what he was doing. Pete was working with the hatchet when he smelled smoke. Some of the powder-dry rotten wood had caught fire! Pete couldn't get out as the fire was between him and the entrance, so John ran to a near-by creek, filled his hat with water, ran back and forced it past the bear's body. John had to make several trips for water before Pete could get the fire completely out. John again pulled on the rope while Pete pushed from within. Finally the bear came out and so did Pete, but it had been a close call. Upon examining the bear they found the reason for all the trouble, the bear's body had bloated during the night. After skinning their prize, Pete and John decided they had had enough excitement for one trip. They returned to the dogs and continued down river to home. One large cougar skin and two bear skins was pretty good "easy money" for one and a half day's effort. They had to admit that the second bear did give them some trouble.

Another time much later in his life John and his two dogs had another narrow escape a short distance south of his home. He was trying to locate a cougar that had been troubling his live stock. The dogs instead startled a bear and brought him to bay on the ground. John did not want to kill the bear and was trying to pull the dogs off. The bear made no distinction between dogs and man and in the midst of the rampage, the enraged bear got John by the leg, biting and tearing it severely. He dared not shoot for fear of killing one of the dogs. John was able to hang onto his rifle and finally one of the dogs got hold of the bear's hind quarters which forced the bear to relinquish its hold on John. This gave John a moment to make a well-placed shot and the bear lost the battle. John dragged himself home and was taken to the Forks Hospital. Four weeks later he was ready for new adventures.

John and Dora Huelsdonk were young and full of ambition and hope when they tackled the seemingly unconquerable wilderness of the western Olympic Peninsula. Many other young settlers who came and made claim became discouraged with the hard-ships they had to endure. They would sell out to timber companies and then disappear. Few stuck it out like the Huelsdonks, and none were as isolated. Mrs. Huelsdonk rarely saw women other than her own daughters. There were no settlers on her side of the Hoh and she seldom crossed the treacherous river.

The partnership of this loving couple was outstanding. Their world was the Hoh River, and here they passed the dangerous currents of the river of life together. The name of "Iron Man and Woman of the Hoh" is well earned by both. However, beneath their "iron" constitutions, beat two hearts of gold. They never refused rest, shelter or food to the occasional stranger or visitor passing their way. The latch-string was always out and your money was no good in their home. I was indeed proud to number them among my tried and true good friends of long standing.

Suspension Bridge, over the Bogachiel River.
Built by early homesteaders, 280 ft. long.

"Lower Hoh Limited" Export Company, John and Henry Huelsdonk, late 1890's

Part III

Preface: Ten Years of Adventure, 1893-1903

A different drummer sounded a call in 1893 and Chris took to sea in search of adventure. In the following three separate episodes he describes a seal hunt with Indians in the open Pacific, a brush with death on a whaling canoe trip from LaPush to Neah Bay, and a three month adventure on a schooner to the sealing grounds in the Bering Sea.

After returning in the fall of 1896 from his great Alaskan adventure, he applied for and was granted, his final citizenship papers in Seattle. Shortly afterwards he was sworn in as Constable of western Jefferson County. This assignment proved to be more annoying than rewarding and lasted six years. He writes of one episode as constable.

An old diary of 1897 and 1898 briefly records three hunting trips up the Elwha Valley. The spelling and grammar are as they appeared in the diary.

On February 22, 1897, a proclamation creating the Olympic Forest Reserve was signed by President Grover Cleveland. This Reserve comprised 2,162,000 acres and included the whole group of Olympic Mountains with their slopes to the north, east, and south and the long slope to the western lowlands extending to the Pacific Ocean, except for Indian Reservations. Creation of forest reserves was the first step taken by the government to conserve, protect and preserve America's forest from waste and destruction, but it was also the beginning of a see-saw fight between the federal government, state government and the private sector over land control on the Olympic Peninsula. Creation of Olympic Reserve was to have a greater impact on Chris's future than any other single factor.

In the spring of 1898 the Department of Interior ordered a Geological Survey of the new reserve and Theodore F. Rixon, a timber cruiser and engineer, and Arthur Dodwell, a surveyor, were hired to do the job. With a crew of four others they worked year-round for the next two years surveying and cruising the lowland areas in the winter, then going to higher elevations as the weather warmed and the snows melted. Their work carried them to many of the mountain peaks, and to the headwaters of every major stream in the Olympics. They mapped and cruised over 3,000 square miles which included parts of Clallam, Jefferson and Mason Counties. The report described the principal rivers rising in the higher mountains and fed by perpetual snow and glaciers. The largest river was the Hoh which drained the central mass of Mt. Olympus, the highest peak of the group, near 8,000 feet in altitude, covered with many

56

glaciers. One of the most important revelations from the Dodwell-Rixon Survey was the denseness of the vast stands of timber and the wealth that lay in this resource. The government credited these men as being trained observers in their profession. Dodwell-Rixon Pass at the headwaters of the Elwha and Queets River Basin was named for them.

After the publicity on the Dodwell-Rixon Survey, Chris's soul was again stirred to adventure. He recounts two exploration trips up the north and south forks of the Hoh River to the foot of Mount Olympus, an Indian legend, and elk and cougar stories. This time frame of ten years from 1893 to 1903 seems to portray a free spirit in search of direction.

Around 1900 Chris took an Indian wife. They had a daughter and a son. Chris's ranger duties took him away from home a good deal of the time. Life was lonely since she seldom saw her family and friends. It became harder and harder to adjust to this harsh environment. After a few years she took the children and returned to the reservation, and the marriage was dissolved in 1907.

Mt. Olympus, looking south from Bogachiel Peak

A fast descent into Seven Lakes Basin

Chapter 12

"Seal Hunting Off the Pacific Coast"

Fur seals migrate between the coast of central California and the Bering Sea off the coast of Alaska. In early March the forerunners of the herds appear off the shores of California, feeding, playing, and traveling in a northwesterly line up the Pacific Coast towards the land of their birth, the Pribilof Islands. The main migration lasts through April and May. Seal hunting by coastal Indians takes place during these two months in the 100 mile stretch of open sea between the mouth of the Queets River and Cape Flattery. Here the seals approach nearest to land, their line of northerly migration being about thirty to fifty miles off shore.

The body of the fur seal is round and streamlined so that it slides through the weather easily. Most swim on their backs and can travel long distances under water from ten to thirty minutes. They live entirely on fish which they have no difficulty in capturing. Mature female seals weigh from forty pounds to one hundred and twenty-five pounds. Males get to be much larger. I have seen exceptionally large old bulls weighing over three-hundred pounds.

The sealing canoe used by the Indians was a smaller version of the whaling canoe and was made out of one cedar log about five feet in diameter and about eighteen feet long. This log was split in two, lengthwise, each half being large enough to make a single canoe. The outside of the log would first be shaped to give it proper seaworthy lines, then the inside of the log would be dug out, leaving about one and a half inches of thickness on the sides and about three inches of thickness on the bottom. Both inside and outside would be made perfectly smooth with a small hand adz and plane. Several braces would be fitted across the inside to add strength. The outer surface and bottom would be burned and charred with cedar faggots, rubbed off with burlap and treated to a coating of hot tallow, which would readily be absorbed by the soft wood. This insured smooth and noiseless gliding through the water when approaching sleeping seals. A mast and sail were fitted to one of the cross braces and this, together with three paddles made of very thin and pliable hardwood in the hands of the crew of three, furnished the motive power.

According to law, the Indians could only hunt the seal the same as their forefathers did before the white man came. They never used firearms, instead their weapon was a harpoon on the end of a spear which was about fifteen feet long. Two hardwood prongs were fitted closely to the front end. Bone sockets fit the spear prongs and attached to the sockets were two harpoons made of steel points. These sockets detach themselves when the harpoon finds its mark. The harpoons are fastened to a stout sealing line about seventy-five feet long and the end of this line is fastened to one of the braces in the canoe. The spear is thrown much the same as an athlete throws a javelin, except he holds a coil of line in his other hand so it will run out freely. When the spear is thrown and the harpoon enters the body of the seal, it becomes detached and the pole floats to the surface to be picked up later. The seal will dive and struggle. Then the spearman will haul in on the line and bring the seal close to the canoe for a fatal blow on the head with a hardwood club provided for that purpose. If the harpoon is only embedded in the skin, it will be a long fight to bring the seal in close for the kill.

In the spring of 1893, I had the opportunity to go seal hunting off the Washington coast with Indian hunters. I was anxious to go for I knew it would be an exciting and valuable experience.

We left shore at LaPush, a coastal settlement on the Quileute Indian Reservation, about 3:00 a.m. with a fresh "mokah" (east wind). After pushing off through the breakers we set sail due west into the Pacific Ocean. After six hours of strong paddling we reached the outskirts of the sealing grounds, some thirty miles from shore. We carried no compass using only landmarks as a guide with the high snow peak of Mt. Olympus as our main landmark.

Indians rarely ventured beyond sight of land. On occasion a canoe might be lost in the fog, lose sight of land or be overcome by a storm and blown out to sea. Some were lucky enough to be picked up by sailing ships or steamers and put ashore near their village or the nearest port. Those that never came back were greatly mourned by friends and relatives and those that did return after many months, as from the dead, were given a great celebration.

We sighted our first seals about ten in the morning. Two of them lying side by side on their backs, with their flippers folded over their breast, were asleep and snoring, gently rocking with the motion of the waves. Our sail had been taken down and the steerman (oputsh) was noiselessly bringing the canoe to the leeward side of the seals. The spearman was poised with spear in hand and one knee braced against the bow of the canoe. Not a word had been spoken and the canoe approached quietly towards the unsuspecting seals. About thirty feet from the seals, the spear was thrown. The lower harpoon buried itself deeply in the seal's body, but the upper prong failed to reach the second seal. Both animals immediately disappeared under the water. The one seal being mortally wounded, was brought up about ten feet from the canoe and showed little fight. When hauled over the side it was easily put out of its misery by a few well-directed blows. The spearman extracted his harpoon, put his line and spear in order, and was ready for another kill.

We saw many seals that day, most of them awake and traveling. Sometimes we saw as many as six in a row asleep; however, one of them usually wakened and all would disappear before reaching harpooning distance. We were fairly successful on this first trip out, taking six seals. Some gave us plenty of trouble and one nearly upset our canoe.

We set sail for shore in early afternoon. The wind was very brisk from the west now and our snow peak landmark grew rapidly larger. The foothills and then the shoreline became visible and we landed through the surf about six in the evening. Dozens of other canoes were also coming ashore.

Five of the seals out of our catch of six were mature females. One of these was slashed opened by the spearman shortly after being taken and disclosed a nearly mature pup. This little baby seal was still alive when we reached shore and was crying like a human baby. All the live pups that were brought in were given to Indian children to play with. The children took them to a fresh water lagoon to wash off the sand and to try to make them swim. The little pups not being able to swim soon drowned, thus being saved from further misery. Some of the other canoes brought in as many as twelve seals. Fully eighty percent of the catch that day were expectant mothers. I have never forgotten the cruelty to the young pups and the almost human moans of the dying mothers.

Coastal Indians hunted very little for the fur seal until the whites arrived to trade for skins. Only a few dozen seal skins were taken by coastal Indians in the mid-1850's. But the number of skins taken grew to 4,000 by 1869 and to 8,000 by 1881. Between 1885 and 1889, the number of seals killed at sea averaged 27,600 annually. More and more sealing schooners were appearing off the coast each year for this lucrative harvest.

Sealing schooners from San Francisco with all white crews would follow the herds from the California coast up to Cape Flattery. They would launch their small round bottom boats and using rifles and shotguns would try their luck killing the seals in the water. The noise of the firearms would waken all sleeping seals for a considerable distance. A wounded or killed seal will sink instantly and by the time the boat got to the blotch of blood on the water, the animal would have gone down lower than the long-handled boat hook could reach. Ninety percent of the seals shot in the water were lost. These white crews soon gave up hunting in this manner for they could not compete with the Indian, his canoe and spear.

Indians then began to work for a commission from the whites. All skins had to be marked and registered by the government. Single skins purchased from the Indians for $6 to $8 were bringing $12 to $20 on the open market.

It became clear that if restrictions were not placed on the fur sealing industry, the wealth would soon run out. The use of firearms was forbidden by law about 1894. Seal hunting after that time was carried on mostly by Indians who had always used the spear and had become very expert with it.

In the early 1890's, the seal population was estimated to be over six million. By 1896, the U.S. Government was granting concessions to fur companies to take as many as 40,000 seals every year. By 1905, the result of this slaughter was near extinction of the herds. By 1910, the Japanese alone had twenty-five sealing ships operating in the Bering Sea. The U.S. took the lead in adopting a fur-sealing convention between Russia, Japan, Great Britain and herself in December 1911. Special provisions were made to the Indians. Under these regulations with enforcement the herds had built up to 2,000,000 by the late '30s.

Chapter 13

"Weathering A Storm In A Whaling Canoe"

Frank Balch had started a general store about two mile above the mouth of the Quillayute River. He had named the place "Boston", which was later known as James' Resort. In the spring of 1895 he was badly in need of fifty sacks of sugar he had ordered that had been delivered by mistake to the trading store at Neah Bay which was sixty miles up the coast and inside the Straits of Juan de Fuca.

David Smith, a pioneer who lived nearby on the Quillayute Prairie, offered to make the trip by whaling canoe, which was the only means possible, and bring the sugar to the store. Smith also agreed to deliver a load of furs, hides and elkhorns to Neah Bay. He rented Indian Chief Jimmy Hoi-Attle's large ocean-going canoe and made up his crew of himself, Allen Wilbur (a stepson of Balch's), a sailor named Hill who had run away from a British Man-of-War, and me. I was 23 years old and looking for adventure.

We left LaPush, the Indian village at the mouth of the Quillayute River early one morning. Chief Hoi-Attle was there and gave us a last word of advice, "Klosh nanich, Mochow mokan," meaning "Look out for east wind!" Smith, who claimed to know all about sailing the winds, remarked, "We will fix the mochow wind!"

When we reached the open ocean a very high swell was running, the aftermath of a heavy southwest gale from several days before. We were sailing along at fair speed, when Hill, the sailor, became seasick and was laid out flat on the fur cargo. The wind was now from the east, but we were under the lee of the shore and did not feel it very strongly.

When we reached Ozette Island we decided to stop and eat our lunch. We had taken no extra food or water as we expected to reach Neah Bay that same day. A schooner was lying at anchor in the shelter of the island and as we approached, the captain waved to us to board and have coffee. He advised us to follow close to the shoreline as there was a strong east wind blowing away from shore. We thanked him and resumed our journey.

As we approached Wi-ach Bay, a wide and deep indentation in the coastline, Smith decided to cut across to save time. We hadn't gone far when the wind struck us hard and we had to scramble to take all the sails down. Smith was steering with a paddle while Wilbur and I were using the oars with all our might trying to pull toward shore. Hill was still unconscious on the pile of furs. We rowed with all our strength towards the last point of land, Tatoosh Island, at the entrance to the Straits, but missed it by about one mile to the west as we were rapidly sliding out to sea.

By now the waves were running high and the air was full of spray. A sea anchor was the only chance of checking our speed of westerly drift. This was made by tying the elkhorns to the sail and a rope from each end of the mast like a bridle. We fastened the bridle to the bow of the canoe and dropped the weighted sail overboard. The mast floated and our sea anchor held the canoe. It checked our drifting speed considerable but when night came we were out of sight of Tatoosh Lighthouse.

Smith and Wilbur were in the stern of the canoe, Hill was still laid out among the furs amidship and I was sitting partly submerged in water in the bow of the canoe. We were all soaking wet and our throats and lips were burning from licking the salt spray. The wind was howling and I was numb with cold. I took off one shoe to bail out the water and although no headway was made the exercise helped keep me from getting stiff.

When daylight came we were in a deplorable condition. We could scarcely whisper as our throats felt scalded and our eyes and faces were swollen. The gale had subsided but a stiff wind was still blowing and the waves were higher than before. The only land we could sight was a small mountain top to the northeast which we thought was part of Vancouver Island.

Smith was now in bad shape, so Wilbur and I covered him with furs beside Hill. Then for the next several hours we worked to pull up the sea anchor and rig a small sail, hoping we might reach that last speck of land. Within a half hour the speck disappeared and with it went all hope of reaching land again. We resigned ourselves to fate and let the canoe drift out on the limitless Pacific Ocean.

I shut my eyelids over my scalded eyes and dozed off. Sometime later I opened my eyes to see a sailing ship heading straight for us, not over a mile away. She evidently had been in trouble, for two of her masts were gone. With hopes of being saved, Wilbur and I livened up and started paddling for the ship. She bore straight down on us and nearly got us under her bow. A sailor was hanging in the rigging shouting and waving his arms as the schooner continued on making no effort to help us. It soon passed out of sight and we again abandoned hope of rescue. The fact is that we would have welcomed the end.

Night came again and I pictured our canoe to be a small chip tossing hopelessly about upon the Pacific Ocean. We could no longer speak to each other as our tongues were too swollen.

Sitting in the water in a reclining position in the bow in the pitch dark, I imagined I saw a reflection of light on the clouds. My eyeballs on fire and it became more painful to keep my eyes open. Now the light was travelling in different directions and seemed brighter. All at once a direct ray hit me for an instant. I roused Wilbur and we watched in a half stupor as the light got closer, frequently hitting the surface of the water and our tiny flapping sail. We both knew a boat was coming our way.

We sat motionless, like two half-dead men as the boat came close to us. We were unable to catch or hold a line or to assist in any way. A crewman jumped into our canoe and secured a line. We were all pulled on board and the canoe was taken in tow.

They carried us to the dining room where we were washed with fresh cold water, fed coffee with a spoon and put to bed. The next thing I knew I was being shaken and told it was ten o'clock in the morning and we were nearing Neah Bay. After more coffee we were taken ashore in a small boat to the Indian Village of Neah Bay. The canoe with its soaked furs, skins and elk horns had also been taken ashore. An Indian took us to his so-called hotel, gave us a room upstairs with two beds and we wasted no time crawling into them. Wilbur and I occupied one and Smith took the other. Our sailor friend Hill was in better shape than any of us and had wandered off.

During the night Wilbur and I were suddenly awakened by a crash. We jumped out of bed, lit a candle and found Smith was not in bed. We found him at the bottom of the stairs bleeding from many cuts. We carried him upstairs, tied him into bed for we knew he was delirious. Next day he remembered nothing of what had happened.

We stayed at Neah Bay four days taking care of our furs and elk horns, waiting for favorable weather for the return trip. We needed the time also for recuperation. Smith was in the worst shape from exposure and loss of blood.

We learned that it was the ocean-going tug <u>Sea Lion</u> of San Francisco that had snatched us from death in the briny deep. It had taken her twelve hours to bring us into Neah Bay from where she had plucked us out of the sea. The ship that had passed us by had been in tow by the <u>Sea Lion</u> but when the storm overtook them the tug let the schooner go to ride it out while the <u>Sea Lion</u> went for fuel. After returning and picking up her tow and returning the schooner to safety, the captain of the sailing ship informed the captain of the tug, about our canoe drifting out to sea and gave him our last known position. It was then the tug started to search for us.

On the morning of the fifth day we loaded the 50 sacks of sugar, took two gallons of fresh water, some bread and several cans of peaches and set sail for LaPush. After sailing around Cape Flattery and across Wi-ach Bay the wind died out.

Hill got sick again and we had no more help from him. We made a bed for Smith as he was too weak and unable to help. For forty miles I stayed at the oars and Wilbur paddled and steered the canoe.

At two a.m. next morning we reached LaPush, bringing the canoe safely through the surf. I held its bow out into the breakers with a pole while Wilbur and a number of Indians unloaded it.

David Smith died shortly after from exposure, young Hill disappeared from the country and no one knew what became of him. For my part I received five dollars for the trip, which had been the agreement. With fair weather the trip should have taken forty-eight hours. Instead it had taken eight days which figured out to 63 cents per day. I tasted fully of the adventure and experience I was looking for but the brush with death taught me many things about the dangers of sea including "Klosh nanich, mokan wind"——look out, east wind! Once more I had cheated the "grim reaper".

Chapter 14

"Fur Sealing In The Bering Sea"

Fur seals are found over nearly all of the Bering Sea area during the summer. St. George, St. Paul and the Pribilof Islands are the principal breeding grounds and rookeries.

In early June, the large herd bulls arrive at the rookeries first on the long migration from California. They select and establish their particular camp by throwing up a ridge of sand marking the private boundary lines of their harem, as they are firm believers in polygamy. The bulls will then be on the lookout to fill their harems. As the females approach the beach, the "big boys" will meet them, grab them by the nape of the neck and more or less forcibly assist them to their respective happy homes. A bull seal is not considered mature enough to be a herd bull until he is eight years old. Some very active bulls will have harems of sixty to seventy cows. These enclosures will fill with expectant mother seals and it is here on these beaches a few days later that the young pups are born. A few days after calving the cows are bred by their particular bull.

Old bulls, will as a rule, respect their neighbor's home, but sometimes a bull will enviously invade the sanctity of another's domain. A fight to the finish very often occurs. If too many young ambitious bulls are about, a great deal of fighting can go on.

The mother seals will swim as far as forty miles out every day to feed, coming back when hunger is satisfied to nurse and comfort their young. As the young seals get stronger, their mothers will take them to tide pools and later to deep water to give them swimming and fishing lessons.

In 1890 the U.S. Government established a sixty mile protection zone around the rookeries in the Pribilofs making it illegal for hunters to take seal in this area. This limit of safe water gave the mother seals the necessary protection for survival while on their daily search for food during the period while nursing their young and teaching them to survive. But hundreds of thousands of young bulls and females would go as far as one hundred miles beyond this protective zone and it was in this outer open water where the greatest capture of seals took place. It was the young bulls and female seals that furnished the most desirable skins for market.

In order to enforce this hunting regulation in the Bering Sea the U.S. Government began using U.S. revenue cutters for patrol duty. The cutter (Bear) played a vital part in this drama in the early 1890's and by the mid-

66

R0L was on board several times! a great thrill for a 16 year old!

1890's other revenue cutters joined the <u>Bear</u> at Dutch Harbor for sealing patrol.

In 1896, Len Whittier, Allen Wilbur, Fred Weston and I, all white pioneer settlers of the western Olympic Peninsula, decided to make a seal hunting trip to the Bering Sea. Our ages ranged from twenty to twenty-five. I was twenty-four.

We came to Port Angeles where a number of schooners were waiting at anchor for crews and hunters. The schooner <u>Bering Sea</u> stood out from the rest and we learned that it had the reputation of being one of the fastest of the entire sealing fleet. We went on board this trim white sailing vessel, signed up and met Captain Lars Larsen, the skipper. We learned that he was an experienced hand at the sealing game and an expert navigator as well.

The next day we were on our way. We put into Neah Bay where our schooner took on sixteen sealing canoes from the Quileute and Neah Bay Indian Reservations and thirty-two Indian seal hunters with their blankets and other personal belongings. All canoes were fastened securely on deck and the entire crew stowed away in the forecastle and other places. Other schooners were collecting their canoes and Indian hunters in the same manner from the many Indian villages along the Washington and British Columbia coast.

Allen was selected as a permanent sailor of our schooner's crew, Whittier, Weston and I were assigned as steermen in three canoes.

We left Neah Bay on July 1, sailing out of the mouth of the Strait of Juan de Fuca. The last landmark we saw was Tatoosh Island lighthouse. For the next twelve days we were in open water until we approached the westerly tip of Alaska at Unimak Pass. We sailed through the pass into the Bering Sea, thence westerly to Dutch Harbor. Here we anchored for about six days filling water tanks and taking on supplies for the six or seven weeks we would be sealing. About eighty other schooners from San Francisco, British Columbia and Puget Sound Ports were also anchored in Dutch Harbor taking on water and supplies for the long stretch at sea. A number of revenue cutters, including the <u>Bear</u>, were also present from America, Canada and Russia.

The six-day layover in Dutch harbor gave me a chance to recuperate from seasickness which had plagued me since leaving Neah Bay. The food consisted of white beans, salt pork, rice, potatoes, turnips, coffee, hardtack, etc. I could not keep any of it down for the smell and continuous roll of the ship made it impossible. After reaching Dutch Harbor, I learned to eat and retain this food and I soon recovered my strength.

While loafing about the trading store in Dutch Harbor one day, Len, Fred, and I met five men who where passengers on a steamer on their way to Seattle from Nome. They told us they had staked gold claims on the Yukon River and showed us buckskin pokes full of it. They said they had lots more in the ship's vault and would return next year to work their claims. They gave us directions and information on where to go and how to stake claims. We certainly were excited but none of us had any money to purchase an outfit or our passage to Nome. After much discussion we decided to steal the ship's lifeboat with a water keg and also steal from the schooner whatever provisions we could. Our plan was to leave the schooner early some morning, get out of the harbor and then go easterly across Unimak Pass to the mainland. From there we would follow the coastline north to the mouth of the Yukon River. We reasoned we could find Indian settlements along the coast where we could spend the winter. In the spring we would make our way up the Yukon River to where the Tanana River flows into the Yukon. When we told Allen of our plans, he tried to discourage us but later agreed to come with us.

One night we were all set to leave ship. The little boat was lying in the water. We had filled the water keg and had managed to steal a thirty pound box of hard tack, a dozen cans of corned beef, ten pounds of coffee, five pounds of lard, twenty-five pounds of flour, ten pounds of pork, blankets, harpoons, a compass, and a few cooking utensils. All of this was cached under one of the sealing canoes along with a sail and paddles where it could easily be transferred to the lifeboat. We wanted to get hold of a gun but it was out of the question.

We were sitting on deck discussing our plans in whispers when the Captain came along, looked about for a minute then went down the ladder, got into our boat and rowed to shore. In about an hour he came back in a different boat rowed by another man. The Captain came on board and the other boat returned to shore. We waited until after midnight but our boat did not come back and suspecting that something had gone wrong with our plans we turned in for the night.

The next morning Captain Larsen called us to his cabin and told us that he knew of our plans to run away and had taken the boat to the Trading Store for safe keeping. He gave us a good lecture, telling us how foolish we were. On maps he pointed out that it was eight hundred miles to Nome and only one small Indian settlement along the bleak and rocky coast. It was another three or four hundred miles on foot to where our friends had staked their claims. He told us that if we had succeeded in getting away, we most surely would have met death. This ended our lust for gold and we gave the captain our word of honor that we would not try it again.

Perhaps it was for the best. This slip up no doubt changed the course of our lives. Had we succeeded in getting up the Yukon River as we had planned we most certainly would have been in on the big Klondike bedrock. We were to learn later that it was these five men with their bags of gold that set off the gold rush when they landed in Seattle that fall. In the spring of '97 the rush was on.

It was now late July and the sealing fleet headed out into the Bering Sea, schooners going in all directions. At first we were only averaging two seals per day per canoe. Part of the work was to skin the seal leaving about one-half inch of fat on the skin. The pelts were then packed in salt and stored in the lower hold of the ship.

Each day as we sailed farther north, the seals became more plentiful. Sometimes fog prevented us from leaving the mother ship for part or all of a day.

About the middle of August, the weather was ideal and seals could be seen everywhere, feeding and sleeping. Our schooner stuck its nose into a light breeze and held her position. Only two other schooners were in sight. All canoes were lowered and spread out for hunting. It was important to keep the top of the mast of the mother ship in sight. Our canoe was about five miles from our ship and we had barely gotten started when we saw a flag being run up to the top of the main mast. This was a signal for all canoes to return at once. Within two hours all canoes were on board and the total count of seals taken for that short time was over one hundred.

Captain Larsen explained to us that by mistake we had sailed fifteen miles within the prohibited zone around the Pribilof Island rookeries and that the revenue cutter <u>Bear</u> had spotted us and had signaled us to stay where we were. The two other schooners near us were also inside the safety zone. One of these schooners we could see about four miles distant with all sails down. The captain explained she was hove to and was under arrest and had been boarded by a crew from the <u>Bear</u>. The <u>Bear</u> was now trying to overtake the other schooner which was under full sail and trying to get away. The revenue cutter fired several shots but the schooner kept going. Soon she was out of sight with the Cutter <u>Bear</u> still in pursuit.

Captain Larsen called us all on deck and told us he believed the revenue cutter's captain could not be certain of our identity as there were several other white boats in the fleet and the cutter had not been near enough to read our name. He explained the seriousness of this predicament saying that when the cutter returned we would be boarded and all canoes, equipment and skins would be confiscated and all hands would be placed under arrest. The captain asked for a vote stating, "Shall

69

we wait for the cutter and lose everything or shall we take a chance and get out of here?"

The vote was unanimous to "get". We hoisted full sail taking a south-westerly course. We sailed all night and the next morning all canoes went out hunting. Seals were scarce and only a few were brought in. Worst of all, one hunting crew did not return. We searched all night and part of the next day but did not find them.

Our schooner kept in a westerly direction toward Four Mountain Pass. For two weeks we hunted in this area as we were afraid to go back to good sealing ground. We reached the western-most tip of the Aleutian Islands when one of our Indian hunters became very ill and died. All the Indians started mourning by beating tin pans and the one tom-tom they had with them. When they found out that the captain was planning a burial at sea, a near riot resulted.

The next day a sealing schooner bore down upon us and returned our lost hunters. The men told how they had gone far from the mother ship. They had killed three seals when they sighted a very large sleeping bull weighing near five-hundred pounds. In spite of the fact that the fur of these large bulls is very course, the hunters were tempted to harpoon him. The harpoon went well into his body and the huge animal dove down instantly to the end of the rope, then surfaced and attacked the canoe. They beat him off with their clubs but the seal charged again and again. Another harpoon was thrown into his breast, but the infuriated beast came madly on. It got a hold on the canoe with its teeth and then got its flipper over the side. One on the men struck him again with a heavy blow on the head. In spite of this the seal started to climb into the canoe and consequently it upset. The Indians were good swimmers and stayed near their canoe. They expected a fight in the water but the mortally wounded seal had had his revenge and was now sinking. The Indians swam to their canoe, righted it, bailed it out and gathered up their floating gear and paddles. It was late in the day and the fog bank had settled on the water and our schooner was out of sight. They drifted until the next afternoon when they were picked up. Had the big bull lasted five more minutes this story might never have been told.

Captain Larsen now set a course for Dutch Harbor three hundred miles to the east having agreed to bury the Indian on shore. We also needed to replenish our water supply and clear the schooner of suspicion of having been near the rookeries.

As we approached the entrance to the harbor we were becalmed. Eight of our canoes were launched and took us in tow. We were hailed by the revenue cutter <u>Corwin</u> which then took us in tow up the bay. In case we

70

would be questioned, our captain instructed us to say we had never seen a cutter and had not run away.

It so happened that the Navigator stationed at Dutch Harbor was also a Norwegian and a good friend of Captain Larsen. Our captain made a trip during the night to shore and returned with another man. They visited in the captain's cabin then our mate took the stranger ashore. Next morning the captain and mate went to shore with the log book to answer charges made by the Cutter <u>Bear</u>. When they returned to the ship we were told the log had proved that we were at no time near the forbidden area and that one of the other white boats must have been mistaken for us. We had been cleared to hunt again, but the best part of the season had been lost.

The next day Fred, Len and I were sent to the trading post to get lumber to build a coffin. It was a very rough box and full of knot holes but we laid our dead Indian in it and nailed it up. In the meantime Captain Larsen went to nearby Unalaska, an Indian Village of about 200 people where there was a Russian Catholic Church. He made arrangements with two priests for space in the grave yard and some prayers to be said. For this he paid the priests $30. Fred and I were told where to dig the grave, but about four feet down we came upon the end of another coffin which was very old and decayed. We continued digging except where the other box was protruding. We had just finished when we saw the funeral procession coming up the hill. It was led by three priests and some altar boys. Following came our Indians and a lot of natives. when the head priest saw the end of the other coffin, he shook his head and refused to go on with the funeral. Captain Larsen and the priests had a consultation and it cost another ten dollars. We proceeded with the ceremony but did not lower the coffin. The priests still were not satisfied with the grave but assured us that it would be enlarged later and our Indian friend buried by the natives.

We returned to the harbor and all hands set to work hauling fresh water from a spring. After the water barrels were filled we got under way to try our luck once more among the seals. It was now early September and storms and fog had become frequent on the Bering Sea. We had lost the best part of the season and accomplished little during the last two weeks of September. The sealing season was nearly over since the animals begin to leave the rookeries in late September and October to return to warmer California coastal waters. On September 20, we secured all canoes and gear on board and started for home. Our haul only totaled 653 seals which, we were told, was about fifty percent of a good catch for our ship.

Two hundred miles south of Unimak Pass a storm struck and we were nearly driven back to shore. We lost two canoes and our foretop mast was broken. I became sick again from the churning of the high seas and the smell of seal meat which the Indians persisted in cooking. I decided to get rid of this smell, so when everyone was below deck except the man at the wheel, I crawled along the deck holding fast to whatever I could to keep from being washed overboard. I made my way to the foremast where the meat barrels were lashed, cut the rope and somehow managed to get back to my bunk. When the weather cleared and the storm subsided, the crew put the deck in order and took down the broken mast. The seas were still rolling very high but from then on sailing was good but slow. There was great consternation and lamenting among the Indians when they found that the storm had torn loose and washed away all the seal meat. Provisions were getting low so we were all put on short rations. It took twenty days to reach Cape Flattery.

Our Indian shipmates with their canoes disembarked at Neah Bay. I'm sure it took a great deal of beating of tom-toms to satisfy Quaty, the Indian God, for leaving one of their tribesman in a far away land among strangers

On returning to Seattle I was sworn in at U.S. District Court as a U.S. citizen. Len Whittier and Allen Wilbur were my witnesses. This was a proud day for me.

We four then took a boat to Pysht, where we hit the forty mile trail for our homesteads. Len, Fred, and I each received $120 for about three months work. We agreed that the trip was rich in experience but we were thankful it was over. I never had any desire to go seal hunting again.

U.S. Cutter *Bear*, San Francisco, 1890.   **Credit: Oakland Public Library.**

Chapter 15

"Elwha Hunting Diary"

This diary, recorded by Chris briefly describes three hunting trips up the Elwha Valley. The spelling and grammar are as they appeared in the diary.

Ed.

The First Trip

Wednesday, Oct. 27, 1897
Left Port Angeles, Went to bridge, slept in wood shed.
Thursday, Oct. 28, 1897
Went up and crossed the river. Kild 2 salmon with a clob.
Friday, Oct. 29, 1897
Went down on bottom and kild a deer. Went to old mans.
Stayed all night.
Saturday, Oct. 30, 1897
Went up Hurrycane mounting. 3 miles to camp. Stayed all night.
Sunday, Oct. 31, 1897
Stayed all night

The Second Trip

June 11, 1898
Ward and I started for Press Vallie. (Footnote) Went to Lost River.
June 12, 1898
Went to Bear Camp
June 13, 1898
Went hunting up the Godkin River. Saw 2 old Bulls with fine horns at lick. I mine to have one of them in fall.
June 14, 1898
Rainy. Stade at camp all day.
June 15, 1898
Plisent the morning. Took our stuff and started up the Godkin Vallie. Began to rain soon after starting and kept it up all day. As we were going up the vallie looking fore a place to camp, I saw an elk crost the river feeding. Sliped out of my pack and steped to the bank of river and when it got brod side on I opend fire at about 20 yards. At the first shot it did not stir so I gave it another which

knocked it down, but it got on to his feet soon after. Then I put in the 4 shoot, and down it went. A large cow and 2 calfs was with it. Went over there and found that I had kild a yearling heffer. Just what we wanted. found that all 4 shoot had gone through the elk. the last one broke its back. Went to work and put up a good bark shanty.

June 16, 1898

Was not rain just now, so Ward and I went up to head of Vallie. Saw 2 bands of Elk in all about 40. This is the finest Elk country in the world. Rainy this afternoon.

June 17,1898

Rainy, laid in camp.

June 18, 1898

Raining like the devil. Have named this "Rainy Camp".

June 19, 1898

Lost River

The Third Trip

(Later that same fall, Chris returned to the Elwha and bagged the big bull.) . . . Editor

Nov. 2, 1898

Kild big Bull neare Goldy. Horns for Fred

(Footnote) : The 'Ward' mentioned in the second trip is Ward Sanders, a cousin of Grant Humes. Ward came from upper New York State with Will and Martin Humes in 1897. He homesteaded on the Upper Elwha between Idaho Creek and the Lillian River. Cousin Grant followed two years later in 1899. . . . Editor

Chapter 16

"A Difficult Experience as Constable"

I was appointed constable for Western Jefferson County in the early 1890's and could not rid myself of this office for six years. During this time a number of difficult and amusing cases fell to my lot. It was not easy to make arrests and transport culprits one-hundred and fifty miles over primitive trails to the distant county seat in Port Townsend.

Enoch Burgess was the man I had to deal with in this case and he lived on the Upper Hoh River. He was a large man with a full red beard. He and I had worked together surveying and building trails.

A neighbor named Stodick had been staying with Enoch and had noticed him acting peculiar. One night Stodick awakened to see Enoch coming toward him shouting, "At last I have you and you will not get away, you are a Catholic High Priest and a hypocrite!". He dragged Stodick from bed and began beating and choking him. Stodick finally got away and ran barefoot in the dark cold night up river six miles to the Huelsdonk settlement. Henry and Cornelius Huelsdonk gave Stodick some clothes and together the three went down to Enoch's house. Enoch was in the act of piling kindling wood in one corner of the cabin to set fire to it. He was friendly with the Huelsdonk boys but became furious when he saw Stodick. He grabbed a butcher knife and began to chase Stodick who took to the woods again. The Huelsdonk boys captured Enoch and calmed him down. Enoch explained he was defending the Protestant Church against the Catholics and he insisted that Stodick was a Catholic Priest and the house in which they were living was a Catholic Chapel. He said it was his duty to destroy both the priest and the chapel.

Next morning Stodick appeared at my homestead on the Bogachiel River to get me to come and take charge of Enoch. When I got to Enoch's house the following night I found the Huelsdonk boys guarding him. Before leaving the Bogachiel I had sent a messenger to Pysht, fifty miles distant by trail, to telegraph Enoch's parents in Tacoma to come at once to LaPush and get him.

Enoch was glad to see me and said, "Chris, I know you came after me, I trust you and will not make any trouble." I told him to come with me to LaPush to see his father and mother. To this he readily consented.

We left for LaPush the next day, hiking the ten miles over the poor foot trail, climbing logs and wading through swamps. We had gone about four miles when he turned and said, "Chris, you are foolish to take chances with me this way, you have not tied my arms and I could run away from you or even kill you." I said, "I know you could, but I know you better than that and trust you, and am sure you will not harm me." "No, I won't," he answered and then took a long cord from his pocket and insisted I tie each arm at the elbow like driving lines for me to hold. He plodded along ahead of me for some time then suddenly said, "Chris, I'm glad you tied me up." I also felt considerably safer for Enoch was in the prime of life and a very big and powerful man.

When we reached the Bogachiel River we had to ford across it arm-pit deep. We stayed at the Flannegan Ranch, a mile down river, for the next two days. Each night I tied Enoch's arms. I also tied him in the canoe when we traveled to Forks where we stayed over night. The next morning I got an Indian to take us the rest of the way to LaPush, fifteen miles farther down river.

The schooner was lying at anchor when we arrived. The next morning many Indian canoes began to lighter the cargo to shore. Enoch and I went out on the first canoe. He seemed glad to see his parents. I stayed about thirty minutes, then took one of the canoes for shore. When Enoch saw me leaving in a canoe he shouted to me to take him along. I waved farewell and when he realized I was not taking him he jumped overboard. Another Indian canoe came to his rescue. At first he refused to go on the schooner but his mother finally persuaded him and he became quiet. I felt greatly relieved after delivering my charge and thought I was through with him.

In Seattle Enoch got away from his parents and was next heard from on the South Seattle bridge where he was standing on a pile of lumber throwing it in all directions. He believed he was destroying another Catholic Church. A policeman undertook to arrest him but Enoch got the best of him and began piling lumber on top of him. He was overpowered and taken away in a patrol wagon. He was eventually placed in the asylum in Steilacoom.

About two years later Pete Bergestrom, a neighbor of mine, came to my house to tell me Enoch was at his place. He had escaped from Steilacoom three months earlier and had walked and begged his way to the Bogachiel River by way of Olympia, Aberdeen, Quinault and the Hoh River, a distance of over two hundred miles. He was laboring under a new hallucination. He had apple seeds and other fruit seeds and planned to follow logging operations and replace downed trees with fruit trees. I told Pete to humor him and tell him we were going to Port Townsend to get work in a logging camp and that we would be glad to have him come along and work with us.

Enoch fell in with our scheme and willingly came along. It was a difficult trip to Pysht as rivers were high, bridges washed out and the trails full of fallen trees. Enoch took the lead in fording and swimming the creeks. He seemed to enjoy showing off. At night we camped at different settlers' homes along the way. Pete and I took turns staying awake all night. We arrived at Clallam Bay in the evening and fortunately a boat for Port Townsend was about to leave, so Enoch and I got on board. Pete made an excuse that he had to get something at the warehouse. I explained my mission to the Captain and he assigned a separate cabin to Enoch. The boat pulled out leaving Bergestrom behind as planned. Enoch saw a mirror in his stateroom and began admiring his full red beard and forgot all about Pete. He took a comb and kept grooming his beard for hours. I locked his door and watched it until we were summoned to breakfast by a bell. I knew Enoch's suspicions were aroused for he asked who was paying for our meals and passage. I told him I was paying for my own and he could pay the Captain when he got work.

At Port Angeles I telegraphed the sheriff in Port Townsend to meet our boat. Enoch wanted to work to pay his fare, so he helped the crew load and unload freight at Dungeness. Upon reaching Port Townsend, he again started to help unload freight. I went to look for the sheriff and not finding him, I summoned a buckboard and explained to the driver that I wanted him to pretend he had been sent from the logging camp but to take us instead to the courthouse. He agreed to help me.

I called to Enoch and we got in the buckboard. He was satisfied with the driver's explanation. But when we pulled up in front of the courthouse and he saw the bars on the jail windows, he yelled at the driver to take us away fast. The sheriff and his deputy had just received the telegram and were coming down the steps. They grabbed Enoch, hand-cuffed him and hustled him into jail. Poor Enoch had now lost confidence in me and everybody and became very violent. I went along to try to assure him he'd be all right. I requested a mirror and comb be placed in his cell as I thought it might quiet him down, and it did. Later guards took him back to Steilacoom and that was the last I heard of poor Enoch.

Chapter 17

"Witness to an Elk Battle"

The fight between two well-matched bull elk for supremacy of the herd is one of the most dramatic occurrences of nature to watch. They fight until one or both are exhausted or one finally dies of wounds from the pronged horns of the other. I had hunted for elk many times as an early homesteader and had observed much about the herd's habits from one season to the next. I had hoped some day to witness one of these great fights.

A full grown Roosevelt bull elk in good order will weigh as much as 1,500 pounds. The horns are very large, some reaching a spread of over five feet at the upper tips. Large horns could weigh over fifty pounds without the skull.

About the first week in September this magnificent animal is in his prime. He has grown sleek and fat and has taken the best of care of himself through the spring and summer months. The dark hair on his neck is seven to ten inches long and the skin is nearly one inch thick. His horns are fully mature. His one ambition now is to be the leader of a band of elk. He will roam through the forest bugling his challenge to all comers. When he finds a band he at once bugles to the leader of that herd. If there is an answering bugle he accepts battle. Some other bulls may be with the herd but these have obviously acknowledged previous defeat with their leader.

One morning in mid-September in the late 1890's, I started out to get meat for my neighbors and myself as I had often done before. I headed up a hill not far north of my place on the Bogachiel River. On reaching the top of the ridge I found tracks of a large herd of elk. They had come out of a canyon and were travelling north along the same ridge I had chosen to follow. The tracks were a day old and indicated about one-hundred in the band. The wind was from the north which was in my favor and I knew that for a time I could stay on their track without danger of alarming them. I found where furrows were dug in the bark and the bark torn off the tree to the height of nine feet. This is done with the prongs of the horns to sharpen and polish the ivory points. It was evident a very large bull was among the band and I decided to go after him. As I followed the tracks I noticed several places where the ground had been torn up and much hair was lying about. I came to a place where the herd had bedded down on the previous night, as the camp still smelled strongly of elk urine. Even though it was open timber and I couldn't see anything of them, I was sure they were not far away.

While I was still examining tracks I heard a faint bugle call in the distance. My spirits fell, for I thought the herd was too far ahead of me. Suddenly to my surprise, a loud clear bugle call sounded about a quarter of a mile away. This was music to my ears for I realized I was hearing a champion answering a challenger and I decided to get a ring-side seat to watch the battle.

I approached very cautiously and could hear the challenger sounding closer each minute. I sneaked on my hands and knees into a thicket of small trees. As I climbed up onto a log I could see the band of elk not far ahead. I found my grandstand seat behind the root of an upturned tree with some small hemlocks screening me. The ridge ahead was clear of underbrush, so I could see the herd and the leader bull to good advantage. He was truly a fine specimen, every bit a champion as he assumed his regal posture. He began to bow his neck and break off small trees with his horns. A few of the cows were lying down, the rest were looking in the direction of the approaching challenger. There were several other large and medium size bulls and calves nearby. None of the herd had noticed me.

Suddenly the challenging bull appeared from behind the ridge, neck extended and head held upwards while bugling. The champion began to tear up the landscape at a furious rate while the newcomer started towards him on a trot anxious to begin battle. Ten feet from the champion he stopped. Both animals held their heads low and somewhat sideways. They approached each other slowly, then with a great crash they locked horns. The champion, standing with his hind legs slightly down hill, was being pushed backwards. With a quick leap sideways he charged at the flank of his adversary who turned and countered with his own horns thus avoiding the savage thrust. However the champion's horns found their mark and sank deep into the side of the challenger. Blood squirted out but the fight went on.

Then the champion stumbled and was knocked to his knees by his opponent. He regained his footing and the battle resumed. Sometimes both were standing on their hind legs, sparring like two boxers. Each was a good match for the other and the fight continued for a half hour. Both animals were now bleeding from many wounds. They seemed exhausted and now did a great deal of walking around each other making threatening gestures with their horns. So far it appeared to be a draw. Then without warning, the champion made a quick and savage charge. The challenger braced himself but his head was too low and the blow had broken off one side of his antlers. No longer could he fully protect himself. As the battle continued he was gored in many places and lost one eye. He fell to his knees and made no more attempt at self-defense. After a few minutes he got to his feet and slowly ambled away, completely defeated and mortally wounded. He lay down about one hundred yards from the battle ground in what was to be his last resting place.

The champion, standing nearby with his four legs apart and his head hanging low, slowly raised his head and sounded a faint victory bugle. To my surprise it was immediately answered by one of the other large bulls in the herd. This new challenger walked slowly towards the champion, made a savage charge that was warded off by the champion with his horns. The newcomer kept charging and pushing the champion down hill. I was angered at this young bull taking advantage of the champion's exhausted condition and since I had come after meat, I decided to end this unfair fight and save a deserving champion. I fired at the challenging buck and the fight was over. I had enough meat for sixty days for the entire Bogachiel settlement.

Since then I have witnessed several such battles from the first challenge to the dying groans of the vanquished. Once I found the horns and skulls of two very large elk locked together. No doubt they had mortally wounded each other in combat and were too weak and exhausted to pull apart.

Chapter 18

"The Magnificent Valley Of The Hoh"

After hearing about the Dodwell-Rixon exploration and survey, I was excited and found myself wanting to make my own exploration trip of the Hoh Valley. I had first seen the Hoh River Valley and Mt. Olympus in 1892 when I stood on Bogachiel Peak where I was treated to an unimpaired view of this vast and heavily forested valley below.

Eight years later in 1900 I was able to follow and explore the main Hoh River to its source at the foot of Mt. Olympus.

John Huelsdonk, "Iron Man of the Hoh", who had settled in 1892 about forty miles above the mouth of the Hoh River, had never gone but a short distance above his homestead. About one mile above the Huelsdonk place the river divides into the north and south forks. It was from here that I started my journey alone up the North Fork into this primeval wilderness.

The Indians knew little about the interior as they did not venture close to Mt. Olympus or the other peaks. They believed the booming sound made by the glaciers to be a warning from Quaty, (God of the Olympics) who threatened death to those going near or onto the mountain.

The level Hoh Valley averages a mile wide. The river, averaging a quarter-mile wide, meanders around broad sand and gravel bars, some a mile long. The waters of the Hoh are a milky color due to the action of the melting glaciers that grind the rock to a sediment called "rock flour". It is believed the name "Hoh" is a derivation of the Indian word "Ohalet" which means "white water", and that the name was given to the river prior to 1893 by the tribe that bears the same name and resided for a time at the mouth of the river on the Pacific Ocean.

A very heavy rainfall, averaging 150 inches a year, supports a dense stand of Douglas fir. Many of these trees have a diameter of ten to fifteen feet and reach a height of 300 feet, which would be an estimated volume of 400,000 board feet per acre. Some are over 1,000 years old. Other species of timber here are Sitka spruce, hemlock and red cedar. The spruce and cedars which grow nearer the river have an understory of broadleaf maples, some reaching heights of over eighty feet with fantastic shaped trunks and branches. A heavy mat of moss covers the trunks and branches almost to their tops. Out of this moss grows licorice fern and long curtain-like streamers of Spanish moss. Vine maples, also draped with Spanish moss form huge arches over clumps of sword fern and blackstem fern growing out of a ground cover of moss and oxalis. Near the river, alder bottoms occur frequently. In many places filtered sunlight struggles to break through. Truly a beautiful, dense, lush forest where the high volume of cool Pacific Ocean rains have worked their magic. I saw no evidence of a fire of any proportion ever having occurred in the Hoh Valley.

Elk trails were going in and coming out everywhere and the moss-covered ground made walking easy, especially through areas where elk had browsed. The distance from the fork of the river to the foot of Mt. Olympus is less than ten miles, yet the ascent through the valley was so gradual I thought there had been none at all.

As I neared the head of the valley the surrounding ridges became more visible and I could see evidence of a huge ice movement that had filled this upper region of the valley centuries ago. It appeared that one prong of a glacier had descended from the Bailey Range leaving smoothly ground rock walls and had converged with another prong that had filled a canyon to the right of where I stood. (Later named Glacier Creek).

I was drawn on through this canyon until I stood looking upwards at a gigantic ice river that seemed to go on forever up the mountainside. The tongue of the glacier, where I stood was dripping water and feeding a tiny rivulet. Here was the beginning of the "mighty Hoh". I was impressed with the immenseness of this glacier, with its masses of clear blue ice showing deep and wide crevasses. A radiant blue light also seemed to be reflected above the surface of the ice. "Blue Glacier" was the name later given to this glacier for its deep blue reflected light. The incessant thundering and grinding noises produced by the ice pushing on the walls and floor of the canyon reminded me of the threatening aspect of this natural phenomenon. I returned to my homestead satisfied that I had been among the first to experience this awesome sight.

Postscript by Chris

I later learned that only two rivers on the Peninsula, the Hoh and the Queets drain the vast ice-fields of Mt. Olympus. The Hoh takes approximately eighty percent of its water from the mountain, while the Queets River on the south side of the mountain takes the rest. Hoh Glacier, which is about five miles long is the largest glacier on the mountain, but Blue Glacier is the most beautiful and spectacular. It breaks over the steep mountainside at between four and five thousand feet leaving many crevasses more than 100 feet deep and showing clear blue ice. The glacier carries very little drift which accounts for the eerie blue reflected light at the face of the glacier.

Since my first exploration trip through this valley to the tongue of Blue Glacier in 1900, there has not been much change. In 1907 some members of the Forest Service, including myself climbed on to Blue Glacier and ascended Mt. Olympus. When I stood on the glacier at this time, I experienced an even greater sensation of grandeur. It was on this trip in 1907 that we saw a natural ice bridge spanning the narrow valley of the upper Hoh. A great mass of ice had broken off from Hoh Glacier and had slid down completely blocking the valley below. Water had eaten its way under it leaving a natural bridge with a tunnel beneath.

In 1912 the Forest Service built a good trail which traverses the entire length of this tropical park-like valley and terminates at the point where the river emerges from a rock canyon with sheer walls as high as three-hundred feet. It then follows the timbered ridge past Elk Lake to open country where Olympus Guard Station nestles in Glacier Meadows. From this point the ascent to the top of the mountain can best be made by following the easy slope of the moraine of the glacier. In late August and September the heavy booming sound of the 'calving' (breaking off of the pieces of ice from the mother glacier) can be heard across the valley for many miles. The lower part of this Ice River has receded a considerable distance since I first saw it but in late summer when it is free of snow it is still an awe-inspiring sight.

Mt. Olympus from Glacier Creek, 1908. Blue Glacier, extreme left; Snow Dome, center top; White glacier, to the right in front of Snow Dome.

83

Chapter 19

"Capturing Four Young Cougars"

In the early spring of 1901 I was locating a settler on a timber claim in the cedar swamp country between the Bogachiel and Hoh Rivers in western Jefferson County. I was running a compass line around a certain 160 acres of timber land while my settler friend was following me, blazing the boundary line to his claim. My line took me over a large old cedar windfall. I clambered to the top, jabbed my Jacob staff into the log to take a view sight and heard a vicious snarl. A very large cougar leaped out from under the log, made two jumps to a clearing where it turned, put its front paws on a small log and snarled directly at me. My partner was just coming up. I warned him about the big cougar and he quickly handed me his gun. I fired one shot at the cougar, it leaped high into the air and disappeared into the jungle. My companion climbed onto the log beside me and I showed him the direction which the big cat had fled. Since it was right along our line of travel, we decided to call it a day and return home hoping to run across the wounded cougar and finish him off.

We were still standing on the log looking at, and talking about the timber near us, when right under us we heard some noises...little whining noises. What could it be? Were there more cougars under the log? We hit the log with the Jacob staff, thinking we could drive out whatever was inside. The log sounded hollow and I suspected that it was the Cougar's den and that the noises were from young ones.

While my companion was watching out for the old cougar, I entered the log on my knees, revolver in one hand, lighting matches with the other. About six feet back from the opening in a nice dry bed were four young kittens. I brought one of them out to show my partner. They were not over a week old as their eyes had not yet opened. We decided to come back next day and get the kittens if the mother cougar had not returned. We went back to my place on the Bogochiel for the night.

Next morning with rifles and pack sacks we retraced our steps to the cedar log, full of mis-givings for having shot and maybe killed the mother cougar. It also occurred to us that the mother cougar might have returned during our absence and cat-like taken her young elsewhere. This thought was soon dispelled for on approaching the log we could hear the little ones whining loudly. Evidently mama had never returned to nurse her young. We placed two kittens in each of our packsacks and set out to hunt for the mother. The kittens being hungry, were whining louder than ever.

84

We circled around the vicinity, pinching the cats to make them keep up their noise. We kept enlarging our circles, but in spite of the kittens whining and the circling we did not locate the mother cat so decided that the one shot of the day before must have found a fatal mark. We took the young cats to my place where we fed them on canned milk which became their principal diet for the next six weeks.

These four young cougars were very tame, cute and playful. They followed me everywhere and in play would jump on anybody's shoulders or grab them by the legs. As they got larger their play was not appreciated. When they started killing the chickens I decided to get rid of them. Two were given to a doctor from Seattle who sold them to a circus. The other two, I gave to a timber cruiser from Tacoma with instructions they be given to the city of Tacoma for Point Defiance Park Zoo. On one of my visits to Tacoma several years later, I went out to see my former pets. They were very well behaved and seemed happy in their adopted environment.

Chapter 20

"An Elk Hunt"

In the fall of 1902, Jim Forest, a new settler on the Bogachiel River asked if he could go on an elk hunt with me. Another settler, Ed Crawford, expressed a desire to go along. Neither had ever been elk hunting before.

I preferred to go hunting alone. Stalking and bagging a game animal is a challenge and a triumph and to the victor belongs the spoils. So it was with some second thoughts that I agreed to this outing.

Both men arrived at my place on the appointed day and we assembled our camping outfit and readied our canoe to start in the morning. Crawford and I were to do the poling up stream and Jim was to do the towing over rapids when it became necessary. I had a new one-half inch rope tied on the canoe. Jim, having been a sailor, did not like the common knot that I had made at the end of the rope so proceeded to make a seaman's splice that would not ravel.

We had poled upstream about ten miles when I spotted signs where a band of elk had crossed the river. We landed the canoe and I followed the tracks where they left the river bottom to a higher bench. The tracks were fresh so I was sure the elk herd was not far away. It was late in the day and I knew the elk would be bedding down for the night so I returned to the canoe and reported what I had seen. The wind was down river so we decided to camp down river out of sight and start hunting early the next morning. This would give us a full day to take care of the meat we hoped to get. We beached the canoe at the mouth of a long slough that joined the river. After fixing dinner we rolled into bed.

Over breakfast we discovered that Jim's gun was only a 22 special. Ed and I thought he couldn't do much with his little gun and suggested that he stay behind to wash dishes and clean up camp.

Ed and I, with our large calibre guns, started up river where we took up the tracks and followed the elk up a hill. Near the top we could smell the elk and I signalled Ed to be ready for instant action. I was looking over the crest of the hill and saw some cows get up, then the most immense bull I had ever seen got up about one hundred feet to my left and was off on a stately run. The woods came alive with elk. I yelled to Ed to pick his bull. Crawford fired and ran after the stampeding herd. I kept my eyes on the large bull as he circled to rejoin the band. He was making long jumps when I fired. He stopped immediately and looked at me. I walked towards him, but he did not move. When I came close he turned and slowly and carefully picked his way down the hill towards the river. I held my fire figuring if I let him get to the river I could finish him off and just load the meat right into the canoe.

The bull Crawford had shot at went off with the herd so he gave up and came back to where I was. I told him to follow the band and if he had hit the elk, as he thought he had, the wounded animal would get out of the band and be an easy target. Crawford took off after the band again.

I went after my bull who by this time had reached the river. He was standing perfectly still in a water hole about four feet deep. I tried to drive him a little farther towards the river but he refused to go. My shot had hit high on his shoulder partly paralyzing him. He sought the comfort of the cool water and did not care to walk any further. I tried poking him with a stick but he would not budge and stood shaking his immense horns.

Then a thought came to me to have some fun with Jim. I stuck a large stick into the sand, took off my shirt and hat and made a scare-crow, hoping the elk would think it was me and stay in the water hole. I went back to the canoe, took the tow rope and came back to the elk. I made a noose, lassoed one side of the antlers, pulled the rope taut and fastened it to a nearby alder tree. This was the closest I ever got to being a cowboy. I put on my shirt and hat, went to the river bar where I could see Jim about two-hundred yards down river and shouted for him to bring his gun and knife on the double, as I had spotted a big elk and was out of ammunition.

Jim came on the run. I explained that the elk was somewhere on the sandbar. We held a council of war as to procedure and decided he should stalk his prey up the slough while I circled the island, that way I figured he would see the big beast and finish him off. I was following Jim and out of sight. I could see the elk still in the water hole and only one hundred and fifty feet from Jim. Afraid Jim would see the rope if he got too close, I came up behind and asked if he had seen anything of the elk and he said he hadn't. We sneaked up the slough a little farther and when it became apparent that he wasn't going to discover the elk, I pulled him to the ground and pointed to it. Jim excitedly asked what to do, and I said, "Shoot, he's getting ready to run!" Jim fired, but the tiny bullet only grazed the thick neck skin and the elk shook his huge rack, tangling the rope which Jim still did not see. I told him to shoot again and this time to aim just in front of the ear. The 22 bullet found its mark, the elk dropped into the water with rope floating to the top. Jim threw down his gun and danced and shouted, "I got him, I got him!". I could hold in no longer and burst forth with laughter and rolled over in the sand. In his excitement he asked why I was laughing so hard. I answered, "I am so tickled that you got him."

Jim rushed into the water to pull the elk out. He still did not see the rope fastened to the antlers until I pulled on it. He just couldn't understand why there would be a rope tied to its horns. I suggested that John Huelsdonk could have come up here from his ranch on the Hoh to inspect his trap lines, brought his tame elk "Dewey" to do his packing and had tied him here while inspecting his traps. Believing me, Jim broke down and cried. I couldn't convince him that I had lassoed and tied the big elk as a joke until I showed him the fancy sailor splice on the end. How I could tie up a bull elk was too much for anyone to believe and he made me promise never to tell about his first elk hunt.

The entire episode did not take over twenty-five minutes and the opportunity for a joke was too tempting for me to pass up. Crawford bagged his elk and by nightfall we had both elk dressed out and packed into the canoe ready to come down-river in the morning.

The antlers of this huge elk were the largest and heaviest I ever shot. This seventeen pointer trophy, head and horns are now mounted and hang in the lobby over the great stone fireplace at Lake Crescent Tavern on Lake Crescent, a gift from me in 1916 to Mr. A.J. Singer, owner of the hotel. (Footnote)

Footnote: Singer's Lake Crescent Tavern is now known as Lake Crescent Lodge. The huge mounted elk specimen still hangs over the fireplace and is an interesting conversation piece to visitors. According to trophy experts this is the largest rack of Roosevelt elk horns ever taken in the Olympic Mountains.

Big 17 point Roosevelt Elk taken by Chris Morgenroth on Bogachiel River, 1902. Now hangs in the lobby of Lake Crescent Lodge in the Olympic National Park.

Chapter 21

"Exploration. The South Fork of the Hoh"

In 1903 with three companions I set out to explore the South Fork of the Hoh River. We followed this glacial stream to its source, which is about twelve miles above where it forks with the main stream. I found the South Fork valley not as wide as the main Hoh Valley and the slopes were covered with a heavy stand of large sized trees and low undergrowth, much of which had been killed out by over-grazing of elk. This made our travelling comparatively easy. We were confronted with many slides that extended from the top of the mountains to the valley floor.

The valley eventually narrowed into a short perpendicular canyon which was passable only on the north side of the river along a narrow timbered shelf about forty feet wide. An ancient well-used elk trail led from the valley through the canyon over this shelf to a low river bottom. The upper or far end of this bottomland was covered with large rocks, some larger than a five-room house. They had fallen from above centuries ago and had been worn round and smooth by the action of the glacial water. They lay piled on top of one another like a load of giant gravel, the water finding its way around and underneath.

An old Hoh Indian friend had told me that his tribesmen had discovered the elk trail leading into this box canyon and utilized it as a natural death trap to secure their annual supply of meat. He explained how the "beaters" would alarm the unsuspecting bands of elk and drive them over the shelf trail where in their frantic effort to get through they would be shoved and crowded and fall to the rocky bottom below. Hunters concealed behind trees at the bottom of the canyon would make their kill at short range using yew bow, spear or musket. He had participated in several of these elk kills and told me that in one of the most successful drives, ten elk were killed.

He also had told me of the great fear the Indians had of the powerful God Thunderbird who lived in the high mountains and threatened death to any who ventured into his domain. The Indians believed they could go upstream as far as it was navigable with their canoes. They did not go beyond this canyon because Thunderbird had many Bald Eagle scouts to report any infraction of his rules. The Indians also told of a fierce race of 'Stick Siwashes' that inhabited the high mountains and to encounter one of them meant death. The Indians respected these stories handed down by their fore-fathers.

A fair sized Indian village had flourished at the mouth of the Hoh River until 1890. But this tribe, a branch of the Quileutes, have slowly died out or moved to join other tribes. As a result of these superstitions the South Fork of the Hoh was a convenient and lucrative area for summer harvest for the Hoh Indians. At various places along the river as far up as the canyon, we saw evidence where they had established summer homes and smoke houses. Some of the old cedar stumps that served as smoke houses could still be seen. They also caught and smoked salmon for winter use. A large drying rack of split cedar and forked sticks about two and a half feet high and covering about one quarter acre was still in evidence when we were on this trip but had partly fallen down. Besides killing game, the Indians built new cedar canoes, gathered long slim cedar branches to be twisted into rope, and stripped the inside bark of young cedar trees to be woven into mats, blankets, and baskets. In late September they loaded both the old and new canoes with their bountiful harvest and returned to the village at the mouth of the river, a distance of some fifty miles. Here they exchanged some of their summer's harvest with villagers who had spent the summer killing whales for blubber and oil.

We made camp for the night on a ledge above a slide where the river emerges from this almost inaccessible canyon. From our camp this canyon looked like a tunnel and appeared to be about one-quarter mile long. The next day after further exploration we found another way through the canyon by way of the rough and rocky north slope which led us into a beautiful oblong basin, the sides of which were nearly covered with snow and glaciers. This was the true headwater of the South Fork of the Hoh. The rim of the basin consists of the south slope of Mt. Tom, the southwest slope of Mt. Olympus and Hubert Glacier, and the north slope of another mountain having no name to my knowledge. It would be very difficult to reach the summit of any of these mountains including Mt. Olympus from this side.

Knowing the past Indian history of this South Fork area I feel a haunting and mysterious respect each time I travel here.

Chapter 22

"Indian Legend: 'The Ark and the Flood'"

Mount Olympus is the highest mountain in the several Olympic mountain ranges. It is by no means the highest in the United States but boasts the longest glacier. It is covered with many great glaciers which are the source of a great river system that nurtures the timbered valleys below its mighty summit. Its 7,965 foot-high peak will waft a last farewell to the departing sailor and extend a welcome to the homecoming sailor. It is named for Mt. Olympus in Greece, which according to Greek mythology was the fabled seat of the Gods. Surely the name is well-chosen and applicable to this grand mountain. However, we don't have to borrow fables from old Greece, for the Indian legend about our Mt. Olympus is as interesting as any Greek myth and possibly as old as Noah's Ark and the Great Flood. The following story was told to me by an old Indian many years ago who said it had been handed down to him by his forefathers.

A great many suns (years) ago, the Indians along the coast were continually fighting and were very bad in every way. This displeased Quaty, God of the great mountain, who threatened punishment to the Indians. A few of the Indians from different tribes were tired of their neighbors' continuous fighting, so loaded their belongings in canoes and poled up some of the rivers and settled far inland in peace and quiet. These Indians were known as the "Stick Siwash" and were seldom molested by their coastal counterparts.

Quaty decided to punish the coastal Indians, but first he warned the Stick Siwash tribe whom he loved, that a great flood would come and they must prepare to save themselves.

Then Quaty caused the Chinook winds and warm rains to come. They continued for many days and nights, never ceasing, melting the snow and ice in the mountains and causing a big flood. All this rain and melting snow caused the ocean to rise higher and higher every day until all canoes were lost and all the Indians along the ocean were drowned.

The Indians far up the rivers had gathered many cedar boughs which they had twisted into a long stout rope. They loaded their canoes with their belongings and the rope and, as the water rose higher, they paddled further inland. The water kept on rising until only the top of Mt. Olympus was above water. The Indians paddled to it and fastened their rope to the highest peak. Then all of the canoes were made fast to this rope.

The top of the mountain protruding above the water resembled an island. Deer, bear, elk, cougar, wolves, in fact every animal native to the Olympics were crowded together in complete harmony. It was some time before the waters began to recede and it became necessary to kill some elk for food. The Indians in their canoes lowered themselves down the mountain with the falling water. The big rope was finally cut and as the water kept receding down the valley, they paddled down river to the beach. They found they were the only ones that had survived the flood. They all returned to their respective settlements at the mouths of the great rivers that flowed from Mt. Olympus.

The Indians still claim to this day that at times when there is not too much snow and ice on Mt. Olympus, part of the great rope can be seen sticking out from under the glacial ice.

Hoh River Valley looking slightly to the southeast toward the Bailey Range. Hoh Glacier on Mt. Olympus in upper right center.

Part IV

Preface: Growing Pains In The Forest, 1903-1909

During the period from 1900 to 1903, 500,000 acres of the Olympic Reserve were thrown open to claim. The majority of claimants that clamored for this free land were not serious homesteaders but individuals who filed on a claim, made final proof as quickly as it was legal, then sold out to the eastern timber speculators who had agents in the field to purchase any timber-land they could get their hands on. In three years these timber agents had acquired most of these claims for $200 to $500 each, which was a tidy profit then for the claimholder, and scandalously cheap timber land for the speculator.

Some established settlers who were unhappy or discouraged also sold out to the timber agents. The settlers who remained were those who had already planted their roots deep in the forest, sacrificed money and labor, and felt they could not afford to abandon their investment. The net gain of new settlers in the forest communities was very small. The possibility of future growth and development of western Clallam and Jefferson counties had been dealt another heavy blow.

Prior to 1903 there had been considerable turnover of supervisors and superintendents in the forest reserve. Many were political appointments given to men unqualified to administer the vast chunks of wilderness assigned to them. In most cases they never bothered to acquaint themselves with the rugged interior but were satisfied to direct their duties from behind a desk in relative ease and comfort.

There was an absence of policy and leadership, and no government funds were being appropriated for development of the reserve. Trails connecting settlements soon deteriorated as voluntary upkeep was too much for the remaining settlers. What little trail building was done was usually to accommodate some privileged or special group. Forest fires were numerous and burned out of control because federal and state governments had no funds for fire-fighting or fire prevention. Practically all that was done by Reserve Rangers between 1900 and 1903 was in settling land claim contests, serving notice of illegal grazing, or protecting timber against theft. The permanent settlers, including Chris, resented the government policy of favoring the timber claimant and began to look upon the Reserve Ranger with resentment.

In spite of this animosity, Chris joined the ranks of the Reserve Rangers and took the oath of office on June 25, 1903 while building trail around the south side of Lake Crescent. He continued as a Reserve Ranger under the Department of Interior until February 1, 1905. At that time

93

President Theodore Roosevelt signed a bill transferring the Reserve to the Department of Agriculture and the Olympic Reserve became known as the Olympic National Forest. Two months later on April 1, 1905, Chris was sworn in as a U.S. Forest Service Ranger.

Fred Hansen was appointed the first official supervisor of Olympic National Forest with headquarters at Hoodsport on Hood Canal. In the spring of 1907 Chris as a Ranger-at-large, was called to Hoodsport to locate and build a horse trail for a wealthy timber baron. He was summoned back to Lake Crescent in July to supervise the fire-fighting of one of the biggest forest fires on record on the Olympic Peninsula.

In 1908 Katherine Spease from Indiana came West to visit her cousins, the Elliotts, who had homesteaded on the lower Bogachiel River. Here she met Chris and the following year they were married making Olympia, Washington their first home. In 1910 the Forest Service office was established in Port Angeles. It was here they made their permanent home and raised their three children Margaret, Katherine and John.

On March 2, 1909, President Theodore Roosevelt issued a proclamation establishing Mt. Olympus Monument within the boundaries of the Olympic National Forest. It contained 633,600 acres for the "protection of certain objects of unusual and scientific interest including the numerous glaciers and the region which, from time immemorial has formed the summer range and breeding grounds of the Olympic Elk." (Cervus Rooseveltii). This decree brought conflicting opinion between forest officials and the public and disputes arose on many issues such as logging, mining, and hunting.

Raymond E. Benedict became Supervisor of Olympic National Forest replacing Hansen in October of 1909, and the supervisor's headquarters office was moved to Olympia, the state capitol. Benedict had mapped out a system of trails which would belt the National Forest approximately on the boundary lines. The theory was that it would discourage forest thievery, but it did nothing to open the back country for the public use. Fortunately this plan never materialized.

In the fall of 1909 Chris attended the University of Washington where he was enrolled in the new Special Short Course in Forestry designed by Francis G. Miller, Dean of the School of Forestry, and taught by Associate Professor Hugo T. Winkenwerder. The course was supplemented with lectures by outstanding U.S. Forest Service officials, and forestry leaders from Washington and Oregon. The primary purpose of the course was to train rangers and guards in the objectives of the Forest Service and the technical skills of forestry. Gifford Pinchott, Chief U.S. Forester at the time, deemed this training necessary and made it possible for these men to be released from their regular duties with pay so that they might attend this three month course.

On completion of this course, Chris was promoted to District Forest Ranger and a district office was established at Port Angeles with him in charge. This would be known as District I and comprised all of Clallam and western Jefferson Counties and included over 600,000 acres. The duties of a District Forest Ranger were many and varied, and for the first time the U.S. Forest Service issued a manual or "use" book.

Chris out for a sail, near East Beach, Lake Crescent

Crew returning from work on Lake Crescent Trail

A piece of trail around Lake Crescent

Chapter 23

"Becoming a Reserve Ranger"

For twelve years from 1890 to 1902 as a pioneer settler, I had some heartbreaks and disappointments but at no time did I lose sight of my objective which was to be a good American, do my share of pioneering and help develop the last great West. I had felled trees and cleared away stumps fifteen feet in diameter in order to plant crops and an orchard. I had built my home and helped other settlers build theirs. With hand tools, I had located and built trails through the jungle-like forest, fought forest fires on my land and my neighbors', served as constable of western Jefferson County for six years, explored much of the interior that lay at my back door, and had become familiar enough with life in this rugged environment to survive. I knew that raising spuds and hay in the leached rain forest soil was a poor means of making a living, so I began to look to other horizons for a livelihood. I hung on as long as I could but deep inside of me was a determination to succeed somehow at something in this magnificent forest that I had come to love and respect.

In the spring of 1903 I learned that Reserve Rangers were getting a guaranteed salary of $60 a month and that settlers were being hired because of their knowledge of the forest.

I wrote to Dr. Close who was Supervisor of the Olympic Reserve, asking for a job as a ranger. He answered my letter saying he was about to turn the office over to a Mr. D.B. Sheller who would consider my application. Mr. Sheller answered and explained that there was no well-defined policy for development of the reserve as it was still in its infancy, and that the few rangers employed were widely scattered. As a Ranger-at-large my first assignment would be to locate and build a trail around the south side of Lake Crescent and upgrade an existing Indian trail down the Soleduck Valley to the settlement of Sappho, a distance of twenty-eight miles. If I wanted the job, I should meet him in Port Angeles June 25 and be prepared and equipped to start on this project the same day. I certainly felt qualified for trail building and I needed this paying job, plus the job location would spare me the embarrassment of ranger and law enforcement duties in my own neighborhood.

I wrote my acceptance and on June 25 met the new superintendent, Mr. Sheller in Port Angeles. He had another ranger named Paul Laufeld with him and together we drove by wagon road to East Beach on Lake Crescent.

Chris kept a diary on the trail building and the first four entries read:

Thursday, June 25, 1903 — In company of Supt. D.B. Sheller and Ranger Paul Laufeld, started to blaze trail at 1 p.m. on the south side of Lake Crescent. Blazed from east end of lake to Sec. 24-T.30-R.9W., and camped at 6 p.m. Distance about 1 1/2 miles. Took oath of office at Rock Point.

Friday, June 26, 1903 — Left camp at 7 a.m. and blazed trail to NW Cor. Sec. 36-T.30-R.9W., company same as day before. About 3 miles through old burn and hard work.

Saturday, June 27, 1903 — Left camp at 7 a.m. company same as before and blazed trail to center of Sec. 34-T.30-R.9W., about 2 miles. Rain, very wet and bad going. Camped at Barnes Ranch, 5.30 p.m.

Sunday, June 28, 1903 — Left at 8 a.m. and blazed trail to west end of lake and returned to east end. Distance blazed, about 5 miles. Total distance traveled, 15 miles. Camped at 7 p.m.

The diary states that two additional rangers, Fred Wychoff, and Charles Nutter joined them on July 5th and for the next 12 days the four men and Superintendent Sheller worked from 7 a.m. to 6 p.m. swamping trail, sawing and bucking logs between the east end of the lake and Barnes Point.

Quoting the diary again:

Friday, July 17, 1903 — started work 8 a.m. swamped all day. Moved camp to Barnes Point.

Saturday, July 18 — Swamped trail around Barnes Point, about one half mile.

Monday, July 20 — Swamped trail about one half mile, returned to camp at Barnes Point.

Tuesday, July 21 — Sawed logs out of trail all day. Returned to camp 5.30.

Wednesday, July 22 — Commenced making rock cut. Returned to camp 6 p.m.

At this point the trail building project is discontinued, probably because of fire hazard in the woods, but before leaving the area, Ranger Laufeld, Wychoff and Chris were dispatched to the upper Soleduck River where they repaired the cable bridge. Chris then hiked the twenty miles to Forks and on to the Bogachiel the next day.

Through July and August the diary relates his ranger duties in the Calawah, Bogachiel, Hoh and Clearwater areas which included fire patrol of fifteen to twenty miles on foot each day, posting fire notices, serving grazing permits, cruising timber, investigating mineral and oil locations and repairing trail.

On September 10, the diary states that a heavy rain ended the fire hazard for the season. The daily log for the next two months records his singular activity of building new trail and repairing and improving existing settler trails in the Bogachiel, Hoh and Clearwater areas and erecting a sixteen foot long bridge. The good-will he was building into the ranger image was to have a long-term effect.

The last ten days of the diary relate a graphic picture of November weather in the woods of western Washington.

Nov. 5, 1903 — Continued stormy. High water in river.

Nov. 6, 1903 — Commenced work 8 a.m. making trail, Sec.6-T.27-R.12W.

Nov. 10, 1903 — Everything covered with wet snow, 3 inches, disagreeable and dangerous in woods on account of falling branches.

Nov. 13, 1903 — Started work 8.30 a.m. cutting trail, Sec. 1-T.27-R.12W., 100 yards. Quit 3 p.m. on account of rain.

Nov. 14, 1903 — Started work 9 a.m. but had to quit on account of rain and snow. Bringing home tools.

Nov. 15, 1903 — Making out report for November, gone to Post Office.

Chris continues:

- - - In February 1905 President Theodore Roosevelt transferred the National Forest Reserve from the Department of Interior to the Department of Agriculture and the Olympic Reserve became known as the Olympic National Forest. Paul Laufeld and I were sworn in on April 1, 1905, as U.S. Forest Service Rangers-at-large. My duties for the next five years centered around the Lake Crescent and Soleduck Valley areas. Paul's area was the Elwha River Valley.

In the spring and summer of 1905 a permanent horse trail to the Sol Duc Hot Springs was built. Rangers Laufeld, Nutter, Wychoff and I worked at intervals during the off fire season that same year to complete the twenty-eight miles of foot trail around the south shore of Lake Crescent to Sappho.

More and more people were being attracted to the Lake Crescent and Sol Duc Hot Springs areas for the scenery, fishing, and curative powers of the waters of the springs, so the Forest Service decided a ranger station was needed.

Rangers Laufeld, Nutter, Wychoff, Ed Brooks and I set about to build this ranger station at Lake Crescent. Axel Ahola, a Russian Finn homesteader, who lived near Piedmont, on the north side of the lake deserves much credit in lending his know-how on using the logs available on the spot. He showed us how to peel and prepare the logs so that they fit tightly together, and how to hand-hew and cross-notch the logs so that they dove-tailed precisely at the corners. This made for a superior fit plus uniformity of design. The cabin was finished the following year and we five were very proud of our efforts; a beautiful one and a half story log structure at the water's edge in the shadow of Mt. Storm King. It was appropriately named Storm King Ranger Station. This ranger station was a link in a chain of ranger stations and guard stations built over the next several years in the Olympic National Forest that served as an early warning system for fire prevention. All were manned and connected by telephone throughout the summer season. Besides protecting the pristine beauty of the forests they played an important part in serving the public.

(In 1982 the Ranger station was determined to be eligible for the National Historic Preservation Landmark List. It was necessary to dismantle and relocate the cabin a few hundred feet from the original site. Some of the original logs and other materials were used in duplicating the old structure. In July of 1987 it was dedicated at a public ceremony by Olympic National Park officials.) . . Editor

Storm King Ranger Station, Lake Crescent, 1905-1906. Building crew, Chris second from left, Paul Laufeld extreme right.

Chapter 24

"Locating Trail, South Fork Skokomish"

The timber barons of the early 1900's deserve some credit for opening up the interior of the Olympics. One such person was Alfred H. Anderson who owned the Potlatch Logging Company near Hoodsport on Hood Canal. (Footnote #1)

The first settlers on the Canal had built nine miles of trail to Lake Cushman. Then as settlement advanced, five more miles were built to the south and west through a heavy stand of timber to Brown's Creek. One early settler named LeBar extended the trail two more miles up river to his homestead. After making final proof on his claim and building a cabin, LeBar sold out to Mr. Anderson who was buying all the timberland below the LeBar claim on the South Fork of the Skokomish River.

Anderson was an enthusiastic sports fisherman and had found the river to be well stocked with Cutthroat and Rainbow trout. He rebuilt the LeBar cabin into a fishing lodge where he was known to hibernate for weeks with his "big shot" cronies while being supplied by pack train from Hoodsport with food and liquid refreshments. The best fishing holes were up river beyond the Anderson Lodge and could only be reached on old blaze lines made by trappers and hunters or on an occasional elk trail.

In the spring of 1907, Mr. Anderson came to the Olympic National Forest office at Hoodsport to talk about building a horse trail from his lodge to the head of the Skokomish River. He said he envisioned extending this trail down the west side of the mountains to Lake Quinault making it possible for sportsmen and mountaineers to have an access to Lake Quinault. Fred Hansen, Supervisor of the Olympic Forest, told him that he had neither funds nor authority to undertake such a project. Mr. Anderson countered by offering to finance building this trail, providing the Forest Service locate and supervise its construction. To this, Supervisor Hansen agreed.

Since I was Ranger-at-large, with headquarters at Hoodsport, it fell my lot to locate and build this proposed horse trail.

First I hired a cook and trail crew of nine. Then I selected a man, part Indian, from the Skokomish Indian Tribe to be my scouting partner, knowing he would be familiar with the area. Mr. Anderson sent to eastern Washington for a packer, six saddle horses, nine pack horses and one mule.

On June 1, our heavily laden pack train and crew were assembled at Hoodsport. It was a novel sight for the natives to see such a formidable outfit about to head for the unbroken jungles of the Olympics.

The first day we traveled about thirteen miles on established trail to the Anderson Lodge where we made base camp. By early afternoon my Indian partner and I had blazed about one-half mile of trail along the river bank. Everyone was raring to get started. Some of the crew had begun construction using brush hooks, axes, crosscut saws and mattocks. Some of the crew chose to go fishing and caught enough trout to supply camp for the next day.

After three weeks of blazing and building trail we reached timberline. We had seen deer, elk and bear and had tested many fishing holes with thrilling results. We routed the trail through stands of timber of great diameter and built several good overnight campsites. We advanced another two miles along open grassy, flower-bedecked slopes overlooking beautiful mountain scenery. Continuing over a low pass of 4,000 feet elevation (Footnote #2) and down the eastern side of the divide we came to one of the most beautiful spots in the Olympics. It was here on the park-like shores of Lake Sundown that we relocated our camp.

While transferring camp gear and supplies the pack train encountered near tragedy in a ravine which had been spanned by a natural snow bridge. When the horses arrived at this point, the packer examined the snow pack and decided it was strong enough to carry the horses. Eight of them got across safely, but the next two broke through the icy crust and went out of sight. The crew, with shovels, opened a trail to the bottom of the ravine and rescued the two frightened but unhurt horses. The rest of the pack train had to be detoured around the lower end of the snowbank.

My Indian partner and I decided that while the crew was grading trail back to where we left off at timberline, we should explore farther west for a route to the Quinault Valley. We climbed a nearby mountain peak where we looked down on a deep and narrow valley winding to the northwest. We estimated the distance ahead and time it would take to scout and blaze this piece of trail as about five days.

We returned to camp and early next morning with five days rations put up by the cook, we started out. We marked several switchbacks down the hillside to the main stream in the valley. This was the rainy side of the divide and the undergrowth and timber was very dense. We followed this stream down the valley and noted that many smaller streams fed into this one. By the time we reached the south footing of Mt. Olsen, we were following a good sized stream at that time known as the South Fork of the Quinault River. (Footnote #3) We continued locating trail along the north side of this stream to its junction with the East Fork of the Quinault River. At this junction we estimated it was about fourteen miles to Lake Quinault. We also found the old O'Neil trail coming down the river. (Footnote #4) From this point we started our return to camp following up the East Fork of the Quinault for a distance of about seven miles on the old O'Neil blaze line made in 1890. Here was one of the finest stands of Douglas fir I had ever seen. We followed up O'Neil Creek to the top of the east shoulder of Mt. Olsen, then to Lake Success, then over very sharp ridges. It was evening when we reached a point where we looked down on Lake Sundown and could see our trail camp. We were very tired after spending five days from daylight to dark blazing and staking out about twenty-eight miles of trail.

We sat in silence on an outcropping of rock looking down on the tranquil scene below. Three tents were pitched near the lake, smoke was curling up from an open campfire, the men were sitting or walking about and the horses were contentedly grazing in the grassy meadows close by. The stars and stripes of the American flag were flying in the early evening breeze from a pole near the cook tent. A long snow finger extended up the hill on our left and here two deer were feeding peacefully. The shrill whistle of friendly mountain marmots could be heard from several directions. This tableau of serenity and beauty with my adopted country's flag flying in the breeze had a special meaning to me and has always remained fresh in my memory.

My friend awakened me from my day-dreaming saying, "Chris, Klosh nesike cooly dupa camp, iskims muka muk." (Let us go to camp and get some eats.) We called and waved to the men down in camp and the picturesque scene came to an end. The two deer ran out of sight, the marmots ceased their whistling, the horses stood at attention and the whole camp came to life.

When we got into camp, Mr. Anderson was there and greeted us enthusiastically. He had arrived that day with a pack train and supplies. Over a wonderful dinner fit for a king, he praised the crew for their work. I was satisfied that my guide and I had accomplished what we had set out to do--find the most accessible east to west route along the South Fork of the Skokomish River to the Quinault River.

I advised that ahead lay nine miles of rather costly work to the juncture of the East Fork of the Quinault with the main river and thence to the O'Neil trail junction. Mr. Anderson said that he had already been repaid by being able to ride and fish and enjoy such beautiful high mountain scenery, and that we should go ahead and finish the project.

Part of the crew began work on the nine miles we had blazed to the Quinault River, while the others and myself made a temporary trail over the ridge to McGravey Lakes and Lake Success. Thence to O'Neil Creek and the old O'Neil Junction.

On July 10, a Forest Service messenger came to camp with orders for me to go at once to Lake Crescent and Soleduck as a forest fire had started in that locality. I left immediately by way of our North Fork trail of the Skokomish to Hoodsport, then on to Port Angeles by way of Seattle. I instructed the crew to finish the trail.

Later I learned that Mr. Anderson had returned with his pack train intending to go through to Lake Quinault via the O'Neil Creek trail. I was informed that one of his mules missed his footing in going over the first ridge and had fallen over a cliff. In another place they were passing over the trail where it was close to the brink of a canyon wall. One of the horses caught his pack on a tree, lost his balance and fell fifty feet into the canyon. The horse, which carried all of Anderson's fishing gear was carried away in the swift water and never seen again. The party kept on, determined to reach Lake Quinault, which they did the next evening. After returning to his lodge on the Skokomish, he ordered the packer to move the trail crew out and dismiss them as he had lost all incentive to go back to the Quinault. Thus a seven mile link of this trail was left unfinished."

Postscript by Chris:

Five years later in 1912, the Forest Service completed this seven mile stretch of horse trail. The Forest Service also built a horse trail to the East Fork of the Quinault River by way of Anderson Pass (elevation 5,000 feet) thence through Honeymoon Meadow and down West Creek where it meets the main Dosewallips trail. Many other horse trails have since been built by the Forest Service and alpine lakes have been stocked with fish in the scenic alpine wonderland on the east side of the Olympic Mountains.

Footnote #1: Alfred H. Anderson was a dominant figure in the lumber industry in Mason County for nearly a quarter of a century from the late 1880's until his death in 1914. Anderson Hall, part of the College of Forestry on the University of Washington Campus, was donated by his wife Agnes Healy Anderson and dedicated in 1925 in memory of her husband.

Footnote #2: Sundown Pass or LeBar Pass, Olympic National Forest Map, 1915.

Footnote #3: It has since been named "Graves Creek" for Colonel Graves, U.S. Forester.

Footnote #4: The first exploring expedition from Hood Canal to Lake Quinault was in 1890 by way of the Duckabush River and down the East Fork of the Quinault River. It was sponsored by the U.S. Government under the supervision of Lt. Joseph P. O'Neil of the U.S. Army. Some horses were taken through but no permanent trail location was established.

Old Marymere Hotel, Lake Crescent, 1906. Chris in white shirt, standing on porch, Mt. Storm King in the background.

Soleduck Burn, 1907.

Soleduck Burn, 1907, Lake Crescent seven miles distant.

Chapter 25

"The Soleduck Fire"

It took nearly a week for me to reach Port Angeles from the trail crew base camp at Lake Sundown. I learned the fire had started as a clearing fire in May on the Mueller Ranch west of Lake Crescent. It had gone out of control and burned about forty acres but had been put out by the homesteader, one ranger and the help of a good rain. A rotten log eighty feet long had continued to smoulder like a charcoal pit for two months unnoticed, when it finally burned through to the end where it quickly ignited dry brush and other tinder. By the time two men and I reached the fire it had crept through green timber for a mile across the Soleduck Valley and a mile west and east.

In the early days of fire fighting there were no well-trained crews, no supply of tools and no telephones. I dispatched a messenger to Port Angeles to bring more men and supplies. Eight men were recruited which took another day and a half for them to reach the fire line, coming by stage, boat and foot.

Our first job was to keep the fire from reaching Lake Crescent. Settlers around the lake loaned axes, shovels and mattocks. Theodore Rixon, who was on the Soleduck River with a railway survey crew, let us have eight more men. The wind was coming from the east so I urged the men to work fast to complete and hold the fire line, hoping that the wind would die down by evening. We were able to make a backfire line from the valley floor to the top of the ridge above the west end of the lake.

I hurried on foot twelve miles west down the trail to Bear Creek where I recruited seven more men and tools. We were returning to the fire line when we saw great clouds of black smoke rising and drifting rapidly towards the Straits of Juan de Fuca. The strong east wind had caught the fire and I knew it had jumped our line and was stampeding west down the Kloshe Nanich Ridge.

I sent one man ahead on the run to warn two families of the oncoming fire. As we neared the fire we could see a great wall of flame coming towards us down the hillside. Cauliflower-shaped smoke clouds were billowing four to five hundred feet into the air. Burning tree limbs, five inches in diameter, were being sucked up into the hot air and exploding like skyrockets, spreading fire in every direction. the sight was awesome and terrifying, making me wonder if it would consume the whole countryside.

By eight in the evening the fire had reached Bear Creek but the wind had died down. Part of the crew had retreated to Bear Creek where we hoped the fire could be stopped. A horse trail up this valley, the creek and a fringe of alder bottoms made an ideal fire line. We worked frantically all night back-firing in spite of having to extinguish many spot fires which jumped the line. By morning we had managed to control the westward march of the holocaust.

Word came through that the settlers and the man I sent to warn them were safe. When they saw the fire was too fast to outrun, they went to a root cellar in the open field, covered it with wet dirt and crawled inside. The fire roared by on both sides of them and they suffered only a few burns and swollen eyes from the smoke.

A crew of seven stayed on the west side to mop up while I proceeded up the Soleduck River to survey the damage. It was rough and dangerous going as trees were falling everywhere. The fire crew here told me that a great gust of wind had funnelled the fire over the line along the hillside and they were helpless to control it. Some spot fires had started across the river and while putting them out we were confronted with ground fire in a deep layer of moss and rotted wood. It was impossible to get a shovel down to mineral soil.

A pack train heading for the Sol Duc Hot Springs happened along with two boxes of stumping powder. We borrowed the powder, cut each stick into two cartridges and with a pole sharpened at one end we made holes eighteen inches deep and six feet apart. By setting the dynamite off, the thick mossy cover of humus was blasted off, exposing dirt and rock. This made an effective fire line and stopped the deep-seated ground fire. This was the first time dynamite was used to build a fire line.

From the time the fire went out of control it travelled eleven miles to Bear Creek in five hours. It burned over 12,800 acres and destroyed between six and seven hundred million board feet of good timber. Although this fire had about thirty miles of outline it was held under control until rain came in September. It was interesting to note that the fire did not eat out into the flat valley to any extent, it burned only the south slope of the ridge which was exposed to the sun and the updraft from the valley floor. It did not slop over onto the north side of the ridge.

Many bear and deer were found along the Soleduck River, some had died from burns, others blinded or had their fur partly singed off. Many grouse and birds were found dead or injured.

This fire is known locally as the Soleduck Burn and was the most destructive fire I ever was to fight. I paid the entire cost of fighting this fire out of money received on my personal note to a Port Angeles Bank. The Forest Service did not have a fiscal agent nearer than Washington D.C., and it took nearly two years before I was reimbursed.

The scars of this fire and the immense timber loss prompted the Forest Service to initiate the first reforestation program in the Olympic National Forest. In mid-October of 1910, a crew of eighteen men established camp and in teams began broadcasting seed by hand from shoulder sacks on the burned mountainside west of Lake Crescent. They worked until mid-December when they were forced to break camp because of winter snows.

The following year it was discovered that rodents and squirrels had eaten much of the seeds and only a small percent of the seed germinated. It was not until 1919 that a sizeable reforestation program was again established by the Forest Service in the Soleduck Burn area. The first shipment of 70,000 young fir seedling trees arrived in April of that year and planting began immediately west of Lake Crescent. Planting was halted during the dry summer months, resumed again in the fall, and again had to cease on some of the slopes that were 3,000 to 4,000 feet in elevation because of an early snowfall. It took several spring and fall seasons before the job was completed. The original 540 acres that was seeded in 1910 was replanted with 360,000 young firs. Each tree planter soon became adept at the art and was planting 700 trees each day, the trees being laid out eight feet apart. This reforestation project ensured an excellent stand of young timber.

In 1923 the Olympic Highway from Lake Crescent to Forks was completed. This road passes through the entire twelve-mile stretch of the 1907 Soleduck Burn. Millions of silver colored dead snags visible on those hillsides to passing motorists were stark reminders for several decades of that terrible holocaust.

In 1924 a carelessly thrown cigarette by a motorist resulted in a fire that burned over one-third of this reforested area before it could be stopped. (Footnote)

(Footnote): By the 1950's the trees planted in the 1919 reforestation project had nearly hidden the scars of both fires, and today only an occasional white snag is visible among the healthy stand of second growth timber.

Ed.

Chapter 26

"Indian Legend: 'Tears of Two Dragons'"

On the cool north fringe of the Olympic Mountains on the banks of the Soleduck River near the river's source, is a group of hot springs. Quileute Indians had given the name "Soleduck" meaning "Sparkling Water" to the river. It is rightfully named for it is a very clear, sparkling mountain steam. They referred to the curative waters of the hot springs as "skukum lemensen" or "strong medicine".

The Indians had stumbled upon these hot springs, that bubbled forth from the ground far up the valley, centuries ago while hunting the great herds of elk that frequented the river valley in the fall and winter months. Each fall they would bring their sick relatives and friends up the river in canoes and by trail to this spot where they were restored to health. At the same time they hunted and cured their winter supply of elk meat. According to legend no Indian ever died at the springs.

Theodore Moritz, a white settler who lived in the Quillayute Valley and was well acquainted with the Indians, is credited with discovering the Sol Duc Hot Springs in 1880. He had befriended a sick Indian who in turn showed him this secret place that had magical healing powers. Moritz, recognizing the potential of these hot mineral springs, came to Port Angeles and filed claim on the land. Soon word spread of the "strong medicine" and many people from nearby areas started going there.

The other hot springs, much larger than the one on the Soleduck River is located on Boulder Creek, a tributary of the Elwha River about twenty miles southwest of Port Angeles. A hunter, Andrew Jacobsen, claimed he first discovered these hot springs in 1892 while hunting in the Boulder Creek area. The springs and their whereabouts were all but forgotten until on June 25, 1907, William "Billie" Everett, Thomas "Slim" Farrell and Charles Anderson, re-discovered them while on a cougar hunting trip into the remote, inaccessible canyon. They named them Olympic Hot Springs, hewed out a cedar log for a tub, flumed in the hot spring water and this was the beginning of what was to become the Olympic Hot Springs Resort.

The following Indian legend about the origin of these two hot springs was told to me in the early 1900's by an old Indian of the Quileute tribe.

A very long time ago the Olympic Mountains were ruled by two large and powerful dragons. One of these ruled all of the country north and east of the Elwha River that drained into Puget Sound and the Straits of Juan de Fuca. The other dragon ruled all of the country on the west side of the ridge drained by the Soleduck River and emptying into the Pacific Ocean. Each dragon ruled over all the Indians within his territory. These dragons had many disputes and fights over the boundary line which was along the top of the divide with the Soleduck River on one side and the Elwha River on the other side. Boulder Peak was the highest point of this divide. The headquarters of these monsters were near Boulder Peak in two great mountain caverns, each one on his respective side of the mountain.

Every full moon during centuries past, these dragons would patrol their domain and had met many times in combat over supremacy of the territory. They attacked each other with their powerful tails and were so well matched that the battle always resulted in a draw, each returning to his mountain home to recuperate until the next meeting. The immensity of these battles is still evidenced by the barren grassy slopes in the area.

One moonlit night the two dragons set out on their monthly patrol, meeting on Boulder Peak. They at once challenged each other for combat. They fought fiercely for many hours on the mountain top in an effort to kill one another, clearing the entire ridge of timber and starting many rock slides. Both dragons suffered greater injuries than before and when completely exhausted, dragged themselves to their respective mountain caves where they sealed up the entrances with huge boulders and in solitude proceeded to shed great quantities of hot tears over their wounds. It is said that when their wounds are healed and they have regained their full strength they will again come forth and renew the battle for supremacy. In the meantime the hot breath and tears of the Sol Duc dragon bubble up in the Soleduck Valley to give health and strength to his people during his convalescence, while the Elwha dragon's hot breath and tears do the same for himself and his people in the Elwha Valley.

I trust that these dragons will continue to shed hot tears to alleviate some of the ills of mankind, for many years to come.

Chapter 27

"Locating Trail, Lake Crescent to Olympic Hot Springs"

In August of 1908, Theodore Rixon, Glyde Chapman and I decided to locate a trail from Lake Crescent to the Olympic Hot Springs. Mr. Rixon was a surveyor and engineer. Mr. Chapman worked for the Forest Service and ran a string of pack horses between Fairholme on Lake Crescent and the Sol Duc Hot Springs when that resort was being built. Both Rixon and Chapman resided at Fairholme. I was the District Ranger.

From the west end of the lake we ascended the steep timbered ridge that skirts the south shore of Lake Crescent. After three hours of climbing we reached a park-like flat with three small spring-filled lakes in the center. A band of elk was retreating up a hill and it was evident that this little park was much in use as a drinking place and sanctuary for many elk.

From the shores of Lake Crescent bald eagles had frequently been seen soaring above this ridge, and at this moment a pair were circling overhead. We named the lakes "Eagle Lakes", ate our lunch and continued east along the top of the ridge past Sourdough Mountain. We were at about 4,000 feet elevation with the North Fork of the Soleduck River in the valley below on the south side of the ridge, and Lake Crescent below us on the north side of the ridge.

A well traveled elk trail through alpine timber and grassy meadows made the going easy. By evening we came into a large open meadow where another band of elk was grazing. Here was a strong spring surrounded by sheltering trees, and since this was the only water we had seen since leaving Eagle Lakes, we decided to make camp here.

The night was moonless and as we lay star-gazing, long streamers of light of various colors began radiating over the peak above us. We thought the lights were searchlights, since a number of Japanese battleships were due to go through the Straits of Juan de Fuca on a good-will visit to Seattle. After watching these rotating beams for a while, Rixon exclaimed, "Battleships, my foot, it's the Aurora Borealis, let's go up to the peak and watch them!"

We climbed up the open slope to the highest point. Here our range of vision was unobstructed across Lake Crescent to the Straits, Vancouver Island and beyond. The lights of Victoria were directly in line with the axis of the Aurora Borealis and the colored shafts of light emitted from a central point far north of Vancouver Island. It was a gorgeous display, to which tickets could not be purchased and we had box seats to see one of nature's greatest shows. This spectacle of light lasted over an hour and after the curtain fell, we came back to our starlit camp and made a pot of coffee.

In the morning over breakfast we were still talking about this wonderful show. To commemorate the drama of the night before we established the names of "Aurora Ridge", "Aurora Peak", "Aurora Meadows", "Aurora Camp", "Aurora Springs", and "Aurora Creek". Such high drama as we three had witnessed would never be forgotten.

We continued on this high ridge which was mostly open country, to Boulder Peak. We saw much wildlife, acres of beautiful flowers and a panoramic view of high mountain scenery. This was the first trip by white man from Lake Crescent to the Olympic Hot Springs without trail or guide. We made a bull's-eye arrival to the Olympic Hot Springs late that afternoon of the second day out.

Two wooden bath tubs, a two-room log cabin, and a small natural hot spring mud pool were all the "modern" facilities at that time. "Chap", Rixon and I celebrated our successful wilderness trek with a rewarding soak in a steaming sulphur mud pool.

Postscript by Chris:

In the years that followed twenty-one strong hot spring pools were located in this immediate area and all contained fourteen well-defined minerals with curative qualities. The resort grew into a very popular spa and recreation hub for hikers going into the heart of the Olympics. During this time good Forest Service trails were built reaching out to Mt. Olympus, Mt. Appleton, the Hoh Valley, Seven Lakes Basin and the Sol Duc Hot Springs. Four miles of trail were built by the Forest Service from the Olympic Hot Springs to Boulder Lake and the lake was stocked with fish. From Lake Crescent to Aurora Springs, the Forest Service had also built trail, leaving a gap of about six miles over very easy country. In 1929 a cooperative Forest Service-County road was built from the Elwha Ranger Station to the Olympic Hot Springs. At the same time the Forest Service established an excellent public campground near the springs that could be reached by car. The Hot Springs now boasted a very good hotel, many housekeeping cabins, a store, individual bathhouses with hot mineral baths and a new Olympic-sized swimming pool fed by the therapeutic waters of the mineral springs. That same year Helene Madison, Olympic Gold medalist swim star, dedicated this new pool. (Footnote)

Footnote: Olympic Hot Springs Resort was acquired by the National Park Service in 1966 from the Harry Schoffeld family and all structures and facilities were completely demolished shortly thereafter. Today nothing remains of this once lovely mountain resort except the original bubbling hot spring mud holes. The area has gone back to its natural state. Few people frequent this area except a handful of hardy backpackers who take time to restore their aching muscles in the hot mineral pools.

- - Editor

Suspension Cable Bridge on Soleduck River.

Chris bringing in much needed rations for trail crew. Old Barnes Cabin at Barnes Point, on Lake Crescent, 1906.

Chapter 28

Historic Notes, Anecdotes and Newspaper Clippings

Historic Notes- 1907 Trail Building on the Elwha (Fromme Memoirs)

"Early settlers and trappers on the Elwha River had in most part been responsible for establishing the first pathways into the interior of the Elwha Valley.

In 1907 the Seattle Mountaineers sent Asahel Curtis, photographer, and W. Montelius Price, to Port Angeles where they conferred with the local banker W.R. Delabarre regarding the possibility of having a trail built up the Elwha Valley to Mt. Olympus. In company with Grant Humes as guide, they scouted the best route for such a trail. Work was started immediately by a crew and the Mountaineers paid for the labor."

Two Anecdotes: From Rosalie Laufeld's diary, Summer, 1908, at Storm King Ranger Station

"...When making the horse trail around the lake, they needed dynamite. Quite a load arrived by launch from East Beach and Daddy and Mr. Morgenroth put it in the tent, about 100 feet from the ranger station. The men had gone to work on the trail at the far end of the lake and would not be back for several days.

There was a tree nearby, and it was burning for clearing. I was afraid the tree might fall on the tent and the dynamite would explode. I went outside in the moonlight and carried all the boxes of dynamite into the house. The tree fell and some of the branches landed on the tent. When the men came from the forest, our Daddy gave me a big hug and Chris gave me a big thanks."

"When the trail crew was at "Rocky Point" widening the foot trail for horses, a charge of dynamite was set off. You could hear the blast echoing around the lake and it sounded like the mountains were coming down. When the dust settled Daddy could not find his sledgehammer. He and Chris decided it must have gone flying into the lake, so they named the place "Sledgehammer Point".

Historic Note: Newspaper Clip, Port Angeles "Olympic Leader"--1909
"Great Scenic Trail;
Government Route Around Lake Crescent
Affords Wonderful Natural Beauties."

Chris Morgenroth, District Forest Ranger announces that the new government trail around Lake Crescent and on to the west coast is open all the way and that it is practical now to ride horseback from this city to Grays Harbor. Mr. Morgenroth states that the telephone line will be in operation within a week from the east end of Lake Crescent around the south shore as far as Fairholme at the west end. This trail opened up by the government for use by the U.S. Forest Service, pioneers the route of the state road that will be extended through the territory as rapidly as money becomes available and affords one of the most beautiful scenic routes in the entire Northwest if not in the world. (Footnote)

Footnote: In 1922 an automobile road was completed on the south shore of Lake Crescent. It follows in most part the original Forest Service trail blazed and built in 1903 and 1904. This road later became part of U.S. Highway 101. . . . Editor

Paul Laufeld at Sledgehammer Point, Lake Crescent, 1908.

Part V

Preface: The Wheels Begin to Turn, 1910 to 1920

In May of 1911 Parish Lovejoy replaced Benedict as Supervisor of Olympic National Forest. With packsack and bedroll, Chris showed him the Olympic back country. Their relationship for a little over a year was a very close one as they plotted and planned together a whole new concept for public use and development of the National Forest and the Monument. They agreed that opening up the interior for public use and fire prevention should have top priority. The district office in Port Angeles became a beehive of activity and administration became a full time job. Written reports of a varying nature consumed much time, and more often than not long hours turned into long days and week-ends of forest-related duties. While Chris was dedicated and thorough in his administrative duties, a necessary field trip into his "backyard of mountains" was always another adventure and a welcome respite from the office details.

After a year of service Lovejoy retired in May of 1912 to accept a professorship in the School of Forestry at the University of Michigan. Chris hated to see him leave, but the wisdom, ideas and knowledge exchanged by these two men was to have a lasting effect on the physical development and administration of Olympic National Forest. Their friendship through correspondence continued for the next 27 years.

Late in the summer of 1912 Rudo Fromme stepped in as supervisor, a job he had coveted since Hansen's reign. Like Lovejoy, Fromme was introduced into the back country with packsack and bedroll and became acquainted first-hand with the expert guidance of Chris. The relationship took root and resulted in fourteen years of solid progress for Olympic National Forest.

The Forest Service was responsible for land management and selling timber, but more importantly they were committed to the protection of the watersheds of the great river system and the expansive forests from fire.

Prior to 1915, forest fires were a common occurrence in the summer season and dense clouds of smoke were expected to hide the scenery and obscure the sky. The Forest Service slowly changed this condition and by the mid 1920's, a smoke-filled sky was the exception rather than the rule. This change resulted from a set of fire regulations for the forest, an intensive program of educating and informing the public on use of the forest, strict law enforcement, prompt communication, adequate and modern fire fighting equipment and quick transportation of equipment and crews.

With timber the main resource, the Forest Service played an ever increasing role in the welfare and development of the Peninsula communities. As the Olympic Mountains unveiled their potential scenic resource, the Forest Service found it was imperative that this scenic wonderland be made more accessible to the mountain climber, backpacker, fisherman, photographer, nature lover and seeker of health. During this period hundreds of miles of trails were built and many resorts were developed on the shores of Lake Crescent and at the two Hot Springs in the mountainous interior.

In this segment Chris relates two exciting animal stories, a trespass struggle between the Forest Service and the landowner of the Sol Duc Hot Springs, a report given by him to the U.S. Forest Service Supervisors meeting relating to the responsibility and importance of the Forest Service to local communities and the forest users.

Since he did not write an historical account of the Forest Service of this period, an attempt to fill this gap had been made by use of exerpts from newspaper clips, Parish Lovejoy correspondence, Fromme Memoirs and other material.

Parish Lovejoy and Charlie Anderson
"On a long hike," 1910-1911.

Forest Service cable crossing.

116

Chapter 29

"A Cougar Hunt"

By summer of 1912 the Sol Duc Hot Springs Health Spa was running at capacity. A beautiful luxurious hotel had been completed which could be reached by motor stage from Lake Crescent over a road completed in 1911. Guests were attracted to this remote resort from far-away places by the curative powers of the sulphur spring water both for drinking and bathing.

The Forest Service had decided to build a trail beyond the resort which would lead into the high mountain country giving guests the thrill of experiencing the spectacular scenery and the vistas of Mt. Olympus. (Footnote)

One day in September of that year a trail crew I had assembled for the job was waiting at Fairholme on Lake Crescent to be transported to the Hot Springs. That same day, some guests bound for the hotel arrived on the ferry at Fairholme. The resort had sent its two beautiful red Stanley Steamers to pick up the crew. Mr. Day, the manager of the hotel, was there in his private car to transport the passengers.

I was in the first stage with part of the crew and left ahead of the others. Mr. Day's passengers, which included my wife and two-year old daughter, left with the second stage shortly afterwards. Charles (Charlie) Anderson, who was to do the packing for the trail job, was in the last stage with his dog "Ky" and the rest of the crew and freight.

Mr. Day's car had gone about eight miles to where the road came near to the Soleduck River. Suddenly a very large cougar bounded across the road in front of his car and went up the hillside out of sight. In that moment all passengers had a breathtaking thrill at seeing the cougar. Mr. Day stopped and waited a few minutes for the other stage, knowing Charlie was aboard with his hunting dog. Charlie put the dog on the hot track and "Ky" was off up the hill and after the mountain lion. As Charlie took off after the dog he yelled to Mr. Day that he had no rifle. No one on the other stage had a gun so it was decided Mr. Day and his passengers would hurry on to the Springs, a distance of six more miles and get Mr. Day's gun. I was waiting on the veranda of the hotel when he drove up in a cloud of dust. He hurriedly told me about the cougar and went into the hotel to get his rifle, which he gave to me. Some adventuresome guests, several bell hops and I climbed on the stage and at break-neck speed retraced the six miles in about eight minutes.

Gun in hand, I started up the hill after Charlie through tangled underbrush. A number of people tried to follow but soon I was on my own.

117

After going a few hundred yards I caught the sound of the hound. Charlie heard me crashing through the brush and called for me to hurry - that "Ky" had the big cat treed. Before I could come close enough for a shot, the nervous cougar jumped to the ground and "Ky" was after him again. His line of flight was back down the hill in the same direction. "Ky" bayed "treed" ahead of us; this time he had the cougar up a tree about a hundred yards from the road where the stages were parked. I placed a shot in the cougar's shoulder where-upon he leaped high out of the tree and headed on down the hill. The sight of the cougar coming their way caused some of the crowd to quickly climb the stages while others scattered up and down the road. With two long jumps the cougar crossed the road and headed for the river. At the river's edge he reversed direction and recrossed the road close to the stages with "Ky" on his heels. Charlie and I were just coming down the hill when suddenly charging toward us was Mr. Cougar. Seeing us he jumped on a leaning tree and climbed to the first limb. My shot had apparently wounded him and he was getting weak. We could see he was losing his hold on the tree. "Ky" was now jumping and barking fiercely beneath the tree. Charlie and I were afraid the cougar would fall and in its last struggle, injure the dog. Everybody on the road could see this drama. I took aim and fired, this time the cougar dropped mortally wounded to the ground. "Ky" made no move to attack. When we reached the cat he was stone dead.

The cougar was taken to the Hot Springs where it caused a great deal of curiosity among the 300 guests. It was a large magnificent specimen, measuring nine feet from tip to tip. Many pictures were taken of it in front of the hotel on the lawn.

On this journey to the Hot Springs I was wearing my "Sunday" clothes. When the hunt began I discarded my coat and vest at the road before starting up the hill. When the chase was over, everything I wore was ripped and torn.

The next day when the cougar was being skinned, the hotel chef, Billy Lenoir asked what would be done with the meat. We told him it would be buried. He asked for the two hind quarters, and that evening the dinner menu featured an attractive delicacy, "Roast Young Cougar with Currant Jelly." It sold out within an hour. The elite among the guests thought it very correct and a real treat to eat cougar in the Olympics. Not me, however; it was still cat in my book!

Charlie and "Ky" got the $20 bounty and I got the head and skin, which I had mounted. It served as a rug in my den at my Port Angeles home for many years and was quite a conversation piece.

Footnote: This horse trail from the Sol Duc Hot Springs to the head of the Soleduck River and down the Valley of the Hoh river was completed by the Forest Service in 1913.
Ch.M.

Big Cougar, shot by Chris near Sol Duc Hot Springs, 1912.

Chris and big Cougar, 1912.

Chapter 30

"A Case of Trespass"

One early day struggle between the Forest Service and private interest took place in 1911 while I was Deputy Supervisor. It concerned Mike Earles, a wealthy timber owner who had acquired the Sol Duc Hot Springs and was developing an ultra modern health spa.

Mike had a road built from his resort to the western end of Lake Crescent, but needed a piece of beach land where the road could terminate with a dock. All of the fine waterfront had been taken for building lots. The only available beach where Mike's road could reach the waters edge was a rock bluff, this would be an expensive and major blasting job and would take valuable time.

Theodore Rixon, a well known civil engineer owned two choice lots at this western end of the lake, right in a convenient location to Mike's road. Rixon had built the road to the Hot Springs the year before and the two men were friends. Mike asked Rixon for permission to build a temporary road over Rixon's property so he could bring in sawmill machinery and transport it to the springs where it would be assembled to cut lumber on the spot for the new 100-room hotel he was building. He would build his bluff road and landing later. Rixon told him it was okay thinking a written agreement was not necessary between friends.

While Rixon was busy elsewhere in the county, Mike was busy grading a road across Rixon's choice future homesite lots and ending it in a substantial dock. When Rixon discovered this predicament, he went to Mike to protest. Mike countered, saying the Rixon lots provided a far better landing than the bluff ever would and he had decided to pay Rixon for the lots, keeping the road where it was. Rixon refused the offer and the case went to court. Rixon was paid for the lots and the damage to his property but Mike felt he had won a major victory since he saved himself the extra cost of blasting down the bluff.

Some months later it was discovered by the Forest Service that Mike had built his sawmill at his Sol Duc resort half on his deeded property and half on Forest Service land and that some choice Cedar and Douglas Fir trees had come right off of government property. In order to prove this trespass, a reputable civil engineer was called in to check the survey lines. The surveyor happened to be Theodore Rixon. The property lines were found to be correct, so a civil suit was filed against Mike in Federal Court. Willful trespass carried a heavy penalty in both fines and jail. I was well acquainted with Mike Earles and all the angles of the controversy. We in the service knew he would use every excuse he could muster to avoid the charges.

He considered himself a friend of the Forest Service. He had boarded our trail crews in his logging camp and had willingly loaned his horses and burrows for packing supplies to our trail crews.

The suit was delayed for over a year during which time Supervisor Lovejoy had been replaced by Rudo Fromme. During this time Mike was arguing between the Portland and Washington, D.C. Forest Service offices. He maintained that his lofty character and good deeds in building such a fine first class edifice to benefit mankind should offset what he considered was a trifling accident in the woods.

The suit was finally settled out of court and Mike agreed to pay for the board feet estimate of the stumps of the forest service trees. Even at that he claimed the cedar trees were hollow. In the end Mike's admission of guilt only cost him $30 and Supervisor Fromme had to make four trips to Mike's logging operations office in Seattle to recover the money owed. The Forest Service learned a few hard lessons from this case.

Sol Duc Hot Springs Resort Hotel, showing umbrella walk to spring house and drinking fountain, 1912.

Chapter 31

"Fire Prevention"

The following excerpts from different sources show how fire prevention measures played a vital role in Chris's philosophy on protecting the forest even to making it unlawful to abandon a camp fire.

Letter to the Editor: Port Angeles Tribune Times, September 21, 1910

"During the last three months some fires were started in the Olympic National Forest, threatening large bodies of timber. But owing to the present system of fire patrol, the adequate telephone system which reaches nearly every outlying settlement, and the cooperation of all right thinking citizens in promptly reporting fires, the Forest Service was able to control every fire before much damage resulted. The total area of land burned over in District 1 for this season will not amount to over 250 acres.

On behalf of the Forest Service I wish to extend my heartfelt thanks to the commissioners, citizens of Clallam County, the Forest Fire Association and all who willingly co-operated by promptly reporting or otherwise helped to control fires. This made it possible to avert calamity, loss of life and property as has been the case in other parts of the northwest."

Chris Morgenroth
District Forest Ranger

From "Lovejoy Memos to Fromme", 1912

"... In regards to fire, the Department of Forestry and other outsiders seem to have assumed that there was not much risk. I think this is a great error. I doubt that there is a 40 acre tract on the whole peninsula which will not show big-fire signs from some time in the past. The moss in the tops makes each tree a Roman candle. When fire comes it comes a terror. I have been told that I am a fire crank but I was in Montana in 1910.

Needed here in Olympic are horse trails up all main rivers as rapidly as funds become available. Some bridges are needed at canyon crossings instead of having to hunt shallow, sometimes non-existent, fording spots to reach the better side of the stream bank. Needed are trails and trails and trails all looping into one another and into roads so as to allow cross cuts. All main trails and roads parallel with phone lines. Patrol boxes not farther than five miles apart on the phone lines. Boxes and lots of tools at or near the patrol telephone stations. Houses, sheds and shelters along the trails where they will serve to shelter crews and patrolmen and where tool cache boxes can be concentrated and protected in winter. We have made a fair start in building shelters this season. Lots of guards are necessary who would have regular beats. Morning tests of phone lines and arrangements for repair.

Then we need lookouts carefully selected with mapped locations showing the country commanded from each. Tools and fire equipment should be kept in top shape. There should be no excuse for dull tools. The Department of Forestry was very generous this year in tool allotment money. I am very proud of the quality, quantity, shape and distribution of tools this year.

My ideas have largely been absorbed from Morgenroth who is the best fire fighter in the country if not the world."

From Letter, Lovejoy to Chris, December 1912

"...Hear from Fromme once in a while. He tells me that you got convictions and fines in the "Elwha Bunch" case. That is some record for you. Bet folks will begin to remember about fires when they leave Port Angeles before long.

He says I may have lied to him about some things but that I didn't lie about you. That means that you are as solid as you deserve - good news to me. It doesn't pay to overlook any bets concerning friends, they are too scarce."
P.S.Lovejoy

Article: From University of Michigan Forester Magazine, Vol. V, No. 1, November 1913. This article is in reference to the "Elwha Bunch" mentioned in the preceding letter.

"At the second meeting of the Forestry Club of this year, Prof. Lovejoy told the story of District Forest Ranger Chris Morgenroth and of his job of getting the first conviction for fire trespass under the federal law in District Six in the State of Washington.

Lovejoy who was Supervisor of Olympic National Forest, first met Chris in his headquarters office in Port Angeles. Chris had gained the respect of the best citizens and had come to be recognized as a dedicated forester and the best fire fighter in the country. He asked, and received from Lovejoy, backing in any move he might make to prosecute fire trespassers. He explained how some man-made fires burned out of control every season since his coming to the west coast and how he was dead tired of it and ready to take almost any measures to stop this wasteful destruction. Professor Lovejoy then told how Chris did put an end to setting fire to timber thereabouts.

One day a fire was reported by a forest guard on one of the river trails. The guard reported to Ranger Morgenroth that he suspicioned two hunters whom he had seen, one was tall and dark, the other common looking. Chris asked the town marshall to be on the lookout for these men if they came into town. He then picked his crew, hired a truck, loaded his outfit, put his foot on the siren and went to the fire, with most of the town helping him to get a flying start.

At the end of the road it was trail, and lots of it! Beyond the trail it was just mountain jungle. Ranger and crew sewed up the fire, then with witnesses the ranger began hunting for the point of origin of the fire. It was found in a temporary camp where the fire had been left alive to eat into an old log and then run wild up the mountain.

About the camp Chris picked up cigarette stubs, wood chips that showed nick marks from a faulty ax blade, and empty shot-gun shells.

Back in town the marshall had located the two strangers by giving them to understand he was a game warden and inquiring concerning the killing of elk. Chris got the men to implicate themselves and even to swear to a statement as to just where they had camped in the mountains. He then arrested them for leaving an unextinguished camp fire.

The U.S. Commissioner did not think he had authority to hear the case, but he heard it. The lawyer for the defendants denied the violation of any law, but Chris had his "use" book. The court refused to allow the introduction of the sworn statements, but read them. The sheriff said he could not lock up the fire setters, but he did it.

The nicks in the wood chips fitted the nicks in the men's ax blade. They admitted they used that brand of tobacco found in the cigarette stubs and the empty shells had been discharged from the guns that the two men had carried. Chris proved these things and the Commissioner sent for the U.S. Marshall. In due time the men pleaded guilty in Federal Court and were sentenced to ninety days. This was the first jail sentence for violation of fire laws in that Federal District.

Lovejoy said he thought it took a mighty good man to be a fire fighter, detective, law enforcement officer, chief witness and prosecuting attorney without any assistance or special training. He said a school certainly did a lot, but it would have to 'go some' if it was able to turn out forest officers of the caliber of District Ranger Morgenroth."

From Fromme Memoirs, Spring 1913

"A 'high fire' which required 'unique' treatment to extinguish, occurred on the lower Hoh River in the Spring of 1913. It was burning in dry moss in the top of a spruce snag fully 60 feet up and had started by sparks from land clearing. In this instance Ranger Morgenroth, who chanced to be on the spot, dropped a tall vine maple against the top of the snag, cooned it up (climbed) the maple while carrying a rope around his waist, then dropped the rope for a series of buckets of water and extinguished the fire."

Storm King Ranger Station about 1910.

Charlie Lewis talking with District Ranger over 120 miles of field telephone line. (Ashel Curtis photo)

Chapter 32

"A Potpourri of Incidents, 1912-1916"

From Rudo Fromme's Memoirs, September, 1912

"What I recall quite vividly as Supervisor of Olympic National Forest is that I performed the feat of reigning for 14 years where it rained 14 feet per year. This forest held the reputation among old-timers in the Forest Service of being the richest in commercial timber values, the most difficult to penetrate, the least explored, and most fireproof of all National Forests. I was impregnated with those heralded slogans while still a student at the Yale Forestry School and had hoped Olympic would by my first assignment. Instead, my first appointment on July 1, 1906, sent me to the Priest River Forest Reserve in northern Idaho. In 1908 I was sent to the Regional Office in San Francisco as Chief of Operations. I kept annoying the Washington, D.C. office big shots with my expressed desires to follow Fred Hansen at Olympic. However R.E. Benedict, of more years' service, beat me to it. Benedict's assignment cooled me down for a time and the switch from him to P.S. Lovejoy, caught me unawares until it was all over. I jumped Charles Flory, my former Yale roommate, who was Superintendent of Region 6 in Portland for not putting me hep to this in time for me to put in my oar.

Late in the summer of 1912 I received a wire from Portland that I could have Lovejoy's job as he was departing for a teaching position. I wired my eager acceptance even though it meant "getting going" within a week."

Letter: From Chris to Lovejoy, at University of Michigan Forestry School, January 26, 1913

"...*Charlie Anderson has been at the Sol Duc Hot Springs for the last month doing logging for a contractor who is building 14 cottages, a large barn and a theatre building for Mike Earles. There is six feet of snow at the springs. A civil suit against the Sol Duc Hot Springs company has been instituted to recover $5640.41 on account of timber trespass. I think Mike will do some sputtering but I guess he will pay.*

I have again been cheated out of seven days of my annual leave and was forced to entirely forget about my annual duck hunt. I was detailed to another forest in December to examine 640 acres of land which had been filed on under the mineral act. I camped at one of the ranger stations for a while, got acquainted with some of the rangers and guards, saw some things and heard some others which I would call mismanagement and I know you would not have stood for them.

I enclose a report on the last Soleduck seeding and hope you will get some information out of it. We now have a ranger station in Port Angeles. $2000 should make a sightly and serviceable headquarters out of it including fences and store house. I have seen more than that spent on some stations where it is far less necessary.

I was asked to make a 20 year improvement plan--they must think I am a prophet to look that deep into the future. I have made up a plan which will keep them busy for about five years. (I enclose copy and estimates of costs for my district for 1914). I guess the Forest Service will be talked about this Congress and if we survive the next five years it will then be time enough to finish my plans and estimates for the next 15 years. I have no fear but what the Forest Service will survive, but will the present policy, administration and management be the same? Anyway, I think some changes would not hurt. Our policy should be open and progressive but we should keep within reach of the people for we are depending on their good will for our success. I meet many people from all over the United States every year; some of them have visited other forests but their general opinion of a forest officer is a man wearing a wide brim Stetson hat, on horseback, looking for a fire or making trouble for someone. I don't wish to brag, but I have made only friends since I have been in the service. Even among men that lost claims because of my adverse reports and those arrested for letting fires get away. It is not the things we do but the way we do them.

You are still well remembered here for you were well liked by everyone who knew you and they wish that you had stayed. You were a good mixer and could listen as well as talk."
Yours Truly,
Chris

Newspaper Article: Seattle Post Intelligencer, February 24, 1913
"Olympics, Place For Short trips"
Probably one of the best known and most popular ranger in the entire Olympic National Forest is Chris Morgenroth who has spent his time on the Olympic Peninsula since 1890 as a settler, cruiser, locater and explorer and for the past twelve years as a member of the U.S. Forest Service. Morgenroth knows every nook and corner of the Olympics and loves the mountains as only one can who has spent this length of time in them. Many interesting articles telling of thrilling experiences have been written by this hardy mountaineer.

The Forest Service has played an important part in the opening of the best hunting and fishing grounds by constructing trails and camping spots throughout the mountains. The sportsman has come to look upon the "service" as his best friend when in the woods. The sportsman will find Morgenroth, as well as any other member of the Forest Service always ready to lend a hand "on the trail." Morgenroth has outlined a list of little tours covering all parts of the Great Range for the man with the camera, the hunter, fisherman, the lover of nature and the seeker of rest and health. Following are listed some of the points of interest and side trips along the way.

1. Dungeness River — scenery, deer, elk, bear, grouse.
2. Elwha River — scenery, fish,bear and elk.
3. Elk Park and Hurricane Ridge — scenery, deer, bear, grouse.
4. Olympic Hot Springs and surroundings — scenery, best cure for rheumatics, deer, bear, grouse, elk.
5. Lake Crescent and surroundings — scenery, fish, deer, bear and grouse.
6. Soleduck River — camping, deer, fish, bear, grouse.
7. Sol Duc Hot Springs — scenery, best resort in the state, best cure for rheumatics and other ailments. Deer, elk, and grouse.
8. Soleduck Park — scenery, bear, deer, elk, and grouse.
9. Sappho and Beaver Lake — fish, deer, bear and grouse.
10. Ozette Lake and surroundings — access to ocean beach, all kinds of water fowl, bear and elk.
11. Bogachiel River — elk, fish, deer, bear and grouse.
12. South Fork Hoh River — elk, fish, deer, bear and grouse.
13. Hoh River valley — elk, fish, deer, bear and grouse.
14. Glacier Creek and Upper Hoh Valley — scenery, glaciers, bear, elk, deer.
15. Clearwater River — deer, bear, elk, grouse, fish.
16. Quinault River and Lake — scenery, fish, deer, elk, bear, grouse.
17. Wynooche River — fish, deer, elk, bear.
18. Hood Canal and Rivers — scenery, fish, deer, bear, grouse.

A trip encircling the whole Olympic Peninsula can be made by steamer, railroad, auto, stagecoach, lake ferry, horseback and foot. This trip offers much changing scenery, opportunity to fish and see some wildlife.

The following three recommended pack horse trips will take the visitor into the interior where spectacular mountain scenery can be viewed.

1. Pack trip through the Olympics, North to South--Port Angeles to Elwha River, up Elwha Valley and across Low Divide to Lake Quinault and Aberdeen, very scenic.
2. Pack trip through the Olympics East to West--From Hood Canal up the Skokomish River and down the Quinault River to Pacific Ocean, very scenic.
3. Pack trip over Soleduck-Hoh Divide--This is perhaps the most scenic and interesting trip. It can be made without hardships by ladies as well as men. A near view of Mt. Olympus and its glaciers can be seen. The trail passes through some of the best virgin timber.

Newspaper Article: Port Angeles Herald, February, 1916
"New Trails Recommended by District Ranger"

Following is a report by Chris Morgenroth, District Ranger in charge of District I, Olympic National Forest, to Chief Forester Graves in Washington, D.C. The report consisted of recommendations for new trails and was given last night to the Port Angeles Commercial Club. Mr. Morgenroth also declared that the more trails and telephone stations installed the less danger of forest fires getting out of control. Trails would provide faster transportation of men and equipment and by following streams where possible, the camper would be induced to extinguish his campfire. The stream would also provide water for fighting other fires.

He stated that trails connecting the Hot Springs country with the high mountains of the main divide are of chief interest. Following are the trails recommended in the report.

"A trail, to be known as the Mt. Angeles Trail, would start at Little River-Ennis Creek trail at the end of the Mt. Angeles wagon road. It would lead to the summit of Mt. Angeles and connect with Hurricane Ridge and open country beyond. This would include a good lookout station. It would confine travel to one trail in the interest of fire protection.

Eleven and a half miles of trail from Lake Crescent to Bear Creek, would be a continuation of the trail near Piedmont and run west. It would provide fire protection of an approximate 700,000,000 feet of standing timber east and west of the headwaters of Twin Rivers, Deep Creek and Bear Creek.

Four miles of new trail between the Elwha and Hurricane Ridge would connect with existing trail and make a continuous scenic high-line trail fifteen miles long at an elevation of about five thousand feet.

129

Ten miles of trail up the Hays River from the Elwha to the west end of the Dosewallips trail, would make it possible to cross over from the Hood Canal country to the heart of the Olympics.

The Snowfinger trail at the head of the Elwha River would lead from the Elwha Basin to the Dodwell-Rixon Pass so that horseponies might be taken over into the Queets Valley.

The most needed trail from a scenic standpoint in the high country is fifteen miles from Dodwell-Rixon Pass to the Divide between the Elwha, Queets and Hoh Rivers, thence down the Hoh River to Mt. Olympus Ranger Station.

There should be a trail from Boulder Creek to the Soleduck Valley thus connecting the two Hot Springs resorts.

The Soleduck Ranger Station should be connected with trail to Sourdough Mountain on Aurora Ridge. Here it would connect with the existing Lake Crescent trail and continue on to the east to the Elwha River. This extension would be known as the Happy Lake Trail.

There are a number of other proposed trails which would, if built in time, be of advantage to those of us now in the land of the living. This will depend upon securing sufficient appropriations from Congress. This rests largely with the people themselves. The greater their interest in the scenic possibilites of the country, the sooner the Olympic Mountains will come into their own as the greatest recreation grounds in the United States."

Letter From U.S. Dept. of Agriculture, Forest Service District 6, February 23, 1916

Dear Mr. Morgenroth,

I have just received a newspaper clipping giving a report of your talk before the Port Angeles Commercial Club, and I wish to congratulate you on the favorable publicity you succeeded in giving the Forest Service and on your excellent grasp of the situation and the policy of the Service as a whole. Your statement of the facts is concise and clear and indicates your work means more to you than simply a dull routine.

> *Yours Very Sincerely,*
> *Charles H. Flory*
> *Assistant District Forester*
> *Portland, Oregon*

News Article: Seattle Post Intelligencer, Oct. 10, 1916
"Fire Threatens Olympic Forest, Ranger Appeals to U. of W. to Send Students to Save Public Property"

"If skilled fire fighters are not available immediately the Olympic National Forest is in danger of being destroyed by fire," said Chris Morgenroth who is in charge of this District.

As yet the National Forest is only fringed by fire, but a continuation of the present winds, which enlarged a three-mile front in three hours to a six-mile front early today, will put the national forest in grave danger.

"I think it would be a fine thing for the University of Washington to help,' said Morgenroth. "The University has many students in its forestry department who are more or less experienced. The students will be getting practical experience and also be paid for their trouble, besides doing their state and country a great service." Cy Johnson, a former ranger who attends the U. returned to Port Angeles today and volunteered his services. Eighteen state fire-fighters and nine from the Forest Service comprises the skeleton crew.

The fire is near Piedmont on the north side of Lake Crescent and burning on state land. Every attempt is being made with limited men and equipment to keep the fire within the limits fixed by Boundary Creek, East Twin Creek and a base line built by Morgenroth a few years ago in anticipation of just such a condition as exists today.

During a three hour wind on Saturday, the fire developed from a "ground fire" to a "crown fire", which jumps from tree top to tree top.

Residents of the lake shore in the vicinity of Piedmont are alarmed at the approach of the fire. Dense smoke hangs over the lake and visibility in only 100 yards.

Cause of the fire was probably careless hunters and an unusually dry forest floor and under-story which is as dry as tinder.

The fire is chiefly in State timber but threatening Puget Sound Mills and Timber Co. timber and U.S. Forest Service timber.

U.S.F.S. Fire Tool Cache Box, one of many, Bogachiel Trail.

Chapter 33

"Treed by Timber Wolves"

Wolves were fairly plentiful during the early days of the Olympic Peninsula settlement. They were rarely known to attack a human but were very destructive to game, cattle and sheep, and other domestic animals. By the early 1900's the settlers had declared war on wolves and as a result the wolf was nearly exterminated. What few that were left became shy and cautious and were seldom seen. They travelled in small bands limited to a family of six or eight. The fact that there were any timber wolves in these mountains would be almost forgotten except for the rare evidence of a big paw print in moist soil or a missing dog or farm animal.

The Olympic gray timber wolf was a most magnificent animal. The peer of his cousins that roam the Russian Steppes or the North American Continent, he was known to attain the age of twenty years. A good sized male would weigh one-hundred and twenty-five pounds, stand hip high and measure about six feet in length. The bushy tail was from ten to fifteen inches long. The fur was long and coarse in winter, dark on the back, gray about the head and flanks and lighter underneath.

It has been said by experts that there was no depth of meanness, treachery or cruelty to which the wolf does not cheerfully descend. They are the only animals on earth which make a practice of killing and devouring their wounded companions and eating their own dead. But in the face of foes capable of defense, gray wolves are rank cowards and when cornered in a den, will not even stop to fight for their own pups. Powerful teeth, strong jaws and a wide gape enable them to bite with great cutting power. Every snap means a deep wound or a piece of flesh torn out.

In June of 1916, I ran into a situation with wolves which sends cold chills up and down my back when I think of it.

Lee Elliott had just started his duties as forest guard for the upper Elwha District and was temporarily camped at the Grant Humes ranch on the Elwha River. This ranch was the only one on the forty miles of wild and remote upper Elwha Valley trail. Humes was not at home but a Mr. Pearson who was staying with Humes, was there.

I arrived about noon on June 13, planning to make an inspection trip with Elliott to estimate the cost for repairs to damaged telephone lines and trails from winter storms. Pearson said that Elliott had already gone up river to repair telephone lines, so I started up the trail to join him telling Pearson I would be back for the night. I walked over the hill to Lillian Creek, which is about two and one-half miles above the

Humes ranch, then down a long, steep new trail into the Lillian Creek Valley. When I reached the creek I did not cross, but went on up to acquaint myself with the general make-up of the canyon.

Returning down the creek, I decided to sit on a footlog that crossed the river and write up my field notes while waiting for Elliott. I began to get cold and decided Elliott had gone home by way of the old trail, so I started back up the long grade. When I reached the level benchland on top I saw what looked like two elk coming toward me. Then suddenly I realized it was two large wolves. I was astonished at their size. One of them was as large as a Shetland pony. They were moving along with their heads down and did not see me at first. I yelled at them as I often had done before, expecting to see them run away. Instead they stopped, exchanged glances, and the smaller one circled off to get behind me. The larger one, supposedly the male, came straight toward me very slowly. I shouted repeatedly at him but he only halted for a moment.

I had met wolves and every other kind of animal in the Olympic woods and had never been attacked, so I was not frightened. I had no gun as I never carried one unless on a real hunting trip. I was in my shirt sleeves and a note book and pencil were my only means of defense.

The bigger wolf kept coming while the smaller one kept circling and closing in. I looked quickly around for a stick or club but every branch I picked up was either brittle or rotten. I started walking backwards down the trail, all the time looking for a tree to climb. A broken snag about twelve feet high and fourteen inches in diameter on the upper side of the trail was the only chance for safety. Two stones the size of hen's eggs were lying at the foot of the snag so I put them in my hip pocket and backed up to the snag.

The large wolf was now about thirty feet away from me. Slowly walking a few paces towards him I waved my arms, threw my hat and yelled, but instead of turning tail, he kept coming towards me. I gave one great yell at the wolf and without any further loss of time shinnied up the snag. It was a mighty tough job hanging on as I had to wrap my legs around the snag and claw my fingers into the rotten bark for a hold.

The big wolf sat down at the base of the snag while the smaller one sat about twenty feet away. Neither made any sound. Both watched me and showed their teeth with their tongues hanging out. The big one had a peculiar snarl which exposed his vice-like jaws.

I shouted a couple of times, thinking possibly Elliott was close behind me on the trail. I got no answer, so gave it up. The big wolf started to pace back and forth now, all the time showing that vicious snarl on the left side of his jaw. I managed to get one of the stones out of my pocket and threw it hitting him squarely on the forehead. It sounded hollow but it

133

must have hurt for he gave a suppressed howl and made several leaps towards his companion. I threw the other stone but it failed to hit him. I tore pieces of bark from the snag and hurled them at him. This kept the larger wolf retreating until he stood by the side of his mate.

They just stood there staring at me. My legs began to cramp so I slid down off my friendly snag and began a backward retreat down the trail, facing my tormentors and talking to them. The wolves were now following me on a parallel line above the trail. I located a rock of about five pounds, also a short cedar limb about two feet long and another stout club about five feet long. I felt considerably safer and started on a run down the trail. I raced the wolves for a quarter of a mile when suddenly with their long leaps and bounds they had closed the gap and were coming straight for me.

I gave a blood-curdling yell, backed up against a large fir tree, dropped the cedar club and rock and stood ready to cut the first wolf in two with the longer club. The smaller wolf stopped fifty feet from me, the bigger one came within twenty feet before halting. I think he was aware that I was not entirely helpless. I did a lot of talking and coaxing to get him to come closer, but he held his ground. I hurled a handful of pea gravel at him and he backed off toward his mate and together they stood snarling.

I gathered up my rock and clubs and again started a retreat down the trail, running at times when screened by bushes. Once more they attempted an attack by backing me into a tree, and once more I won out.

After catching my breath this time I started running with the hope of putting more distance between me and the wolves. A huge mud hole was in the trail, with a leap I hit it but once right in the middle. The trail switchbacked down a long steep hillside which I did not take time to follow but proceeded straight to the bottom. The wolves still in pursuit were about three-hundred yards behind me. I did not stop but raced to a clearing where I jumped a fence five feet high and landed on top of a large stump. I dropped my rock and short stick and prepared to welcome my oppressors with my longer club. To my disappointment they did not appear again.

The Humes house was only one-quarter of a mile further down the trail through the clearing and after catching my breath, I figured I could make it safely on the run. When I entered the cabin the first thing Pearson asked me was, "Did you see any wolves?" He told me they had repeatedly been seen and had killed a hunting dog at the nearby Olympic Hot Springs, and that Elliott was now packing a rifle. He wanted to know why I carried clubs and the rock and then I related my experience.

134

Elliott was now coming across the clearing, so Pearson asked me to go into another room so he could question Elliott without his knowing I was there.

When Elliott came in, Pearson asked him if he had seen any wolves. Elliott said, "I didn't see any wolves but would like to as I am ready and looking for them. I see tracks every day but I saw something I could not make out while coming down the trail just now. Do you remember that wet place in the trail? Well, it's now about twenty feet long and ought to be fixed. There is something funny about it, some large animal stepped right in the middle. Elk or bear would have left other tracks but I could find none. The track is fresh, for the mud and water are still oozing in."

I came out of the back room and told him I was the large animal. I told him my story and asked if he had heard me calling. "I remember hearing calls but the noise of the river destroyed the sounds. I expected no one out there so I thought it a couple of trees rubbing together." We calculated that if I had hung on another five minutes to my first snag, he would have been there and it would have been too bad for the wolves.

When Grant Humes came he wanted to know all the details about the wolves and being a stickler for exactness, he insisted we go back over the ground after supper. We looked at all places where there were wolf tracks. He took measurements of distances and tracks and examined shoe nail marks where I went up the snag. He also took a picture of me hanging onto the snag.

Next morning my arms were swollen and stiff. I was also nervous for a few days after the episode. I have been in the woods for twenty-five years but have never seen wolves that aggressive until now. These two were big fellows, with shaggy coats and big ruffs. They meant mischief, and I think myself lucky to have escaped them.

I have always felt the woods were safe from wild animals. Time and again I have laid down in the woods and gone to sleep with no firearms and without fear. But I shall take no more chances. I must say that a revolver has the same value in the Olympics today that in once had on the Texas border. You may never need one, but should you, you will want it mighty bad. (Footnote)

On my next trip alone over the mountains to the Hoh Valley I carried a six-gun, but since I was not accustomed to carrying one I promptly forgot it every time I took it off at the Ranger Stations or camps. The gun was always in transit being forwarded to me.

Grant caught a very large male wolf in a trap the following winter. It was six feet long. One of its canine teeth was missing and the upper left lip had been torn but had healed in such a manner as to give the appearance of him continually snarling. Humes said an elk could kick an attacking

135

wolf with such a smashing blow to the jaw as to cause such injury. It is presumed this was the same wolf that stalked me for whatever purpose I do not care to dwell upon.

Footnote: The Olympic timber wolf is apparently now extinct as no sign of them has been reported for the past forty years. (Ed.)

"The Morgenroth Stub," upper Elwha Valley, 1916. Picture taken by Grant Humes. Chris reenacting on the same snag, his encounter with the wolves.

Elwha Ranger Station, 1910.

Chapter 34

"More Potpourri"

Letter: Parish Lovejoy, U. of Michigan, to Chris, December 21, 1916
"Dear Chris,

I hear about you pretty regularly even if you don't write. Last summer three of our boys from the forestry school scattered through the country out there and sent in clippings from their local papers about your 'wolf' business and the fire where you wanted to call out the University of Washington Forestry students to fight fire. The boys recognized that this must be 'the Morgenroth' that they heard me talk about so much in classes. Anyway I was glad to see that you still had your pep and knew what so few folks do--how to get good and proper free advertising. It's the right stuff and helps the Service and the man too.

Remember when we located the Elwha Ranger Station? How has it come along? That was always my sort of hobby, ever since we drained the pond and I prophesied that the lime would show up white. Did the apple grafts on the old fruit trees ever come through and do business? That was the first time I'd ever seen that done. Did our little new fruit trees, bushes and vines go into action properly? Remember how I juggled my expense account to buy them. I still think of that station as the best location I ever saw. And did you get the lower meadows slashed and pasture enough? I noticed the little scar on my foot where the axe got me that March you showed me the elements of swamping alder. It near cost me a split foot, but it was worth a nick and a cut shoe string to see the place coming up out of the brush. That was the time I dug the big wood-tick out of your back. Remember the time I patched your ear on the Soleduck?

Yours very much, Lovejoy"

Letter: Chris to Lovejoy, December 31, 1916
"Dear Lovejoy,

Your welcome letter of December 21 is received, and I am glad to know that you are still interested in what I might be doing. I have not forgotten you, for I often recall with pleasure the little trips and talks we had together. I am sincere when I tell you that you are the only supervisor I ever had that I liked from the first. I admired your frankness and aggressiveness.

I like Mr. Fromme, he has greatly changed of late years. He has adjusted himself to the country and local conditions instead of adjusting local conditions to suit his ideas as to what would be best for Olympic. He

137

found out early that he needed the co-operation and good will of his rangers and local communities. Since a Washington D.C. order came out asking all forest officers to take an active interest in community advancement and development and to freely mingle with other human beings, distrust and friction between the public and forest officers has almost disappeared. Fromme is now well liked and has the good will and confidence of all his subordinates and the public.

Only one of the apple trees we planted at the Elwha is bearing fruit, some that I grafted are large now and bearing. The elk are now very plentiful on the north and west side of the peninsula and are becoming a nuisance where they are invading settlements and destroying crops and fruit trees.

Yes, I remember your split foot, also the wood tick operation at the Elwha and the split ear at Littleton Ranger Station. I think those were the days of real sport.

Yours Truly,
Chris Morgenroth"

Newspaper Clip, Port Angeles Daily Herald, 1917
"The Alps Have Their Edelweise,
Why Not A Flower For The Olympics?"

"The Klahanne's should adopt a flower for the Olympics and make it as well known as the Edelweise," was the rather startling suggestion made last week by Ranger Morgenroth, himself a member of the Klahanne Hiking Club. "We have ten times the flowers here and more beautiful ones, many grow high up on the rocks but the public has never seen them." He went on to say, " Over in Switzerland every little feature has been made the most of. The people live off the tourists and they advertize every town and mountain to the limit. They chose the Edelweise and advertise it as growing in inaccessible places on the cliffs, soon everyone has to have a piece of it as a trophy to prove that they were nervy climbers.

"Possibly the most distinctive, beautiful and rare plant belonging to the Olympics alone, is the Viola Flettii, first found by Professor J.B. Flett, noted western botanist. It has small round leaves, purple-green above, purple beneath, with each plant bearing from two to six royal purple flowers. It grows in the tiny crevices of the rocks and cliffs of Mt. Angeles. This would be my nomination as the official flower of the Olympic Mountains."

From Fromme Memoirs, 1917
"You've Got Two Germans Working For You, Investigate 'em."

"That was an order I received through the U.S. District Attorney's Office in Seattle, as the U.S. entered the First World War. The names funished me were Chris Morgenroth and G.A. Whitehead. These were both experienced, capable and loyal district rangers, at Port Angeles and Quilcene respectively, as I well knew. I also knew that both were born in Germany and had come to this country in their teens. However, the order was to investigate.

Certain army officers stationed at Forts Worden and Lawton near Port Townsend, supplied me with affidavits as to the loyalty of Whitehead. Affidavits from forest users served as my principal defense for Ranger Morgenroth.

Dropping into the District Attorney's Seattle office sometime later, after this file was closed, he smilingly remarked that one of his subordinates had mildly protested my evidence, saying, "How can you expect any trustworthy results, when you have two German-born men investigated by their own boss, who bears a German name?"

Newspaper Clip: Port Angeles Herald, March 1917
"Study of First Aid Methods"

At a recent convention of the Forest Service Supervisors in Portland, Oregon for District 6, Chief Forester N.S. Graves of the U.S. Forest Service, called attention to the valuable aid the Forest Service can give the government in connection with national defense (WWI). First Aid Service is of great importance in time of peace as well as war.

The Herald is informed that Chris Morgenroth, Ranger in charge of this part of the Olympic Forest will take up the study and when he has perfected himself he will be asked to teach the first aid methods to the high school pupils of Port Angeles.

The practical arts are coming more and more into their rightful place in the public schools. Young people are quick to learn and the instruction in the methods of first aid to the injured provides an excellent foundation for efficient hospital and Red Cross service.

Letter: From E.E. Harpham, Acting Deputy Supervisor, September 13, 1917
To: Forest Supervisor, Olympia Washington
"Dear Sir,

During District Ranger Morgenroth's absence on an inspection trip to the west end of the Port Angeles Ranger District in the early part of

August this year, I was detailed to take charge of the office at Port Angeles. A bad fire got started in the Little River country. I notified the guards a few miles from the fire but the country being unfamiliar to me, I was at a loss to know how many men to send from Port Angeles. Also it being Sunday, I did not know how and where to get the equipment and supplies necessary for the fire fighters. Mrs. Morgenroth gave me all the information necessary, not only in furnishing the equipment, but also directed me to the right parties to obtain transportation for the men and supplies. She also informed me as to the character of the country where the fire was burning and that was very helpful in supplying the proper number of men. As a consequence, the fire was stopped in the edge of green timber, after getting an excellent start in an old logging operation adjacent to the National Forest.

I am informed the above is only one of many instances in which Mrs. Morgenroth has materially assisted the Forest Service in matters not only of fire protection but in directing administrative work as well. From the spring of 1910 to the spring of 1917, District Ranger Morgenroth's office has been at his residence at Port Angeles, and up to the season just past Mrs. Morgenroth has been his assistant in that office during his absence.

The Port Angeles District comprises approximately 600,000 acres, is visited by about 12,000 tourists annually, has numerous small timber sales, issues many special use permits and has other various administrative duties. During the summer ten to eleven guards and patrolmen are employed in the field and these men make their reports directly to this office. Besides the business involved in these activities, the Port Angeles Headquarters, located as it is, is a bureau of information to the travelling public.

From these facts it can readily be seen that the work during the summer and autumn months requires the constant attention of someone from early morning until late night. During Ranger Morgenroth's absence numerous fires have occurred, and some of them bad ones at that, which have been successfully handled by Mrs. Morgenroth.

For practically six years she has served at numerous intervals in the capacity of Assistant Ranger without compensation.

Very Sincerely Yours,
E.E. Harpham
Acting Deputy Supervisor"

Chapter 35

"Our Responsibilities To the Forest Communities"
By Chris Morgenroth

(This paper was presented at a U.S. Forest Supervisors meeting at Portland, Oregon, in March 1917.)

The responsibility of the Forest Service to serve local communities and forest users is of the greatest importance. Co-operation is the key in solving existing and new problems as they continue to arise.

In 1890, six months after homesteading on the Bogachiel River, some of my pioneer neighbors and myself saw the need of a trail from Forks to our homesteads on the Hoh and Bogachiel Rivers. We organized a crew and in two months had built eighteen miles of trail through Olympic jungles. Other settlers followed this trail and in about five years most of the bottom land had been settled by young, and enthusiastic men. All had honest intentions of developing their claims for farming and planned to build homes to which they could bring their families. Clearing this heavily forested land by hand into farm land was a Goliathan task in the 1890's. Many settlers did not have the physical strength to prove up on their claim.

In 1897 President Cleveland ordered most of the Olympic Peninsula set aside as a Forest Reserve with no further settlement. This meant county revenue would never increase to sufficiently fund roads, schools and other necessary improvements. About ninety percent of the settlers became panic stricken and began to pull up stakes. Half of them did not wait to make final proof, the other half who had proved up were glad to sell to scrip speculators for $200 to $500. By 1900 the only settlers who remained were those who had families or had made such physical and material investments they could not afford to leave. The few existing trails which connected settlements and constituted the only artery of transportation soon deteriorated as there was no county aid and voluntary upkeep was too much for the few who remained. The feeling of resentment and antagonism of the remaining settlers towards the Forest Reserve action was intense and Reserve officers and rangers were looked upon with suspicion and as a common enemy.

In 1905 the Forest Reserve was transferred from the Department of Interior to the Department of Agriculture and in June of 1906 the Forest Homestead Act was passed. The purpose of this congressional legislation was to eliminate wholesale acquisition of land by the timber speculators. It partly served the purpose for which it was intended by bringing new permanent neighbors to the older forest communities. County revenue

141

increased, providing new roads and hundreds of miles of trails along which telephone wires have been strung connecting every settler with civilization.

My experience for over ten years as a pioneer settler and for the past fourteen years as a forest ranger have taught me a great deal on how forest problems affect the settler, communities and the public user. In the past ten years the Forest Service has worked hard at gaining the respect of the community and individuals who have carried a grudge against forest officials. We have made every effort to foster goodwill through knowledge and understanding of the Forest Service policies and regulations. We have endeavored to work harmoniously among ouselves as well as taking an active interest in individual and community problems. As a result we have won respect and confidence and have been able to mold public sentiment favorable to the Forest Service. This constructive and practical public relations policy is now apparent. Enemies of the Forest Service are now the exception rather than the rule.

The following activities are carried on within Olympic National Forest. The volume of these activities vary depending upon surroundings and resources of the individual forest. Timber sales are now welcome, with the Service giving preference to the small operator. Lease of grazing land has increased and is now an established success. Prospecting and mining is allowed on a bona fide basis. Settlement on National Forest land that is more valuable or suitable for agriculture than a timber crop is encouraged. Water power development for industry and domestic use is being expanded on a conservative scale.

Much has been accomplished to make the National Forest accessible, safe and attractive for the camper, sportsman and tourists. More trails are continually being built with mile post and destination signs appearing on all trails and roads. Free maps are available at most Ranger Stations. Fire regulations and danger signs are posted along the trails and at trail heads. Summer homesites and campsites for public use are available. Resort, hotel, and organizational facilites, are all encouraged.

An industrial and recreational survey of each forest area is being made and the information gained should be of great help to forest communities in stimulating industrial enterprise and providing conservation guidelines for all the resources. The Forest Service welcomes all users.

The Forest Ranger is now a respected and trusted friend. We have gained the confidence and support of the public and as long as this exists we can count on the public for their co-operation and support of any fair policy or regulation.

142

Excerpt, Newspaper Clip, Port Angeles Daily Herald, March 1917
"Interesting Paper Read by Chris Morgenroth
At Convention of Forest Supervisors"

Forest Ranger Chris Morgenroth who attended the convention for District 6 at Portland, Oregon, March 19 to 25, appears to have made a hit with the forest service with a paper he read on "Our Responsibilities to the Forest Communities" because the paper has been ordered mimeographed and copies sent to all members of the Federal Forest Service. The paper was written by Mr. Morgenroth who knows much of the relationship between the Forest Service and the settler within and near the forest, and the larger communities on the fringe of the forest.

He was able to give ideas of the evolution of the national forest from the time of the first reservation orders, which aroused the hostility of settlers, to the present time when, as he declared, "the Forest Service has now become the best co-operative agency for farmers, settlers and industrial communities." He pointed out how the Service was able to help by locating new settlers and building new and maintaining old trails, etc. He concluded by stressing the importance of aiding these people and the communities and how, in return, these settlers and communities have aided the Forest Service in fire prevention and co-operation of forest regulations.

Douglas Fir, 11½ feet in diameter, Upper Hoh River Valley.

Chapter 36

"A Chew on the Kaiser and a Chew on the Bogachiel"

Letter From Chris Morgenroth to E.E. Harpham (Forest Ranger), 20th Engineers, A.E.F., France, April 19, 1918

"Dear Sergt. Harpham,

I was thinking of you this morning and thought that you may sometimes wonder as to how things are going on in your old stomping grounds. This is a fine morning, such as you know we can have only in western Washington when things are in bloom and everything is getting green, with plenty of spring sunshine and breezes from the mountains and the sea. Things here seem peaceful enough on the surface for we are a long way from the scene of battle, but the heart of the people is with the boys in France. While the little news we get about the big doings just now in France is not to our liking, we are all confident that the allies with the help of the U.S. will turn the tables on the Kaiser at the right time. The people of Clallam County surely are with you, they are doing everything to help the fighters at the front. Clallam County's share in the new liberty loan was $101,000. We went over the top the first week by raising $125,000 by voluntary subscription, not bad for a sparsely settled county like Clallam.

I do not know whether you are still in England or over in France, however I know you will do your share in driving the Kaiser back and keeping him on his own dung pile. Trusting that you are in the best of spirits and health and that you will come back home with a feeling of having done your full duty to your country. Every American citizen is with you. As you know, I am German born, but I am glad and proud to be a loyal citizen of the good old U.S.A. and a believer in the principle for which she stands. Best of luck and a safe return."

> *District Forest Ranger,*
> *Chris Morgenroth"*

Excerpt: Newspaper Clip from Port Angeles Herald, February 1919
"Morgenroth Spending Week in Olympia"

Chris Morgenroth, forest ranger of Olympic Forest will spend all this week in Olympia with forestry heads, voicing his plans and needs for the coming year for Olympic National Forest. As this forest is one of the pets of the department and is visited by so many thousands of tourists each year, it is reasonable to expect Mr. Morgenroth's plans will receive satisfactory consideration.

Anecdote from Rudo Fromme's Memoirs

Ranger Morgenroth and I had walked up to Bogachiel Peak from the Sol Duc Hot Springs the summer of 1920. We had planned to hike down the west side of the peak and follow the river some fifteen miles to river bottom trail country. We would be intercepting the trail crew on the second night so our provisions were at a minimum. I was carrying my lightweight feathered sleeping bag but Chris had only one blanket in a roll on his back. He always seemed to consider all of the rough country back of Port Angeles as just a part of his backyard and, except for hobnailed shoes, he made no more preparation than if he were going out to split a bit of wood for the kitchen stove.

The second day out was even rougher than the first. By the time we reached river bottom it was getting too dark to follow elk trails, so we took to sand bars out in the river where we had more light. Darkness was fast overtaking us and since we hadn't caught up with the trail crew camp we decided to flop by a small creek outlet for the night.

As we toasted our aching feet in front of a cheery campfire, feeling a bit hungry, Chris remarked, "Gosh, I wish now that I had saved one of those overstuffed Hot Springs sandwiches which I gorged myself with on the snow-field."

"Second the motion," responded I. "But I haven't even got a piece of Swedish hardtack." "Aw-hah," I uttered hopefully a minute later, as I drew two sticks of gum from my Filson shirt. "With a little imagination, we could make these do for a seven or eight course dinner."

"Sure," came Chris, "Let's pretend we're parked in the grill room of the Butler Hotel in Seattle." "O.K.," said I, "Here's your first order," handing him the stick of gum and removing the wrapper of the other as I poised it artfully, and hungrily in front of my open mouth.

"What will we start with?" "Well, why not make it a Manhattan cocktail?" came Chris's suggestion. And then we went from soup to nuts, not even overlooking a sip of wine now and then. We were very deliberate with each course, having no place else on the agenda for that evening. And we carefully removed the chewed gum at the end of each suggested course, ready to plunge it in again with renewed gusto for the next mouth yearning debauch.

Believe it or not, this really helped considerably toward soothing the inner man. At any rate, it immersed our minds in pleasant thoughts and started our slumbering dreams in a happy direction.

It was the early dawn of another day on the Hoh River. "Get your camera ready, I see some elk!" came this remark from Chris in an excited whisper. This gave me the requisite courage to give the final tugs to my toe pinching boots. I cautioned him to wait until I could get both the

145

Kodak and my eyes opened up, then we stepped gingerly together towards the animal shadows a few hundred yards downstream. "Oh, hell! It's the pack horses!" came Chris with requisite chagrin. Apparently, they had been nibbling and sleeping within our immediate proximity all night, hence the trail camp must be close by. Sure enough, it was not more than a quarter of a mile from where we had flopped for the night without food. Furthermore, we had paralleled a full mile of finished horse trail when taking to the river bars for better light the night before.

"Why didn't you answer our shouts last evening?" Chris asked of the trail crew. "Didn't hear any," was the concerted reply, "Maybe we were playing penny ante too hard," said another. "Well, for one thing," concluded the ranger, "You're camped by too noisy a creek. But we'll excuse you this time if the cook will just hurry up that breakfast."

Chris trying to get his supper, 1919.

Chris and friends on the Hoh, 1916.

Part VI

Preface: Final Years In The Forest Service, 1921-1927

On July 1, 1920, Chris was promoted to Deputy Supervisor. Chris continues to narrate the dramas that occur between man and nature. The big "Blowdown" of 1921 ushers in the roaring 20's. His description of this destructive cyclone is a very personal one.

Beginning in the early 1920's and for almost ten years the U.S. Pacific Fleet visited Port Angeles Harbor. This was their base while they conducted maneuvers in the Straits of Juan de Fuca. This was in the summer and thousands of service men with shore leave headed for the cool, green forests to fish and hike. A massive education program was put into effect by the Forest Service. The majority of these fine young officers and enlisted men had never been in the forest before, knew nothing of forest fire safety and most of them wanted to pack a gun for target practice or whatever. The navy cooperated one hundred percent with the Forest Service and by the second summer all navy personnel were given an intensive briefing on board ship regarding rules and regulations for safety in the forest. So successful was this endeavor that no accidental fires or personal injuries occurred during those years due to any sailor's or officer's fault.

Chris relates his close brush with death in an airplane crash on Mt. Constance and a tale of a tragic death on Mt. Olympus.

He was so respected by the public, the timber industry and the government that when he attempted to retire in July of 1924, he was dissuaded from doing so by a wide variety of people and his request was turned down by William Greeley, head forester in Washington, D.C. Said one local newspaper at the time, "To mention the Olympics without coupling with them the name of Morgenroth will not sound right, somehow." Eventually he did retire in 1926 to start a new phase of his life devoted to the Olympic Mountains.

Again newspaper articles, letters to and from Parish Lovejoy, his longtime friend, Fromme Memoirs, Forest Service historical notes and anecdotes are used to round out the narrative.

Chris and Supervisor Rudo Fromme playing croquet at Rosemary on Lake Crescent, early 1920's.

Chapter 37

"Olympic Blowdown"

On January 29, 1921, an unprecedented windstorm of cyclonic proportions swept up the west side of the Olympics racking destruction in an area seventy miles long by thirty miles wide in the most heavily timbered region in the nation. Timber thrown down in the path of this storm is referred to as the "Blow-Down."

Emery Ware, the first man to reach Port Angeles to spread the news of the storm said, "I left Forks on foot early in the morning and did not get to Fairholme on Lake Crescent until after seven that evening. At times I ran into walls of fallen timber forty feet high. I did not dare leave the road, because I knew I would lose my bearings and never get out. At times I was compelled to crawl on my hands and knees to feel for the gravel in the roadway."

Immediately after the storm I made my way to Forks. This was a most difficult trip. Twelve miles west of Lake Crescent the road became almost obliterated with fallen and uprooted trees. I had built most of the original trail from the Lake to Forks through pristine forest but that day I travelled over strange country.

When I reached Theodore Rixon's home at Beaver, eight miles east of Forks, he reported that he had noticed his barometer dropping to almost nothing in late afternoon, then at 6:30 p.m. with a mighty roar the wind came, felling everything before it. "I immediately put out all fires on my premises and it was well I did for the storm destroyed my windmill and waterworks system shortly thereafter. Trees fell like tenpins and the roar was thunderous, the storm beggared description."

On reaching Forks I learned from first hand accounts that the wind struck there at 6:30 also, preceded by a complete eerie calm. As the wind increased it was accompanied by thunder-like explosions. People ran out of their houses into the open spaces listening with terror to the crashing of nearby stands of timber going in a body. Some trees broke off in the mid-section and some were completely uprooted. World War I veterans, who had seen service in France, likened the noise of the wind and falling timber to being worse than the hottest battle of mortar and cannon-fire on the Western Front. Since Forks is somewhat protected by a hill on the south side of town it had escaped the full force of the wind, however several homes and eighteen barns were blown down with a loss of twenty head of stock.

The storm came from the south, cutting off about thirty families from the outside world in the Clearwater, Queets, Hoh and Bogachiel

Districts. Their only means of communication had been by trails, a few wagon roads and telephone lines which were now blocked or destroyed by downed timber. The storm then swept on north in Forks, Pysht, Clallam Bay, Neah Bay, Lake Ozette and the Hoko River areas. Also the Soleduck and Calawah River Valleys suffered heavy damage. Information was completely lacking on the fate of the settlers and Indians in the coastal communities. An Indian from the Reservation at LaPush on the coast managed to break through the fallen timber barrier and reach Forks to report that six houses had been completely destroyed, one burned and nineteen more damaged. Among the homes blown down was that of William Penn, the Indian who had discovered the wrecked sailors of the Chilean ship Pirrie recently wrecked near LaPush.

For the next few days crews were at work everywhere, opening roads, trying to reach settlers and trying to asses the damage. I made my way back to Port Angeles and gave a preliminary report to the Forest Service and to the local and Seattle press. My initial estimate was that six billion feet of timber had been blown down with immense damage to roads, railroads, trails and telephone lines in the path of the storm.

As the days passed more details and reports on the intensity of the wind began to pour into Forest Service headquarters in Port Angeles. It was learned that at 3:32 o'clock on the afternoon of the storm the wind reached a velocity of 126 miles per hour at the North Head weather station on the Pacific coast near Grays Harbor, Washington. The force of the gale tore the wind measuring instrument, the anemometer, to pieces. The wind vane was torn loose and smashed a moment later and the sunshine recorder soon followed. The wind velocity continued to increase and weather observer Perry R. Hill estimated it reached 150 miles per hour. The anemometer, at Lone Tree Bureau at the entrance to Grays Harbor, registered a velocity of 140 miles an hour for three minutes before it was torn to pieces according to official report.

Two weeks after the storm, Rudo L. Fromme, Forest Supervisor from Olympia, Jack Pike, Clallam County Game Warden and I started out to get more detailed information from the Bogachiel and Hoh River country where a number of families were reported to be hemmed in and had not been heard from.

We left Forks early in the morning and got as far as the Bogachiel River where we stayed the first night at my old homestead. This area had no storm damage. However, The Bogachiel-Hoh trail had much timber down and our progress was slowed to about one mile an hour. After two strenuous days travel we got to the Hoh River. We reached the Carl Fisher place but found no one home. The door was open so we moved in, built a fire in the kitchen stove and made ourselves comfortable for we were very

149

wet and tired. The tea kettle on the stove was empty so I took two buckets and went to the well for water. Coming back I saw the roof on fire. My shouts brought out my partners who quickly found a ladder, laid it up against the house, and with an axe they chopped a hole in the roof and we extinguished the fire with about ten buckets of water. We saved the house but made an awful mess inside.

While we were cleaning up the house, Fisher came home. He and I had been friends for many years. I told him about our trying to burn his house down to which he answered, 'Chris, I don't care about the house but how in --- did you get here, I have tried for a week to get out but never could get more than a mile from the place, and I'm sure glad to see you." Fisher was a bachelor, but he made us comfortable and soon had a great pot of Mulligan stew on the stove for our supper. After a good night rest we started up the river six miles to check on the next three families.

At one place on the Hoh we came to a tract approximately one mile square where only twelve trees were left standing. I felt as if I knew every tree in that territory. Some of them were young saplings 500 years before Columbus discovered America. As I stood alongside one fallen giant that I estimated to be 900 years old, a rush of tears came into my eyes.

We took to the sand bars and river bottoms as much of the trail had been obliterated. Further up the Hoh I gazed on more of the terrible destruction wrought against the forest through which I had travelled for the past thirty years. I looked at a lone stump that had broken off thirty feet from the base and was standing alone like a dead sentry on duty over the thousands of fallen troops. The desolation of it affected me and again tears streamed down my cheeks.

At John Huelsdonk's place at Spruce, we stood and looked out over the devastation. For miles in every direction you could count the few trees left standing. We found everyone on the Upper Hoh all right and not in want of food as reported. We continued on as far as Jackson Ranger Station then worked our way for the next three days, back to Forks where, by now, more reports had come in from the coast and from the north and east.

One could stand at Quillayute Prairie and see the Soleduck River a distance of three miles where a vast area of hemlock had been mowed down. In the Hoko district where the government got its best airplane spruce, the storm had felled the best trees, leaving in most cases the scrubs. I estimated 450,000,000 board feet of choice spruce and half of the fir in the same area was down. Some patches of timber escaped the fury of the wind but not many. Putting this all together with what I had seen on the Bogachiel and Hoh, I now estimated that 7,000,000,000 board feet of timber had been blown down.

After comparing notes some weeks following the storm with T.F. Kennedy, special agent and timber cruiser for the Milwaukee Land Company, we agreed that 8,000,000,000 board feet was more likely the correct amount of down timber. By basing this estimate on value of logs in the water, at an average of $18 per thousand, we arrived at a total timber damage of $150,000,000 for the thirty minutes battle between wind and timber. For instance one downed giant spruce on the Hoh that I measured was 90 feet of clear log and would contain almost 50,000 feet of first class lumber, and the finished product being valued in excess of $4000. The downed timber was nearly a total loss to industry and the taxpayer, for not over one percent was ever salvaged. Ninety-nine percent was left on the ground to rot.

This storm was the greatest catastrophe to natural resources that had occurred in living memory in the state of Washington. An area of one thousand square miles was more or less affected. The damage was not continuous but rather in narrow swaths running south to north. The timber was some of the finest in the Northwest. Nine tenths of the downed timber was owned by the State and private holdings, the other one tenth being on National Forest land.

Besides the billions of feet of timber down that could never be replaced or salvaged, the main problem looming like a monster on the horizon was the fire risk. I trembled to think of the fire danger that would surely come with the summer dry spell. The brush, limbs, and broken tree tops that lay on the ground represented millions of gallons of turpentine which could explode into one of the worst fires in the history of the country, and I knew that some drastic measures would have to be taken to try to prevent such a holocaust. Roads and trails would have to first be cleared and repaired before over 100 miles of telephone wire could be restrung. The federal and state governments made immediate special emergency appropriations to reopen all lines of communication and transportation as fast as possible.

No human lives were lost but I was told about many hair-breadth escapes. Automobile travel on the road in the vicinity of Forks at six-thirty the night of the storm was light, but had the wind delayed until eight o'clock, loss of life would have been certain as a dance had been scheduled in the neighboring community and many cars would have been on the road.

Just before the storm struck two cars with men in each left Forks. When about a mile out on the road and in tall timber, they heard the roaring of the wind and noise of crashing trees. Suddenly, a very large tree fell directly in front of the first car. As they all jumped out, the roar of the wind became closer and more terrifying. They ran, taking shelter under a nearby bridge. Here they found safety as no timber fell across the bridge. One of the cars was cut in two and the other was totally hemmed in between two fallen trees.

Two other men were walking together a quarter of a mile from their homes when overtaken by the storm. Trees began falling all around them. They sought shelter behind a very large fir tree. When they felt their shelter tree going over, both moved to one side and let the great tree fall. They then took refuge under the uprooted trunk. They were completely buried under branches and falling debris, but came out unharmed.

Many similar escapes were told to me. Tom Newton and one of the Peterson boys were on their way to Shuwah Prairie. Trees five to seven feet through were falling all about them with a roar like continuous thunder. They were jumping from side to side as trees crashed to the right and left. Realizing they would surely be killed they ran climbing and jumping over fallen trees and eventually reached the open prairie. One tree top plunged so close in front of Tom, he ran, bang, into it, the top was driven four feet into the ground!

A man trying to cross the clearing of his farm kept being knocked down by the wind. He tried to make it on his hands and knees but finally had to crawl on his belly to safety.

Five automobiles were on the road between Forks and Fairholme on Lake Crescent when the storm broke. M.E. Klahn was driving his car with a friend, Joe Gaydeski. The two men abandoned their car and crawled under some fallen trees for safety. Klahn's car was smashed by fallen trees. In another instance W.C. Klahn and Eddie Konopaski abandoned their machine and saved their lives by taking shelter under the Calawah River bridge for three hours.

A great tragedy of the blowdown was the immense loss of the elk herds. The Forest Service had several years previous made an estimated census of over 5000 elk that wintered on the west side of the Olympics in the lower valleys of the Queets, Clearwater, Hoh and Bogachiel Rivers. The elk herds on the lee sides of the ridges no doubt survived. We had to assume those caught in the path of the storm were either killed outright or starved to death from being trapped by fallen timber. No count could ever be made of this tragedy.

One settler told me of coming out of Forks on the trail a few hours before the storm broke and sighting four bands of elk. The wind had reduced that area to a mass of criss-crossed logs piled ten to forty feet high with only an occasional glimpse of the ground. The settler managed to reach his home several days later but only saw one lone elk standing on the sand bar in the river, hemmed in by a mass of logs--doomed to die where he stood.

The spring and summer of 1921 found special rigid forest fire preventative and suppressive measures inaugurated and enforced. This included the most up-to-date fire fighting equipment. Tank trucks carrying water, a gasoline pump, several hundred feet of hose, axes, shovels and mattocks were installed at strategic points along the main highways within the storm area. Foot patrolmen on the trails carried fire fighting tools while caches of other tools, water bags and gasoline pumps with hose were maintained at intervals along the route. Each patrolman averaged 15 to 20 miles on foot every day and the more dangerous trail sections were covered four times daily. Both the Secretary of Agriculture and the Governor of Washington prohibited smoking within the storm area except at designated safe places. No camp fire permits were issued within the blow down area except in camp grounds. Anyone entering the storm area was subject to personal registration at Fairholme. Co-operation of all settlers and the general public was solicited and while some of these regulations seemed rather harsh, very few complaints were recorded. This rigid enforcement of regulations prevented perhaps a calamity of even greater proportions than that wrought by the tornado itself.

By the mid 30's, fifteen years later, nature had produced a young forest which had begun to grow through the windfalls, thus hiding the fallen trees. The fire danger had been practically eliminated by reason of this dense young growth holding moisture, thus preventing wind and sun from drying out the forest floor.

January 1921 blowdown, south of Forks, Washington. Chris looking for the trail.

Blowdown, January 1921, highway west of Lake Crescent.

Chapter 38

"Two U.S. Marines and One Red Squirrel"
A lesson in Conservation of Wildlife

The first visit of the Pacific Fleet after World War I was in the summer of 1921. A contingent of forty ships of all types anchored in our spacious harbor of Port Angeles for two weeks of practice maneuvers in the Straits of Juan de Fuca. This was the first of many visits to follow.

During this time thousands of officers, sailors and marines had shore leave and many took advantage of the scenic surroundings, taking to the trails to hike, camp and fish in parties from two to twenty-five men. To camp under the open sky in the wilderness gave them a feeling of freedom from disciplinary restraint and the rules and regulations of shipboard. At times in this two-week layover as many as two thousand men would find their way into the Olympic National Forest in widely scattered localities.

Few, if any, of these men knew anything about safety in the woods or fire precautions. Some built campfires in unsafe places or neglected to extinguish them when breaking camp. All were allowed to carry revolvers or rifles and a lot of ammunition, and of course, they did much shooting of birds, squirrels, and other small wildlife. A cow belonging to an Elwha settler was killed while standing in the bushes and many fishermen and trail travellers reported hearing bullets whistling over their heads.

Complaints about abuse of fires and firearms flooded into the Forest Service office. About all we could do at this date was send word out to all forest patrolmen and guards to caution and advise all navy personnel about fires and firearms regulations.

The following summer about forty-five ships of the Pacific Fleet came again to Port Angeles. We decided it would be more effective to have forest regulations and instructions issued to the men before leaving ship. I sent a letter to the Admiral extending an invitation to all officers and enlisted men to be the guests of the National Forest, to enjoy fishing, hiking and camping; but, that the following regulations would be in effect: "No firearms were to be taken into the forest; all camping parties before leaving Port Angeles were to report to the District Ranger's office to register the names and number in the party and what ship they were from; all parties were to receive a campfire permit and instructions on handling campfires; all parties had to indicate their destination or designated camping spot and length of stay; and one member of the party was to be responsible for the proper use of campfire."

Next morning I received an answer from the flagship by special messenger. The admiral thanked me for the kind invitation and stated that many servicemen would no doubt avail themselves of the hospitality of the Forest Service. He assured me of full co-operation in fire prevention and suppression.

A few days later lightning started several fires in the hills directly behind Port Angeles. These had been visible to the battleships' night watch crews and were reported to the Forest Service office thus enabling us to extinguish them before spreading. Another instance of the Navy's co-operation concerned a five acre fire up Little River. We had a forest service crew there fighting the fire. One ship heard about it and sent twenty Marines to the office insisting on helping to fight fire. I hired a truck and when we arrived the fire was nearly out. However, the Marines insisted on the mopping up. They felt indebted and wanted to do something constructive. I thanked them all and their captain.

That same summer of 1922, week-end hiking and camping parties were numerous. I was coming down the Elwha River trail when I met two young Marines. They were carrying their blanket roll and camping equipment and looked very hot and tired. We stopped and exchanged greetings and one of them said, "Oh, oh, here is where we have to show our camping permit. Are you a ranger?" "Yes," I said, "Where are you going?" "To Griff Creek, here is our permit." I looked it over and noted that they had passed their destination two miles back. I offered to change their destination to a good place further up river, but they were tired and wanted to go down hill back to Griff Creek. They asked if they could walk along with me and I agreed. I let the taller of the two set the pace. They told me they were from Missouri and asked a lot of questions about the woods and trails and animals.

Suddenly the first Marine held his hand back and stood still. "Look, a squirrel, let's watch him." The squirrel had just jumped from the upper slope down into the middle of the trail about 15 feet ahead of us where it sat on a projecting root, its bushy tail curled over its head. With its front paws it was twirling a fir cone, biting out the seeds with its sharp front teeth. This is a common and amusing sight for any forest traveler to see, but to the seamen it was something new. It seemed to give them a great thrill. The tall Marine exclaimed "Partner, I've never seen anything so pretty. I wish all the boys on shipboard could see this!" At this, he released his hold on his partner's arm and started pointing at the squirrel. This motion alarmed the little animal, its tail came down, but with cone still in its mouth, it sat there poised to run. The big Marine exclaimed, "God, if I only had a gun! I could knock the eye out of the little son of a -----! Look at him run up that tree!"

I stepped up to him a little angry and lectured him that this harmless little squirrel was part of the wildlife and had a right to be here and that we were the intruders. "One minute you got a thrill out of watching it and wished all of your shipmates could see it, and the next minute, the savage of your nature comes out and spoiled it all. If you had killed it, it would lay and rot and the next passerby would have the unpleasant task of kicking it out of the trail."

We continued on down the trail to Griff Creek in silence. I showed them a good camping place and wished them a pleasant weekend. The tall Marine extended his hand to me and said, "Ranger, I want to apologize. I know I shall never kill anything again for the mere pleasure of it." I continued my journey and in time forgot about the incident.

Five years later Frank Fountain, a Boy Scout leader in Port Angeles, asked me to come to a meeting and lecture to his scout troop on behavior and conservation in the woods. When I finished my little talk, Mr. Fountain told a story about a hike he had taken that summer. He was returning from a climb up Mt. Angeles when he overtook six sailors on the Heart of the Hills trail. He joined them and as they walked along together a squirrel ran out to the middle of the road carrying a seed cone. It hesitated, then sat up for a moment and looked the group over. One tall Marine halted the party and said, "Mates, that beautiful little creature taught me the best lesson of my life." Mr. Fountain and the other five sailors listened while the Marine told his story...."It happened over on the Elwha River trail about five years ago. . . "

Mr. Fountain went on to tell the story of how the marine had met a ranger and the rest of the incident with the red squirrel. Mr. Fountain, a great lover of nature himself, wanted me to know that the little lecture given that Marine by some ranger had made a lasting impression.

Trio of young Elk going to a lodge meeting.

Chapter 39

"Jeffers Loses Life on Mt. Olympus"

In 1924, a friend of mine, Joseph Jeffers, a commercial photographer from Olympia, lost his life on Mt. Olympus. I had made two trips with him into the mountains on previous picture-taking expeditions and found him to be extremely knowledgeable about the Olympics with a growing passion to photograph the hard-to-reach places. He was very venturesome and many times took risks that I advised against.

On this trip, in company of his teenage son Vibert, he had planned an ascent of Mt. Olympus from the north side, crossing Blue Glacier to the Queets side via West Peak. This was relatively unknown country on the Queets side and Jeffers hoped to capture spectacular scenery never before photographed.

On the eve of the 23rd of August, the two had camped near the foot of the glacier where a Forest Service trail crew was building the Glacier Creek trail. Early the following morning the pair assembled their gear including crampons and ropes, and departed. Late in the afternoon the son came running back to our trail camp almost unable to talk to tell us that his father had fallen into a crevasse. He told us that his father had tried to lower himself by rope to a shelf below the surface of the ice but that the rope was not long enough, so he had tried swinging and letting go with a jump, he had fallen short of the shelf and went down between the rock and glacier. He said he had shouted to his father for some minutes but had gotten no answer.

At daylight some of our men went back with the young boy to the place where the accident had happened but found that nothing could be done from above. The accident had occurred on the southwest ridge of Mt. Olympus just above the basin that feeds the South Fork of the Hoh.

I at once notified the Forest Supervisor's Office in Olympia, and they in turn notified the family of Jeffers. The Olympia Chamber of Commerce engaged two Swiss guides from Mr. Rainier to attempt a rescue. These two guides with about ten local mountaineers and Forest Service men with experience left for the scene of the accident by way of the South Fork of the Hoh. They arrived in the west glacial basin on the third morning out from Forks. Here they made visible contact with two men I sent up the mountain by way of Blue Glacier to the place where Jeffers had fallen into the crevasse. After trying all day to get into the crevasse from below, these expert Swiss mountain climbers admitted defeat for at no place could they get near the opening to where Jeffers

157

went down. The ice had melted away from the rock making a crevasse of unknown depth. Jeffers was no doubt killed instantly. The son had used good judgement by not following down the rope to assist his father, for the same fate would have awaited him.

The family and friends had offered a liberal reward for recovery of the body but Mt. Olympus had claimed its victim for all time and the picture records he had made remain a secret. Since this tragic accident this glacier has been known as Jeffers Glacier.

Theodore Rixon, Surveyor and Chet Howser, Assistant District Ranger, Port Angeles office, 1920's.

Chapter 40

"Wrecked In An Airplane In The Olympics"

What started out to be the first aerial fire patrol flight over the Olympic mountains ended in near tragedy for pilot and passenger.

Early in September 1924, after an unusually long dry spell, the interior of the Olympics was visited by an electrical storm which started many lightning fires in all parts of the forest. Most of these fires were quickly located by Forest Service foot patrolmen and extinguished while small. One fire at the headwaters of the Elwha River was not discovered until one week after the storm. The fire had started on top of a ridge between the Goldie and Elwha Rivers and was burning down both slopes toward good timber, especially on the Elwha side.

Chet Howser, my assistant, was sent up with a crew of eight men to assist Ranger Harold Lee, in whose district the fire was located. The walking distance to this fire was forty miles from the nearest road, a two-day hike for the crew carrying blankets and food. Two pack trains with tools and supplies were also dispatched. After the men and supply train had left, Ranger Lee telephoned the headquarters office that at least twenty more men would be needed. It was not easy to get men to walk forty miles to their jobs, but I managed to hire eight more men and with a forest guard in charge sent them as reinforcements to the fire.

On the third day Howser phoned that there were two fires but he could not get around them on account of the dangerous and inaccessible country. He also thought that there might be other fires. I instructed him to concentrate all efforts on the Elwha side and try to keep the fire out of the valley, retarding its progress until the long overdue rain should come. I advised him that I was planning to make a flight over the mountains to survey the fire situation of the Elwha, locate other fires, if any, and take a close look at a large fire in the Quilcene District. The Quilcene fire was being fought by a large crew directed by Ranger William Vallad and Forest Service disbursing agent Clarence Adams from the Olympia office.

Fire patrol by plane had never been tried before in this area and I thought it might prove to be an efficient means of fire control. The only government airfields near Seattle were Sand Point Naval Base and Fort Lewis Army Base near Tacoma. Their equipment was mostly World War I machines used for training. Reconnaissance and commercial flying was still in the future. Pilots knew relatively little about the Olympic Mountains as none ventured into this air space.

I made arrangements by telephone with the Sand Point Naval Air Station in Seattle to fly over the Olympics, and I left Port Angeles on the

15th of September, arriving in Seattle that evening. The next morning at the Base I met Lieutenant Theodore J. Koenig, Commander of Sand Point Naval Air Base, who was to be my pilot. I described the Olympics as being a jumble of mountain ranges. Those nearest Seattle, which he had flown close to from the airbase, were jagged and rocky and lacked the heavy blanket of timber that we would see on the more westerly ranges. I outlined the trip to him as follows; up the Dosewallips Valley to the Divide, then to the Elwha Basin, thence over the Elwha-Hoh Divide, down the Hoh Valley, then northerly to the Bogachiel River, Forks, Lake Crescent and Port Angeles, thence to the Quilcene fire and return to Sand Point. We would fly at lower elevations through the valleys.

On the morning of the 16th of September it was somewhat foggy and misty over Lake Washington. Lieutenant Koenig did not approve of the weather and said we could not go unless it cleared. I telephoned the Elwha Ranger Station by way of Port Angeles and was informed that is was very warm there and not a cloud in the sky. I explained this to my pilot and he said, "I have never flown over the Olympics but will go if the weather clears by afternoon." The weather did clear about one o'clock leaving only a few scattered clouds.

A large DeHavelin plane was readied and we donned flying clothes. Lt. Koenig climbed into the front cockpit and I took the after one. I was strapped in and told if there was anything I wanted to say to the pilot that I should do it in writing, so a pencil and paper were put in a convenient place in front of me.

We left the ground shortly before 2 p.m., circled over the north end of Lake Washington, and headed west over Puget Sound toward the Olympic Mountains. I had an altimeter in front of me and could see that we were flying at eighteen hundred feet. With the exception of a few white clouds it was very clear. I began to relax and enjoy my first airplane ride very much.

We entered the Dosewallips Valley and had gone about ten miles. The altimeter read 2000 feet and I could see a cloud of fog rolling over the ridge ahead. We were heading straight up the valley towards this fog bank. My altimeter now read 2200 feet which I thought much too low since the divide ahead was about 3000 feet high. I started to write a note to the Lieutenant to tell him to "go higher". We entered the fog bank and all visibility vanished. I never finished the note nor did I ever know how much of the message I had written as my mind became a blank.

How much time elapsed before I began to regain consciousness, I do not know. When I did come to, I imagined I was sitting in a comfortable chair feeling cozy and happy. Pain totally absent. Looking down I saw blood on my feet and much more on the floor. For some time I wondered where so much blood could come from. Slowly I moved my head and could see long strings of congealed blood hanging from my face and clothing. I began to realize that all this blood was mine. In a half daze I stared straight ahead at a wall of rock. A large fir tree thirty inches or more in diameter partly broken and torn up by the roots lay along the right side of me on a steep angle up a hill. I gazed at it a long time through tangled wires and broken lumber. A big blue star was wrapped around the old tree. Nothing made any sense. How long it took me to realize where I was I do not know. I tried to get up but my left leg and arm were helpless. Now everything began to rush back into my mind. What had become of the pilot?

With my good right arm and leg I dragged myself out of the cockpit and over the wreckage to the front cockpit. Lt. Koenig was bent over with his head under the control panel. I tried to speak to him but my mouth seemed glued shut. I got a hold on his collar and pulled with all my strength. He fell back in his seat, face upward, and I thought he was dead. One of his eyes was black and swollen and his lower lip was badly lacerated. I kept trying to talk to him while I stroked his forehead and hair. He finally opened his eyes and looked slowly around. After staring at me for some minutes he said, "Chris, we had a wreck and you are badly hurt." Since I felt no pain I said, "No, I'm not hurt much." He moaned and cried, "Chris, you are hurt, half of your face is gone!"

We helped each other get clear of the wreck and sat down together upon the rocks. Outside of being bruised and black and blue, my pilot was not severely injured and he had no broken bones. We looked around and sized up the situation. The plane had collided on a steep and rocky ridge on the side of Mt. Constance. The wing had caught a tall snag which had spun the plane around easing the impact. We had struck a rock shelf and luckily we were right side up and had not caught fire. The plane was a total wreck, and if it had struck any other place it might have rolled down into a canyon.

We decided to make an attempt to get off the mountain. Since it was all strange country to the pilot it would be up to me to find a way down. After looking over the country and getting my bearings, I found we were on the divide between the Dosewallips and the Quilcene Rivers. If we went down on the Dosewallips side of the divide we should hit a Forest Service trail that would take us to the Corrigenda Ranger Station in the valley and a ranger or hiker would surely find us.

We started down, Koenig assisting me all the way. An old forest fire had burned through on this side of the ridge and the steep rocky slopes were covered with dead brush, blackberry vines and charred logs and limbs. We dragged ourselves, rolled and slid over rocks and through

161

brambles. Temptation to rest was with us constantly, but we knew if we stopped for only a few moments we could never regain strength to go on and death would surely overtake us. I was also very weak from loss of blood and my torn face was full of sand, dirt and briars. My injuries had numbed every nerve in my body, so luckily I had no feeling of discomfort.

About dusk, after hours of this tortuous descent, we heard someone calling from below us, "Are you from the aeroplane?" The pilot answered "Yes", and a man soon appeared. He was the Forest Service Patrolman and helped me to the trail which was close by. He partly carried me for a mile and a half to the Corrigenda Ranger Station and set me down on the edge of the bed. I knew I had gotten us down off that mountain and proceeded to pass out.

When I awoke next afternoon Clarence Adams of the Olympia Forest Service Office was with me. He refreshed my memory and the horrible experience came rushing back. He related to me that It was Forest Ranger Jerry Neihart who had been coming down the Dosewallips trail to Corrigenda on his regular patrol when he heard the buzzing of an airplane in the fog above him. He heard a crash, then all was still. With frightening thoughts rushing through his mind he ran the four miles back to the ranger station where he telephoned the Quilcene ranger and reported the crash. Adams was there and remarked, "If it is an airplane in that area it must be Chris, as he was to fly to the Elwha and the Hoh and back over this area on a fire patrol trip today."

Adams immediately telephoned the hospital in Port Townsend to dispatch a doctor and nurse and ambulance to come to Quilcene. He then organized a search party, placed a mattress in a forest service truck and set out for the Corrigenda Ranger Station. In the meantime Patrolman Neihart left a note of instruction at the ranger station and hurried back up the trail to locate the wreck. The rescue party had to travel over a narrow winding road for twenty-five miles from Quilcene. Ranger Neihart had gotten us to the ranger station before the rescue party arrived. We were driven in the pick-up truck back over this same winding road to a hotel in Quilcene where the doctor and nurse were waiting. They used two rooms in the hotel as a hospital and surgery. The doctor, assisted by the nurse, performed the operation on me and Clarence Adams administered the anesthetic.

After cleaning my wounds, and sewing up the ragged lacerations on my face, the doctor assured Adams that I was not dangerously hurt, so Adams decided to telephone my wife in Port Angeles. He told her we had made a forced landing near Quilcene and would not be home for a day or two. She knew of the forest fire near Quilcene and just supposed we had landed nearby to look over the fire. Later in the evening, Clarence got to

162

thinking that the Seattle newspapers might print something about the crash next morning. He again phoned my wife, telling her that we had an accident in which I was slightly hurt but would be home in a couple of days and not to worry. We were then taken to the hospital in Port Townsend.

Three days later a bed spring and mattress was placed over the seats of an open touring car and I was secured with straps to this bed and driven to Port Angeles. It took three hours to make the fifty-mile drive over rough, unpaved road. I still had no feeling in my whole body.

We drove up in front of my home and my family came running out to meet me. When my wife saw the men unload me on a mattress she fainted, and it was indeed a solemn procession that followed me into the house.

A local doctor came to look me over and make me comfortable. He assured me that the Port Townsend doctor had done an excellent job of sewing me up and setting joints and bones. The skin over my entire body had turned dark blue and green and I still had no feeling.

I later learned the sum total of my injuries. My left shin bone was cracked, the left knee cap was out of socket, the left elbow chipped, the left shoulder muscles torn loose, the lower lip torn down to the chin, the right cheek torn from the corner of the mouth to the right ear, the right lower jaw was broken and four lower teeth knocked out. It took three months before I was able to get out of bed and almost that long for the terrible bruises, which covered most of my body, to go away.

About two weeks after the crash, mountain climbers found the wreckage and someone sent me photographs. Later the government sent some soldiers to burn the fuselage. They reported that the altimeter read 2800 feet and that if we had been 200 feet higher, we would have been clear. They also reported it was a "total wreck--tree tops, wires, wings, lumber, and rocks--a cat had no business getting out of a mess like that alive!" Crash pictures showed that the wing had topped a tall snag which spun us around and eased the crash. Once more I had cheated "The Grim Reaper"!

A year after the crash, Lt. Koenig came to see me. He told me what had passed through his mind after entering the fog cloud. "I thought it a short cloud like others we had passed through over the Canal, but I immediately sensed it to be a long one. My first impulse was to turn and come out of it, however, I was afraid of the valley being too narrow to give us enough swinging room, so I tilted the plane up and gave her full throttle, perhaps 120 miles per hour, as I knew our safety lay in elevation. I was bending over, holding the clutch stick with a death grip and that is all I remember."

I know that my pilot made the wisest decision otherwise we would have slammed full bore into that mountain of rock with fatal consequences for both of us. However, I regret I did not read my altimeter sooner.

I kept in touch with Lt. Koenig for many years after and he urged me to fly again as soon as possible so that I would not be afraid in the future. I am not afraid of riding in airplanes and will be ready to go again if the need arises, but I know the pilot must stay out of clouds over mountains. I marvel now how I ever dragged myself, even with Lt. Koenig's help, down that rough mountainside. My mind had worked clearly for I knew at all times where we had to go to get out. If Lt.Koenig had crashed alone he surely wouldn't have known which way to go.

I am in good health for a man in his early fifties. That Port Townsend doctor surely worked miracles in sewing my face back together, as I have hardly any visible scars.

I might state that the fire fighters held all lightning fires to the high country, and none of them reached good timber in the valleys. Three days after our 'forced' landing near Mt. Constance, a heavy rain extinguished all the forest fires in the Olympics for that season.

Airplane reconnaisance flight ends on Mt. Constance, September 1924.

Chapter 41

Historical Data, Excerpts From Newspapers, Memoirs, Letters And Forest Service Publications, 1921-1927

Historical Data As Seen From the Pen of Clarence Adams Administrative Assistant, U.S. Forest Service, Olympia, Washington, Written August, 1946

"Chris Morgenroth's first duty assigned to him by Supervisor D.B. Sheller, upon entering the Forest Service June 15, 1903, was the locating and building of a trail along the south side of Lake Crescent and along the Soleduck River to the settlement of Sappho. There it connected with the wagon road from Clallam Bay to Forks.

I feel this is of historic value because this trail was used as part of the present U.S. Highway 101 which connects Port Angeles with the west end of Clallam and Jefferson counties and is a link in what is known as the Olympic Loop.

In 1921, when that part of the highway around Lake Crescent was being built, Chris was interested in preserving the beauty along the edge of the lake, so tied rags to small alders, maples and fir trees and asked the contractor not to cut them down or cover them up, so that they might live for the benefit of future generations."

Summer, 1922,

"I believe it was in the year 1922, when I was learning the forest by taking two-week trips, that Chris Morgenroth and I, with a party of eight from Seattle and Port Angeles, made a trip up the Soleduck and down the Hoh. When we reached the snow on the north side of the Soleduck watershed, one of the men gave out and said the high altitude affected his heart. He just couldn't make it with his pack. So, Chris and I divided his pack between us and went merrily on our way. When we reached the top, trodding over about two miles of snow, the sick heart became well all of a sudden, so we refused to carry his pack any further.

Then we descended the two miles of shale rock trail dropping into the Hoh Valley to Olympus Ranger Station where Charley Lewis had a fine dinner for us. (It tasted like elk meat to me). After we had taken a dip in the icy waters of the Hoh just below Blue Glacier we were sitting on the front steps of the ranger station's one room dwelling and Chris says, "I just happened to remember something." We went to the back of the cabin where he removed a board, reached his hand in, and sure enough, there it was after eight long years, a bottle of Sunnybrook and the seal not broken. All of us, except the two minors who were with us, had a drink, then another, well--I don't remember how many, but it certainly made us feel good after that cold dip in the Hoh.

On the same trip, Chris developed a large boil on his back, near his spine. On the way from Jackson Ranger Station to Spruce (Huelsdonk's) he stopped, took out his jack-knife, handed it to me and after he stretched himself across a log, says, "Open that damn thing, I can't stand it any longer." I didn't profess to be a surgeon, but I did as instructed and when the core popped out it almost hit me in the eye. Chris felt better, of course."

Summer, 1923,

"In the summer of 1923, shortly after the highway had been opened on Lake Crescent, Chris and I turned two pair of mountain goats loose near Storm King Ranger Station. Chris didn't think of what might happen when they were unloaded, so he just stood there waiting to see what they would do. I was near the truck. One of the big he-goats looked at Chris, sized him up, and then with his head down, bolted for him. Chris being near an old snag, reached as high as he could and pulled himself up just out of reach of the ram's butt. Goats must have a tough head, because if Chris had been between the goat's head and the snag, there wouldn't have been much left of Chris. The ram then shook his head, looked around a bit, and scampered up the side of the mountain.

These goats increased quite rapidly as they have been seen on different watersheds quite some distance away. The next year after we turned them loose on Storm King Mountain, two of them were seen by us from the ranger station on a ledge where we thought it impossible for them to get off. The next day they were gone. When it comes to mountain climbing, they can do things that no human would ever think of doing."

1923,

"On another trip with Morgenroth in 1923, we were enroute to Forks. We passed a truck that was stalled and so stopped to see if we could give any assistance. The occupants were two boys from Forks and just as we got up to the truck, one of the boys flipped a live cigarette to the side of the road. Both boys were pretty well lit up with liquor, and Chris asked one of them to pick up the cigarette and put it out. One boy replied, "Who's going to make me?" Well, after quite an argument, the boy picked the cigarette up and stamped it out in the middle of the road. No action was taken in the matter as the Forest Service had dealt with this family and their relatives on many previous occasions. Chris handled the situation in a calm and friendly way, and about a week later the boys apologized to Chris for the way they had acted."

Newspaper Article: Port Angeles Evening News, September 1923, By E.B. Webster, publisher

"Sampson Leveled A Temple,
Mr. Morgenroth Has Reduced Mt. Angeles to a Mole Hill"

"There is no part of the trail as steep as the hills on the road to Klahanne Lodge and much less effort is necessary. On the old trail I had to stop every fifty feet to get my breath. I had walked up the new trail without stopping. I lost sight of the fact that I was climbing a mountain; my interest was concentrated on the general excellence of the trail itself, for it was wide, level and soft underfoot. There are no roots and no rocks to make for discomfort. Chris Morgenroth, Deputy Forest Supervisor of this area, was largely responsible for the building of the new trail up the mountain. Mt. Angeles has been flattened out into a hill, and not much of a hill at that!"

Newspaper Editorial: Port Angeles Herald, September 1923

"Fire Prevention a Matter of Common Sense", by William D. Welsh

"When all the northwest seems ablaze with forest fires it is well at this time to point to the great stretch of timber known as the Olympic National Forest from which no curl of smoke or dart of flame has shown within the past two months.

Organizations of men, a system of trails and roads, plenty of sane equipment, education of the public and last of all regulation of the forest to the nth degree will keep 95 percent of the fires away from the timber.

It is in the Olympic National Forest that the great storm swept down trees several years ago. It is in the Olympic National Forest that 300 miles of trails and miles of telephone lines have been built. It is in the Olympic National Forest that fine equipment, modern pumps, capable men and a wonderful organization are maintained. So with a fire hazard greater than in other forests and a record of very few fires, this common sense sort of prevention certainly gets results.

Education of the tourists and citizens generally is another vital matter. In this, Ranger Chris Morgenroth has made a fine reputation. He appeared before every club in the city, has always sought and received co-operation from this paper, and has capable men at the registration station at Fairholme to advise tourists against fires.

It takes a long while to grow trees. It takes a few hours to destroy them. The old axiom that "one tree will make a million matches and one match will destroy a million trees" holds good now as it always has."

Newspaper Article: Port Angeles Evening News, June 30, 1924
"Chris Morgenroth, Veteran Forest Service Official
Resigns Post July First"

Just twenty-three years since he entered the employ of the U.S. Forest Service, Chris Morgenroth, Deputy Supervisor of the Olympics, steps from that post tonight.

To mention the Olympics without somehow coupling with them the name of Morgenroth will not sound right somehow. Chris was roaming the Olympics, stomping out fire and protecting timber when there wasn't a vestige of trail, an inch of telephone line or a foot of hose. The only method in the early 1900's of communicating news of fire and sending for help was by male runner who took days in their journey through the forests. Today as a result of his supervision, 195 miles of telephone line stretch through the forest lanes to mountain tip and ranger stations. Three hundred miles of horse trail now lead to all parts of the forest. Ten ranger stations with men and equipment are placed at convenient points from which men, pump and hose can be taken at a minutes notice to forest blazes.

Mr. Morgenroth's resignation was not accepted in Olympia, it was not accepted at Portland. It is now in Washington, D.C. where no word has yet been received. Morgenroth has checked over supplies and equipment to Chet Howser, his assistant in the local office and announces he will step out at five o'clock. To watch him in the closing hours of his administration is to make one absolutely know that his going is the hardest task he ever performed.

Newspaper Article: Port Angeles Evening News, July 10, 1924
"Morgenroth Will Remain With The Forestry Service"

". . . When his resignation reached the hands of Forester Greeley in Washington, D.C. that official realized the necessity of keeping the hand of an experienced veteran on the wheel in this section of the world, in other words, Mr. Morgenroth's resignation was not accepted and his return to the service was solicited.

He said he is glad to be back in the harness; happy to be able to trot the trails and ford the streams. The Olympic Forest has been his life. He would have been lonesome without it. "

Letter: Lovejoy to Chris, March 26, 1925

"Dear Chris,

Last night in the Saturday Evening Post I saw a little picture of Lake Crescent and it sure set me to thinking about a lot of things. I always liked that country better than any other.

First time you took me up the Elwha we ate up the pie the Guard had made for himself. The next morning he lit the fire in the little cabin stove and went to the creek to get water, and while there he gaffed a two foot salmon and brought back steaks for breakfast and the grease in the pan was just beginning to smoke!

I quit being a professor in 1919. They starved me out and I got tired of their damn pretenses and high brow foolishness. Then I took to writing for a living.

I hope you will try to write a book. I've often said that you had lived a life with more "book adventures" in it than anybody I ever knew. You are a very unusual man who has had some very unusual experiences which ought to be recorded. Try writing a chapter or two, then send it along for me to read."

Yours truly,
P.S. Lovejoy

Letter: Chris to Lovejoy, May 12, 1925

"Dear Lovejoy,

The Spruce Railroad is open for business but no camp has as yet started along the line. However a large camp is contemplated on the Calawah River for the near future.

No timber was ever salvaged from the "Blow Down" and the hemlock and spruce is now about 60% total loss.

The Olympic Highway is completed from Olympia to the Bogachiel River by way of Hood Canal. It is also completed from the south to a point ten miles north of Lake Quinault. The rest of the way is all cleared but not graded. This will take about five more years.

The old Elwha dam is in full use and a new one to develop more badly needed power for industries in Port Angeles is going to be constructed very soon. This new dam and power house will be located about one mile above the Elwha Ranger Station. Port Angeles has now two large pulp and paper mills as well as a large saw mill and a cooperage plant and other smaller wood-working plants. Population of the town is about 10,000.

Many of my friends have also urged me to write a book. One of these days I will give it a try."

Yours truly,
Chris

Letter from the United States Battle Fleet, Division Three
U.S.S. Pennsylvania, Flagship, July 7, 1926

Mr. Chris Morgenroth
District Forest Ranger
Port Angeles, Washington

My Dear Sir;
Your letter addressed to the Commanding Officer of the Pacific Fleet assembled in Port Angeles Bay has been received by the undersigned. The letter itself has been quoted to the vessel's present senior officer with instructions to comply strictly with its provisions and the matter will be turned over to succeeding senior officers on their arrival.

I am sure that everyone thoroughly appreciates the necessity for care of our natural scenery, etc., and that they will do their utmost to protect it by co-operating and following your instructions.

Very Sincerely Yours,
H.J. Ziegemier,
R. Adm., U.S. Navy

Letter from: U.S. Navy Young Men's Christian Association
July 21, 1926

Mr. Chris Morgenroth
U.S. Forest Service
Port Angeles, Washington

Dear Mr. Morgenroth;
I want to thank you again for your share in helping to make the Camp Conference of the Triangle Service League on the Elwha River, an outstanding success. This is the first event of its kind ever attempted by the Army and Navy Y.M.C.A. and will be long remembered by those present. Your talk at our luncheon the first day had a marked effect upon every man present and a number of them have since spoken very highly of what you had to say.

You will be interested in knowing that there was a total of 67 men registered at this Conference and they represented fourteen different ships.

We have all received a new impression of the beauty of God's great outdoors and after meeting you have a greater respect than ever for the men who are dedicated to making that outdoors safe.

Sincerely yours,
Howard G. Eddy
Religious and Social Work

Letter of Resignation: December 1, 1926

Forest Supervisor
Olympia, Washington
Dear Sir:

I hereby hand you my resignation from the Forest Service to become effective on January 1, 1927, after being with the Service for nearly a quarter century.

Owing to many accidents in the line of duty, I find that I cannot now endure the hardships and physical exertions required of me. I am taking this step, after due deliberation for the purpose of finding employment better suited to my present physical ability.

Trusting that you will promptly relieve me of all responsibility of any official nature by the date mentioned, I am,

Very respectfully yours,
Chris Morgenroth
Forest Ranger

The following report was submitted as part of a summary of improvements and inventory required of U.S. Forestry officials upon retirement.

Statistical Report, Form 446, Year ending 1926

The following improvements were made in Region I of Olympic National Forest between 1903 and the year ending 1926.

31.71 miles of Forest Service roads (not major roads) at a total cost of $63,031

494.57 miles of trail, at a total cost of $187,554

11 bridges at a total cost of $13,299

541.98 miles of telephone line at a total cost of $39,630

2 lookout houses, cost: $979

6 dwellings with four rooms or more, cost: $5,840

30 dwellings less than four rooms, cost: $6,854

4 barns, cost: $501

3 offices, cost: $1,431

31 other structures, mostly trail shelters, cost: $4,888

11 water projects, cost: $783

3 wing dams, cost: $5,699
30 camp buildings, cost: $1,910
For the calendar year 1926, $5,154 was spent for trail maintenance
and $3,181 for maintenance of telephone lines.

Signed--Chris Morgenroth
Forest Ranger

Article: Taken from U.S. Forest Service Publication, Region 6, Portland, Oregon, December, 1926.

"Chris Morgenroth Resigns"

Effective December 31, 1926, Chris Morgenroth leaves the Forest Service which he has served so long and well. Almost a quarter of a century has elapsed since Chris first became a guardian over the vast timber resources of the Olympic Forest. While his present appointment dates from February 1, 1905, he had for several years previous to this date been in the employ of the Interior Department, which makes him one of the oldest, if not the oldest, Forest Service man in years of service.

Among many sterling qualities it is perhaps as a fire fighter that Chris was pre-eminent. Veteran of many a battle that was usually won gave him a fund of experience that other forest officers have drawn upon for two decades, and in that way much of his valuable experience will remain with the Service. As a Public Relations man, Chris was one of the pioneers. His talks have done much to enlighten the public of his district in regard to the purpose and aims of the Forest Service and his successful handling of thousands of sailors roaming the woods, without a single fire, is an enduring monument.

Morgenroth resigns to enter private work, in which the Olympic personnel wishes him a long, happy and prosperous life.

J.H. Billingslea
Assistant Supervisor
Olympic National Forest

Editorial: Port Angeles Evening News, January 4, 1927, by William D. Welsh

"Twenty-five years in the service of one employer is the honor that goes out of office with Chris Morgenroth who, on Saturday, resigned from the U.S. Forest Service.

That twenty-five years covers a quarter century of real development in the Olympic National Forest where Morgenroth served. In that time there has been built a system of trails, roads, ranger and guard stations and telephone lines. This network has provided protection against the ravages of forest fires.

Morgenroth risked his life at least a dozen times for the service. Blinded by smoke, he fell into a pit during a fire that swept over the Soleduck area. He lay stunned while flames snapped at trees above him, and was given up for dead but escaped. He was at one time treed and chased for hours by two timber wolves. Making an airplane reconnaissance of an Olympic Peninsula fire, the plane struck the side of Mt. Constance in the fog and Morgenroth was seriously injured. He has been a good servant and we wish him success in his new venture. We welcome his successor and offer the same spirit of co-operation we have always accorded Mr. Morgenroth."

Chris, having guided a party of over 400, mostly sailors from warships in the Port Angeles Harbor, to the top of Mt. Angeles, 6000 feet elevation, is here (standing at extreme left), giving a talk during the lunch hour on conservation of the great out-of-doors and its wildlife. July, 1931.

Part VII

Preface: Campaigning For A National Park, 1927-1938

Mt. Olympus National Monument contained 633,600 acres when it was set aside in 1909. Mining and timber interests and other developers had pressured, over a period of six years, to get the size of the Monument reduced. By 1915 it had been whittled down three times by simple Executive Orders until its boundaries included only 298,751 acres, half of its original size.

During Chris's long career in the Forest Service he had remained loyal to the principles set down by that branch of the government. He touches briefly on the five year period serving the forest products industry in the private sector, and the year and a half in the Civilian Conservation Corp. Both experiences helped to keep alive his ideas on conservation and use of the public domain.

By the 1930's a great deal of open discussion was developing for establishing a National Park in the Olympic mountain region. Transferring the Monument from the Department of Agriculture to the Department of Interior in 1933 opened the door to a park campaign.

From this time on Chris dedicated his time to explaining how a National Park would boost tourism on the peninsula and how with a sustained timber yield, the mills could run forever. One of his greatest concerns besides protecting the timber resources from fire and over-harvesting was the threatened species of mammal, the Roosevelt Elk. For years he had warned of the declining numbers and had advocated strong measures for preserving the herds. He drew up guidelines for a National Park on the Olympic Peninsula and presented the facts and logic supporting such a park. He went to work in 1934 for the National Park Service and became involved in the greatest adventure of his life.

The first bill to establish the park was introduced by Representative Mon Wallgren from the second Congressional District of Washington and the "battle over boundaries" began. In the spring of 1936 Wallgren submitted another bill, H.R. 7086, to the Committee on Public Lands. Hearings for this bill were called for April of 1936. Excerpts taken from those hearings and from some correspondence during and after those hearings are set down here.

Chapter 42

"Post Forest Service"

Early in 1927, after retiring from the Forest Service, I went to work for the Washington Pulp and Paper Corporation in Port Angeles. Since I was familiar with all the territory inside and outside of the national forest boundaries on the Peninsula, it was my job to cruise and acquire private timber tracts, and purchase pulpwood from independent pulp cutters. I was also consultant on reforestation, fire control, tree farming and pulpwood harvesting methods.

Excerpt from "The Olympic Howler" (Newsletter, O.N.F.), Olympia, Washington, Feb. 1, 1927, Written by Clarence M. Adams

Former Ranger Chris Morgenroth called at this office on January 25. He was here in Olympia as his company's representative in connection with the fight at the present session of the Legislature between Clallam County and Grays Harbor Port Districts over who will control the timber interests in the west end of Clallam and Jefferson Counties. Naturally Clallam County is vigorously opposing the measure and a big delegation from Port Angeles is in Olympia looking after their interests.

Incidently, we learned that Morgenroth is now Chief Lumberman for the Washington Pulp and Paper Corporation of Port Angeles. The same party also told us that Chris now occupies one of the finest offices the corporation maintains at the plant and is furnished along with said office a most beautiful stenographer. Although he had to buy himself a new Dodge Roadster for use in his present work, it is stated that the company furnishes him with a first class chauffeur, since his duties keep him on the road a great deal for the purpose of purchasing pulp wood.

We also learned that his salary is fairly doubled what he was receiving in the Service, with all expenses paid while away from his headquarters. This statement alone only proves more conclusively, as has always been the case in the past, that the Forest Service serves as an A-1 school for its students who later enter into the service of the privately owned timber companies.

This writer joins with the Olympic force in wishing Chris the best of success in this his new undertaking.

When the Olympic Loop Highway is completed in 1931, it will skirt the entire Olympic Mountain range for approximately 320 miles and will attract annually many thousands of visitors. Climatic conditions and low elevations will permit travel over this road at all seasons. But only an occasional far-away glimpse of a mountain peak will be visible from the highway.

A plan to build an Olympic Mountain Loop Highway permitting tourists to drive within a short distance of Mount Olympus glaciers was proposed at a joint meeting of the Peninsula Chamber of Commerce and the board of directors of the Port Angeles Chamber of Commerce.

The plan, put forward by Chris Morgenroth who has spent a lifetime in the Olympic mountains, is as follows:

"Leave the Olympic Highway at the Elwha bridge and continue along the Elwha River crossing the Elwha at the Soldiers Bridge. Continuing up the hillside to Lookout Point, where, at an elevation of 2000 feet one may view Mills Lake, Hurricane Meadow, the Straits of Juan de Fuca, the Upper Elwha Valley and mountain peaks. This ten miles of road would terminate at the Olympic Hot Springs.

The proposed road would take off over Boulder Mountain from the Hot Springs to Crystal Ridge, a distance of six miles. Here open meadows, waterfalls and mountain flowers abound. Another seven mile stretch to Soleduck Park would traverse a scenic mountain side covered with blueberries and wild flowers and where marmots and bear frequent the area.

A five mile stretch around the Soleduck-Hoh Divide would take you to Bogachiel Peak. Here one has a 360-degree view including an unobstructed picture of Mt. Olympus, a mere seven miles across the Hoh Valley. From here the road would descend for four miles through Bogachiel Park which is great game and fish country with a beautiful small lake. Another four miles down hill would bring you to the Sol Duc Hot Springs Resort, one of the largest health resorts in Washington.

An extension of this loop road from Bogachiel Peak down into the Hoh Valley for eight miles would bring the visitor to Glacier Creek Canyon. From here a four mile hike would take you to the top of Blue Glacier on Mt. Olympus. This spur road could exit down the Hoh Valley a distance of 21 miles through virgin forests where elk and deer could be observed. This road would connect with the Olympic Loop Highway 101.

Mt. Rainier and other national parks have a good start in road development and these roads are crowded with tourists. The Olympics can truly be called the Switzerland of America and such an interior road loop along the feasible route suggested would make accessible some of our outstanding scenery to the ever increasing annual tourist crop."

Letter: Chris to Lovejoy, May 2, 1932
"Dear Lovejoy,

You may know I quit the Forest Service January 1, 1927 and have since been in the employ of the Washington Pulp and Paper Corporation of Port Angeles as timber, land and pulpwood buyer. I also took care of their fire protection and reforestation planning. All of these projects are now finished and my job with them ended May 1, 1932.

Not having anything in sight just now, I decided to write the story of my early pioneering and Forest Service experiences. All parts of the story are factual. I am sending the manuscript to you as you suggested some time ago. If you are still interested, I want you to give it your honest criticism. Go after it with any changes you think should be made.

Yours truly, Chris "

Letter: Lovejoy to Chris, May 14, 1932
"Dear Chris,

I don't think you have had a clear idea of what you want to do. You have been using a shot-gun and have scattered your charge. You need to use a rifle, get and hold a steady aim at what is going on today about you. Tell more about your experiences when you hit the Pacific Coast and how homesteaders like yourself were attracted to free land you thought could be developed as farmland. Tell how the timber barons were able to grab cheap timberland from discouraged homesteaders. Tell how the timber industry started from hand and ox team logging and went on to the present high-speed destructive and wasteful method. A history of the Forest Service should be told beginning with the earliest years of contesting land claims and the friction and ill-will that resulted between the settlers and the Forest Service. Tell about the growing pains the Forest Service went through and the part you played for twenty-five years struggling to make conservation become a reality. Such a book would have historical value and added to this would be the physical adventures you have written about which is what make most auto-biographies "go". That, as I see it is your main job now. Together we will find the shake logs and work on some of them. Take out some chips and see how the grain looks.

Yours truly, P.S. Lovejoy"

Letter: Chris to Lovejoy, June 12, 1932

"Dear Lovejoy,

I have received the manuscript as well as your letter of comment. I only tried to cover the highlights of my life. Many things occurred but to record them all would make the book too long and monotonous.

I am afraid that writing such a book as you suggested would be too complicated. It would take me no end of time, and since I still have to keep the pot boiling, I could not even find time to make a start. Perhaps some day together we could shape the information into a book, If not I know much valuable material will pass out with me.

You are in a very interesting department. Game, wildlife, and Forest Protection. I am going to try for similar work with the State out here. I am now sixty years young, but as long as I can keep my present health, I am not afraid to face to future.

Yours as ever, Chris"

Chris continues-

On May 1, 1932 after five years with the Washington Pulp and Paper Company the purpose of my job had been fulfilled. The necessary timber holdings had been acquired and the company had a timber management program which would guarantee the mill's future operation. I was convinced this industry could survive forever and thus be a permanent economic asset to the community.

The great Depression had a grip on the country and jobs for my age were scarce, but I seemed to be in the right place at the right time. A CCC (Civilian Conservation Corps) camp was to be established near the Forest Service Ranger Station on the Elwha River. The government would be giving young unemployed men a chance to make a living building trails, roads and campgrounds in the forest.

I was hired as a foreman to teach a crew of young fellows the skills of building trails and roads, falling trees and snags, making fire breaks, and reforestation with transplanted seedlings. This camp was 936 Co. CCC, Camp No. 17, Camp Elwha, and opened in May of 1933 with a full commitment of 200 young men mostly from the northwest and some coming from the midwestern states. The camp was run jointly by the U.S. Forest Service and the U.S. Army and Navy. From 8 a.m. to 5 p.m. work projects were under the direction of the U.S. Forest Service and from 5 p.m. to 8 a.m. the camp was under the surveillance of the U.S. Army and Navy. These were frustrating times for both camp personnel and the young recruits but many lasting friendships resulted from this experience. I served for over a year teaching the skills of the woodsman to experience. I served for over a year teaching the skills of the woodsman to a crew of some forty men. I soon learned not to take for granted anyone's knowledge of how to use a mattock, a cross-cut saw or a double bladed ax. The city boys gave me the most trouble since they didn't have the foggiest notion how to use any of these tools. The work had its rewards and the most exciting accomplishments for me was the road we constructed from the Elwha Ranger Station up Hurricane Hill to Idaho Camp and beyond to Obstruction Point. It took the better part of two years before it was finished and on July 15, 1935 it opened and for the first time the public could drive by car to see some of the splendid back-country scenery.

(The National Park Service built a new road from Port Angeles to Hurricane Ridge in the mid 1950's. The original road up the back side of Hurricane Hill was closed off at that time. However, about five miles of this old road is still used to reach the foot trail head at Whiskey Bend which leads the backpacker into the beautiful upper Elwha Basin. The spur road from Hurricane Ridge to Obstruction Point is still maintained by the Park Service. This road takes the motorist to some fantastic views of the interior mountains.) . . . . Ed.

Summer of 1931. Church under the trees at
the Elwha River C.C.C. Camp. Chris adding
a little inspiration on the great out-of-doors.
Clive McLeod photo. Courtesy of the *Seattle
Times*.

Chapter 43

"Framing The Picture"

The Monument boundaries eroding prior to World War I convinced me that the only answer to permanently protect the timber resources and beauties of part of the Olympic Mountains was to establish a National Park. This idea was not original with me but had surfaced many times by others over the past 25 years.

In June of 1933, Mt. Olympus Monument was transferred from the jurisdiction of the Forest Service to the Department of Interior. It was placed under the guiding arm of Mt. Rainier National Park Superintendent Major O.A. Tomlinson. This Executive Order gave the Monument a new preservation status and the proponents of a national park now had a nucleus to work with. Many others felt as I did, that a part of this mountain grandeur should belong to everyone and be safeguarded for all to see and enjoy. This was our cue to push for a park.

I had remained loyal for twenty-five years to the principles of the Forest Service and for another half dozen years of employment with private industry and the government. At this point in my life I had no ties and decided to go public with my long standing views on a national park for Olympic. I knew the Forest Service and the logging industry would be among those opposing such a park but I was optimistic that they might even be convinced there was room for all three concepts of resource management to coexist.

Following are some observations that I had made over the past forty years. Many logging camps and saw mills had come and gone. Much of the timber they cut was destroyed by wasteful logging practices. By 1930, high speed logging technology, with its wasteful methods, was taking large bites of timber even faster than before. In the coastal areas the Douglas fir was fast disappearing and in the upper valleys and on the mountain slopes it would soon be in reach of the logger's saw. I had watched many of these forest giants come crashing down in a matter of minutes and knew that in a few more decades the remaining stands of Douglas fir would be gone forever. Even now it is too late to advocate sustained yield for this species, for it would take 100 to 200 years to produce any appreciable second growth of this forest giant.

During the five years I was with the pulp and paper industry I became aware of additional mistakes being made in the forest that would have to be rectified if nature and man were to survive on the harvest of trees.

More efficient methods of harvesting and utilization of the forest should be practiced. For example, by cutting trees into pulpwood size in the forest rather than bringing the whole log to the mill, twenty to twenty-five additional cords of pulpwood per acre could be salvaged. This could be possible by using stumpage, broken trees, tree tops and the smaller trees that are under logging size. Shingle mills should also be located in or near the cutting areas as much of the older cedar is hollow, short bodied, or spike topped, and waste always results when whole trees are sent to the mills.

In order to perpetuate our wood consuming industries on a sustained yield basis the logging industry would have to be re-educated. To cut and market the whole virgin log as a major industry would soon come to a screeching halt. And no longer could we afford to tear down and waste undersized trees in order to get out the choice larger trees.

Along the western coastal lowland areas of Washington the dominant original forest cover was spruce, hemlock, amabilis or white fir and western red cedar. These species have a fast growing cycle in this area owing to plenty of rain, a long temperate growing season and the very light fire hazard. Harvesting operations for either saw or pulpwood timber should be based on clean or clear cutting. Slash burning is not necessary where hemlock, spruce, white fir and cedar are to reproduce, as it is a known fact that these varieties will germinate quickly in shaded decaying logging debris, moss and other vegetable material. Under such natural conditions these species would reproduce commercial saw timber every eighty years and tree size for wood pulp in thirty to forty years. This regrowth, together with the available standing supply would keep ten pulp mills running forever. Many other commercial forest crops, such as evergreen Christmas trees, poles, ties, props, etc., can be grown in much less time.

It should be mandatory that all federal, state, and private forest land be reforested where needed, so as to produce new forest cover. It is my opinion that with a sustained lowland yield, efficient harvesting and utilization, the forest products industries could have a healthy permanent survival and the tourism industry could one day run a close second.

Until conservation in the woods penetrates below the skin and reaches the heart of the average logger, any sustained yield policy would have tough going.

Many local organizations and industries supported the idea of a park, but it was the Port Angeles Chamber of Commerce that became the prime mover. They set up a "Mt. Olympus National Park Committee", and I was appointed a member. It was decided that the people who lived and worked on the Peninsula, county and state government, environmental groups, sportsmen, outdoor groups and the timber industry would all need to be informed. They would need facts and figures so they could voice an opinion on what would be best for the peninsula and the counties involved. As a pioneer and forest official for the past forty years of Clallam and Jefferson counties, and one who had come to know all of the area well, the Chamber of Commerce felt I could best describe the area and give a knowledgeable opinion on the size and benefits of such a park.

The following is a brief description of what the Olympic hinterland has to offer. The rugged ranges of the Olympics rise from close to sea level to nearly 8000 feet in altitude. The highest and most prominent is Mt. Olympus which is 7965 feet in altitude. Nearly 200 more peaks and pinnacles range in altitude of 5500 to 7000 feet in elevation. Glaciers and snow fields are numerous at the higher elevations and collectively these cover a large territory. At timberline, which varies around 5000 feet altitude, there are great tracts of open country that shed their deep snowpack by mid-summer to become beautiful flower-bedecked grassland meadows.

This mountain mass is drained by many snow-fed, swift flowing rivers that head in or near the central mass and radiate outward to the north, south, east and west. The principal streams flowing to the east that empty into Hood Canal are short with deep descents and are the Quilcene, Dosewallips, Duckabush, Hamma Hamma and Skokomish Rivers. To the south into Grays Harbor, flow the Humptulips, Wishkah, Wynoochee and Satsop Rivers. To the west into the Pacific Ocean flow the Soleduck, Bogachiel, Calawha, Hoh, Queets, and Quinault Rivers, and to the north into the Straits of Juan de Fuca flow the Dungeness and Elwha Rivers. The streams that flow into the Pacific Ocean along with the Elwha, which flows into the Straits of Juan de Fuca, are much longer than the others and have a less rapid course. The numerous glaciers in the center of the mountain chains help to maintain a continuous waterflow during the summer season.

Salt water and mountain breezes seldom permit the thermometer to register above 80 degrees in the summer, and winters are tempered by the Japanese Current, a warm easterly flowing Pacific Ocean current. On the extreme northwesterly part of the peninsula at Cape Flattery, the rainfall can measure 188 inches per year. Twenty to thirty miles inland, in the high mountain ranges, this falls in the form of very heavy snow thus causing glaciers that remain year 'round. Because of the temperate coastal climate, snow rarely lays on the ground in the lower coastal areas more than a few days, being melted by heavy rains and warm (Chinook) winds. Sixty miles to the northeastern portion of the Olympic Peninsula the average yearly rainfall drops to eighteen inches per year. The western slopes of the mountains receive the heaviest dump of rain, up to 130 inches, leaving the mountains on the eastern side of the peninsula somewhat arid, or in what is called a "rain shadow".

Before the white man came, the Olympic Peninsula was covered with extensive forests estimated to contain 150,000,000,000 board feet timber. Between 1880 and 1930 forest fires and wasteful logging practices had reduced this timber stand to 70,000,000,000 board feet, half the estimated original stand. Much of this primeval forest remains in the upper valleys and slopes of the western flowing rivers. Many trees tower 300 feet into the air and measure ten to fourteen feet in diameter. The forest cover consists of Douglas fir, Alaska and western red cedar, Sitka spruce, hemlock, white fir, noble fir, and white pine with a sprinkling of other varieties. Underbrush is very dense in the western regions near the ocean and the straits and includes salal, huckleberry, salmonberry, vine maple, devil's club and others. Big-leaf western maple, cottonwood and alder grow along the river bottoms in the western "Rain Forest" areas.

When I stood on Bogachiel Peak that first time in 1892 and looked out at the sea of mountains with their inspiring beauty, I knew that they could easily take their place as the Swiss Alps of the United States. Now forty years later I was being asked to draw maps and describe what areas should be included in a national park. To encompass a portion of nature's grandiose plan would not be an easy task.

I envisioned a park of 650,000 acres. The existing National Monument of some 298,000 acres with Mt. Olympus and its many glaciers, would be the nucleus. It would include the jumble of surrounding mountain peaks with their glaciers and flower bedecked meadows. Added to this would be the hundreds of waterfalls, river canyons, mountain streams and lakes. Completing the picture would be the vast river valleys with the hillsides supporting dense virgin forests. These forests are needed to prevent erosion, equalize stream flow in the lower valleys and provide forest cover for a variety of wildlife including the great herds of Roosevelt Elk.

We must not forget that Mt. Olympus National Monument was set aside in 1909 with the explicit purpose of preserving the majestic Roosevelt Elk. Now today those boundaries have shrunk by over half and the elk herds are diminishing in ever increasing numbers. The only solution to elk preservation is the proposed park that would include the high mountain meadows where the elk can be observed and photographed in summer, as well as some lowland range so necessary for their winter browse and cover. Such a park would protect about 1500 elk where they could never be hunted.

183

Two or three stub roads to high points should be built to afford tourists the enjoyment of distant views. One short loop road which had been planned by the Forest Service and is wanted by the majority of local people, would extend from the present Olympic Hot Springs road and connect with the present road leading into the Sol Duc Hot Springs. It would skirt Boulder Mountain, Cat Creek Basin, Sol Duc Park, Seven Lakes Basin, Deer Lake and exit at the Sol Duc Hot Springs Resort which is connected by road to the Olympic Highway 101. On such a road one would have a close-up view of Mt. Olympus in all of its magnificent glory, and one would be able to look down on the mighty Hoh River winding its way for forty miles, like a silver ribbon, to the sea. Such a loop road would make it possible for old and young and all disabled to enjoy the thrill of being in the Olympic Mountains---'Home of the Gods'.

Cat, Grader and Truck one mile from Idaho Shelter, elevation 5230 feet. Hurricane Ridge, November 28, 1933. Road construction with C.C.C. labor, Forest Service equipment and supervision. Chris Morgenroth, foreman. Bailey Range in background.

First official party reaching top of Hurricane Ridge by auto over newly completed C.C.C. road from Elwha Camp. November 28, 1933. Chris second from right.

Chapter 44

"Showing Macy Around"

In June of 1934, a year after the Monument's transfer to the Department of Interior, Preston Macy, Assistant Chief Ranger at Mt. Rainier, arrived in Port Angeles to "keep a weather eye on the National Monument." He chose Rosemary Inn on Lake Crescent as his headquarters and a few days later Rose Littleton, owner of the resort, arranged for Mr. Macy and me to meet. He explained that his principal duty that summer was to get acquainted with the Monument and he wanted me to be his guide. On July 6, I went to work for the Park Service.

I met with Park officials on July 17 to discuss the Monument and the National Forest. On July 20, in company of Mr. Macy, George A. Grant, Chief Photographer for the National Park Service, David M. Madsen, Wildlife expert of the Department of the Interior, Charlie Lewis, the packer, and six horses, we left Jackson Ranger Station on the Hoh River and travelled to the new Olympus Ranger Station in the upper Hoh Valley. Mr. Grant took many pictures along the trail. Next morning we went on foot up onto the mighty glacier where Mr. Grant took more pictures. We returned to base camp at Olympus Ranger Station about 8 p.m. The following day, July 22, we returned down the Hoh Valley, left the horses at the Lewis Ranch and went by car to Forks where we stayed all night. We talked with many people in Forks about a national park and Mr. Grant took more pictures.

On August 11, I took Macy to Lake Quinault to a meeting of people in that area who were interested in a national park. We camped at the Quinault Ranger Station then drove twenty-eight miles next day to the North Fork Ranger Station and hiked the two and a half miles to Wolfe Bar.

On August 13, Macy and I, a packer and three horses went up the Elwha Valley to Elkhorn Ranger Station. The next day we went on to Dodger Lookout then back to Elkhorn Ranger Station. On August 15 we went on to Hays River, Hayden Pass and the Dosewallips Meadows cabin where we stayed all night. From there we went to Lost River, where we had to clean out parts of the trail before going on to the Monument boundary in Grand Valley. From here the trail took us to Obstruction Rock and thence to Idaho Camp and down Hurricane Hill to the Elwha Ranger Station.

On September 13 and 14, Macy and I went up Bogachiel Peak and down the Hoh Valley to Jackson Ranger Station. On this trip we had to do some trail work again. The Forest Service had built some mighty good trails but neglect for the year that they had not been maintained was much in evidence. On this trip we finalized plans for building a Lookout house on top of Bogachiel Peak.

On September 16 I left for Bogachiel Peak in company of Charlie Anderson. Minnie Peterson had set up our camp with a cook in an adjoining meadow and her string of pack horses did all the packing of building materials and other gear and supplies. It took Charlie and I six weeks to build Bogachiel Lookout. This was the first construction job in the Monument under the Department of Interior.

During that summer and fall, in between trips with Macy, I completed two maps for the Park Service showing fire districts and fire protection plans for the Monument that the Forest Service and the National Park Service had agreed on. I also drafted several maps for the Park Service showing timber estimates, winter and summer habitat of the various elk herds and showing suitable boundaries of areas for inclusion in a national park.

In November of 1934 I completed a detailed map showing the Monument boundaries and the additions and extensions that had been discussed and approved by both the National Park Service and the Chamber of Commerce Park Committee. This map prompted the Chamber of Commerce to make the following "Resolution".

See Copy of Resolution at end of Chapter

In December of 1934, I sent a copy of this map to Major O.A. Tomlinson, Superintendent of Rainier National Park. I stated, *"The additions will in no way retard development or handicap industry and prosperity of the northern and western portions of the Olympic Peninsula. The Port Angeles Chamber of Commerce does not care to take the responsibility of recommending additional area to the south of the Monument because the greatest objection to adding any territory in that vicinity comes from Grays Harbor County timber interests. The resort and summer home owners of private property on Lake Crescent are willing and anxious to be included in a park, but want to be assured that their property rights are safeguarded. Also included in this area are two highly developed hot springs resorts and several other recreational resorts. The owners of these have likewise expressed their approval of a park but want assurance of retaining their full property rights. The present monument with suggested additions will make a good sized National Park of unusual recreational value for the entire nation to enjoy."*

A few days later that same month our Chamber of Commerce National Park Committee met with Congressman Mon Wallgren in Everett to discuss the proposed park and suggested he draft a bill to establish a national park and that it be presented for approval at the 74th Congress early in 1935. We suggested he use the map with the proposed boundaries that the park officials and our Chamber of Commerce Park Committee had agreed upon. Congressman Wallgren did not confer with us during the preparation of his bill until after it had gone to committee. He had included much more merchantable timber than we had mapped out. Due to the protests that arose on the peninsula, the House Committee on Public Lands tabled the bill for further study and Congressman Wallgren promised to modify the bill and introduce it at the next session. He also promised that all factions would be heard before a definite decisions was made on boundaries. It took another year before boundaries could be compromised and another bill submitted to committee.

Excerpt From: Newspaper Article, Seattle Post-Intelligencer, January 15, 1935

In a letter written to the Port Angeles Chamber of Commerce and the citizens of the Olympic Peninsula, a copy of which was received by this paper, Chris Morgenroth former national forest ranger and for 45 years a resident of Clallam County, sets forth his views on the proposed Olympic National Park as follows:

". . . I think it is greatly desirable to change the Monument to National Park status; however the present area should be enlarged in order to make it a more desirable biological unit. I have indicated on maps additional areas which include some forests where examples of giant trees of all species native to this locale could be preserved. It is my opinion these areas can be included without materially affecting the life of our present and prospective local industries. In a very few years all of our remaining stands of virgin Douglas fir timber will be gone. These additional areas include only a few small tracts of commercial timber which will have a much higher value for scenic and recreational purpose and as sanctuaries for elk and other game.

The suggested boundaries for a National Park are for the north side of the Monument only and extend only as far south as the upper North Fork of the Hoh River. Additions to the south side of the Monument should be decided on by those communities and people directly affected.

The Olympic hinterland holds great possibilities. Let us get this National Park if possible and develop its recreational resources. It can be made a second Switzerland for the entire nation. Think of that little country which is smaller than the Olympic Peninsula; its population has nothing much to sell except recreation and scenery, and yet they are the most prosperous and happy people in Europe. Once we get started we can sell it every year and still have it to pass on to our children.

I would suggest that all interested parties, such as local industries, merchants, sportsmen, timber owners, power companies, etc., be invited to a meeting to try and iron out differences of opinion. I think this is a matter of great importance to the north side of the Olympics. Let us find common ground and then all work together."

PORT ANGELES CHAMBER OF COMMERCE

H. B. MOLCHIOR,
Secretary-Manager

Member of
United States Chamber
of Commerce

PORT ANGELES, WASHINGTON

RESOLUTION

WHEREAS, the Mount Olympus National Monument, now under jurisdiction of the National Park Service, embraces an abundance of those characteristics which measure up fully to National Park standards; and,

WHEREAS, this rugged area is of inestimable value in perpetuating the pioneer spirit so typically American, in contributing to the health and character of American youth, in contributing to the spiritual and physical welfare of all who enjoy its recreational advantages; and,

WHEREAS, in our estimation, its commercial value as a recreational area far surpasses the commercial value of its natural resources; and,

WHEREAS, the members of this organization, through their own familiarity with the area, through information furnished by officials of the National Forest Service, officials of the National Park Service, and by those whose commercial interests are concerned, feel that they have full knowledge of all matters of importance concerning the area; now,

THEREFORE, BE IT RESOLVED, that the Port Angeles Chamber of Commerce endorse the creation by Congress of a National Park, which shall consist of the present Mount Olympus National Monument with such additions in the adjacent high mountain country as the National Park Service deems advisable, and which additions shall not interfere with the eventual industrial and commercial development of the Olympic Peninsula.

BE IT FURTHER RESOLVED, that copies of this resolution be sent to: The State Planning Board, the North Olympic Peninsula Chambers of Commerce, Mr. O. A. Tomlinson, Superintendent of Mt. Rainier National Park, the Resort & Hotel Owners Association and the Good Roads Association.

Resolution by Port Angeles Chamber of Commerce, November, 1934.

Chapter 45

"Battle of the Boundaries"

In April of 1936, Representative Rene DeRouen, Chairman of the House Public Lands Committee, sent word to the Port Angeles Chamber of Commerce that a new bill, H.R. 7086, had been drafted by Congressman Wallgren and that hearings would be held in Washington D.C. on April 23, 1936. Joseph H. Johnson, Prosecuting Attorney of Clallam County, M.J. Schmitt, owner and operator of two cedar shake mills on the Peninsula and past president of the Port Angeles Chamber of Commerce. Major Arthur Vollmer, U.S. Army Retired, and I were chosen by the Mt. Olympus National Park Committee to attend and be heard at these Congressional hearings. During the nine days of the hearings, many different factions were represented and heard, some for and some against the bill.

Following are excerpts from the testimony given by we four delegates from the Port Angeles Chamber of Commerce before the Congressional Committee on Public Lands.

Statement: Chris Morgenroth, Port Angeles, Washington

". . . Industry is not hurt or handicapped or never will be by any National Park that may be created here. I am talking about the West coast of Jefferson and Clallam Counties. In the lowland coastal areas there are 42,000,000 cords of pulpwood type of timber that would support 10 pulp mills for 40 years. God Almighty will take care of the sustained yield in this belt where rains are excessive, the growing season is long and there is no fire hazard to speak of. Here there is a rapid regrowth of hemlock, white fir, and spruce which is the kind of timber used for pulpwood that goes into making cellulose, newsprint and rayon.

On my homestead in this same area in the early 1890's I cleared and planted potatoes on a quarter of an acre. A few years later this garden was abandoned and young spruce seedlings took root. Recently I had the trees on that particular quarter acre harvested and they measured out at 32 1/2 cords to that quarter acre and the trees were only 38 years old. Therefore, the pulpwood industry is your permanent community builder since it would thrive on the sustained yield.

One of the reasons the timber interests do not want a national park here is because there is an area of Douglas fir running up this valley (pointing to the Hoh Valley), and according to Forest Service statistics, which were made about 25 years ago, there is 8,000,000,000 board feet of virgin timber up in there on that watershed and it is one of the most unique forests you can find in the United States. It is entirely different from the redwoods in California because it is Douglas fir. You have trees there up to 1,000 years old, some of them 300 feet high and measuring 14 feet in diameter. These are trees that you will never reproduce by sustained yield. It is in this area where the Roosevelt elk spend the winter browsing under these forest giants. Here they browse on the understory of maples, mosses, brush and ferns. The biggest elk species in the U.S. are roaming all over the Olympics. They are called the Roosevelt elk for Teddy Roosevelt."

Question: By Rep. Robert F. Rich, Pennsylvania

"Do they have as good elk there as they have over in Wyoming?"

Answer: Mr. Morgenroth

"I have seen specimen over there in Wyoming I would call cripples against the Olympic elk." . . . .

Morgenroth continuing: "The way the boundary lines are drawn, there are possibly 10,000 acres within these lines of privately owned land. The rest of it is public land, your land and my land and everybody's land. This is where they want to get into and cut the timber. We want to save a small area of this unique timbered area here and have it for posterity and for your children and mine."

Question: Rep. Fred Crawford, Michigan

"What would happen to this pulpwood industry and the ten or twelve mills that were built, if this country imposed a tariff against the importation of newsprint, and at the end of 40 years all that timber was cut?"

Answer: Mr. Morgenroth

"As I stated before, pulpwood species for the size usable for a pulp mill, will reproduce itself in sufficient quantities here to keep those ten mills running forever. You are in a fast-growing belt here."

Question: Mr. Crawford

"Then you would have a perpetual industry insofar as pulp-mill operations go?"

Answer: Mr. Morgenroth

"Yes."

Question: Mr. Rich

"I should like to make a statement here and should like to have it incorporated in the record immediately following the statement of Mr. Morgenroth. I think, if his statements are correct, on pulpwood production, we should give every consideration to growing our own pulpwood in this country, especially in the State of Washington."

Statement: Joseph Johnson, Prosecuting Attorney, Clallam County, Wash.

"The logging question is becoming a tragic one. The logging companies of which there are about four or five, have the same viewpoint, all of them want no park. All want to cut the last tree. We have had their bitter opposition from the beginning and expect to have it until the end.

If we can get a park there, so that the person in New York and in Florida will know about it, they will know it must be worth going to because it is a national park. Thousands more will come for the same reason. These tourists will take the place of the falling logging industry that is going to wreck the community. If you removed Yellowstone and Glacier National Parks from the map and put national forest all over that territory, the people would not go and look at it. We do not want to injure industry and we value the Forest Service highly. But we do believe we can have a park with logging and pulp mills outside the boundaries. We want them all, not complete domination by one. Each one has something worthwhile for our community. We ask you to create a national park for future generations, not just ourselves."

Statement: M.J. Schmitt, Cedar Shake Mill Owner, Port Angeles

"The economic future of the Olympic Peninsula depends more on pulp and paper production and the utilization of those woods. For instance outside the proposed boundaries of this park is a wealth of cedar which can all be used at some time that will provide employment to a great deal of people. I believe the future of the Olympic Peninsula does not depend on logging. I know there is a splendid opportunity for people on the Peninsula to make a living without a great deal of further logging as it has been practiced in the past."

Question: Rep. White Compton, Idaho

"Would it be better for the interest of Washington and the lumber industry if those boundaries were not so extensive and were revised and brought more in line with the mountainous section, the part that is not so heavily timbered?"

Answer: Mr. Schmitt

"There is a possibility that that would aid."

191

Statement: Major Arthur Vollmer, Secretary-Treasurer, Mt. Olympus National Park Association

"I fell for National Parks a long time ago. Here is a region that can take its place in the great sisterhood of national parks on a parity with any of them. It is unique in that you have a complex of mountain peaks to be found nowhere else except in Tibet. You have the last primeval forest of Douglas fir and here is the home of the Roosevelt elk whose horns are much heavier than the horns of elk in other parts of the country. Here are most and the largest glaciers in the U.S., and here would be the only park that overlooked the ocean. There are mountains and lakes in there that have never been seen by the eye of man, but a road could be thrown in there so that people could enjoy and see it.

I would like to submit a petition with 900 signatures which reads as follows: 'We the following citizens living on the Olympic Peninsula, urge the immediate creation of a National Park on the Peninsula in accordance with the Wallgren Bill H.R. 7086, as introduced or amended with the proviso that Section 4, restricting it to a primitive wilderness area, be revised so as to permit construction of such stub roads as will enable the general public to see and enjoy it.'

As yet 'sustained yield', 'selective logging', and 'reforestation' are but fancy phrases. When Mt. Olympus National Park is created, the sustained yield policy can still be put into effect in the National Forest which would surround it."

During the nine days of hearing many different factions were represented and heard, some for and some against the bill. Among those heard were Harold Ickes, Secretary of the Interior; Henry A. Wallace, Secretary of Agriculture; Mon Wallgren, Congressman from Washington State; Martin F. Smith, Representative Third District, Grays Harbor; Fred J. Overly, Park Service Ranger; Arno B. Cammerer; Director National Park Service; Asahel Curtis, Seattle, Washington; H.M. Allbright, former Director National Park Service; Mr. Robert Marshall, Wilderness Society; F.W. Mathias, Grays Harbor, Hoquiam and Aberdeen Chamber of Commerce; Mr. L.F. Kneipp, Asst. Chief of U.S. Forest Service; E.F. Banker, Director of Conservation and Development of State of Washington.

The following excerpts are taken from just a few of the lengthy presentations given at these hearings. No individual or group that was represented at these hearings or went on record through written letter or otherwise, was against a National Park being established in the Olympic

Mountain area. The unanimous concern was over the size and boundaries of such a park. . . . Editor

Statement: E.F. Banker, State Director of Conservation and Development, State of Washington

"I agree with everything that has been said about the beauties and the status of the country. I believe if a vote were taken by the people of the State of Washington they would vote overwhelmingly for the creation of this national park and I do not object to formation on a national park, but we do feel you should be exceedingly careful in fixing those boundaries. We feel you should not include too much timber."

Statement: Arno B. Cammerer, Director of National Park Service

"One of the obstacles we run across in the establishment of national parks, and it is a serious one, is the fact that the Forest Service pays 25% to 35% of its receipts to the State and counties. In connection with the national park here proposed, that is an expectancy which the counties, of course, hesitate to forego. We believe, however, with the establishment of the park, that direct loss will be more than compensated by the indirect income from the tourist business.

Now, gentlemen, these national parks, when they are established, draw people from all over the country. They serve to create a large travel movement. Let me just read briefly an excerpt from the Saturday Evening Post of several years ago, on national parks and the tourist industry.

'What is the commercial value to a community of a national park? It is an investment of a small percentage of natural resources in one of the steadiest and best paying industries in the world. Tourism, like other crops, has to be cultivated. How do you cultivate the tourist crop? You have to have something to bring him there and after he is there he must have the facilities to enjoy what he has come to see. A good example is the primitive and distant resort in Central Africa, where in the great Kruger National Park there is a sanctuary for wildlife where wild animals in natural conditions will be presented as one of the world's great spectacles. California has gone into the tourist business in a big way, and it is the best crop she has, bar none. When the national parks are bringing several hundreds of thousands of people into a state or into a community each season, bringing nice, new outside money to leave there, you have an asset you would do well to protect as jealously as possible and to

193

cultivate with all your might and main so as to produce a nice big tourist crop.'"

Excerpt: from Brief Submitted by Hon. Representative Mon Wallgren to Committee On Public Lands.

"We believe that the evidence submitted in this hearing has established the following:

I. That a real need for the creation of additional national-park areas exists. (The foregoing by uncontradicted evidence submitted by Secretary Harold Ickes and Major Vollmer.)

II. That the area in question is national park quality. (The foregoing reiterated in testimony, charts, and maps submitted throughout the hearings.)

III. That the area proposed by H.R. 7086 is the optimum area, the one which represents the most favorable result when a choice is offered in a conflict of opposing considerations. (The foregoing is in part self evident and/or testimony of National Park Service Director Cammerer, and Messrs, Horning, Morgenroth, and Vollmer.)

IV. That the creation of this park as proposed would constitute a restoration, a fulfillment of promise, and a climax to unsatisfied yearnings whose history is long. (The testimony of Dr. T.S. Palmer, formerly of the Dept. of Agriculture, and Mr. Horace M. Allbright, former Director of the National Park Service.)

V. That the assignment to national preservation--use for all time--of this resource as against destructive, immediate, local use is the conclusion of every consideration of common sense and humanity. Inasmuch as ownership is as yet in the Nation and not in individuals or corporations, then we would be unworthy of our trusteeship as national servants not to effectuate such assignment."

Chris continues:

H.R. 7086 had embraced a territory of 1,017, 000 acres. Everyone on the west coast knew a park this size contained far too much commercial timber. We braced ourselves for a long fight.

In February of 1937, Rep. Wallgren introduced H.R. 4724 which only reduced the size of the Park by 100,000 acres. It was evident that eastern conservationists were very much in the picture pushing for a big park.

There was so much flack from the State of Washington that the bill was tabled before it even reached committee.

On September 30, President Franklin D. Roosevelt and Mrs. Roosevelt, their son James and his wife, daughter Anna and her husband John Boettiger of the Seattle Post-Intelligencer, came to Port Angeles to take a look at the proposed new national park. Roosevelt was no doubt impressed even though he saw nothing of the dynamic scenery of the interior. The itinerary, the people he met and talked to, and what he saw was arranged and hosted by the U.S. Forest Service. His view from a car window for the 200 miles from Lake Crescent to Lake Quinault was mostly of lowland forests and some logged areas. After passing several logged-over areas he stated, "I hope the lumberman who is responsible for this is roasting in Hell." On returning to Washington D.C. he recommended that the Bogachiel and Hoh River corridors be included in a new bill Rep. Wallgren was drafting.

When our committee with the Port Angeles Chamber of Commerce got word of this, we knew the battle over boundaries was far from over.

Letter: Lovejoy to Chris, 1937

"Dear Chris,

Remember when you let me see the manuscript of your autobiography some years ago? If you are still interested in trying it, I'm still interested in helping. I understand from your last letter, your doctor tells you to take it easy. If you wonder what you can do that would be inside your physical limits, how about working up the manuscript again?

My idea would be for you to sketch out a tentative set of chapters and a general summary of what you would put into each. Let me see it and then you'd go to work on the drafting of the text.

Your recent interests and experiences in the National Park phase of Olympic affairs would be a final chapter, I think. I figure that there's a real chance that you can do something of very real and permanent value in an historical way. You know more of the real Olympics than perhaps any man ever will. It is no small thing to have that said of one, but it is nothing compared to having it said that one has done more for the forests, the game and the people of the Olympic National Forest than any other...as I believe can be said of you.

Yours,
P.S. Lovejoy"

Chapter 46

"The Final Push"

After President Roosevelt's visit in September 1937 it was evident that in order to secure boundaries of practical proportions in keeping with the economic stability of the region, another trip to Washington, D.C. would be necessary. Once more on behalf of the Port Angeles Chamber of Commerce and the Mt. Olympus National Park Association, Mike Schmitt and I were sent to confer with Congressman Wallgren and Park Officials.

We arrived in Washington, D.C. on February 21, 1938 and immediately met with Congressman Wallgren on his new bill H.R. 10024. Mike and I had two conferences in Wallgren's office with park officials and another conference with National Park Director Arno Cammerer, which was pretty "hot going". We convinced them all that the two long arms of the Bogachiel and the Hoh should be eliminated. In lieu of taking these two corridors we suggested that the Government purchase a strip one quarter to half mile wide along the ocean beach between Ozette and Kalaloch, excluding the Indian reservations, and establish a marine drive that would connect with the Olympic Highway near Ruby Beach. They also agreed to drop Section 4 from the bill which would have locked up Olympic as a "Wilderness Park". Thirty-five hundred acres on Boundary Creek west of Piedmont were also eliminated. We were also successful in persuading park officials to consider completing the mountain highway between Deer Park and Obstruction Point, a route that had already been surveyed by the government, and building the long proposed road between Olympic and Sol Duc Hot Springs.

Letter: From Chris to his family, February 28, 1938

"This is sure a tough assignment, for everyone here is arguing for what we don't want. I am afraid the Angeles people think I have a sweet job and it will be easy to get anything out of these Washington Brain Trusters. The cards are stacked against us from the President down. They are disappointed because I am standing "pat" on what I and the majority of the people at home think is right. Everyone is trying to convince me that everything is being done for our best. Wallgren is trying to get me in with him to a conference tomorrow with the President.

I have more talks this afternoon with the Park and the Wildlife Division. Wallgren, I think, is doing the best he can for us. He would like for me to modify our demands. I told him I came here in the interest of our industries and for fully 90% of the sentiment of our state. I know he is in a tough spot. I don't think they can ride over us entirely and I am hopeful for some adjustment. Should we fail I think we still can fight in the Senate Public Lands Committee, where their minds are more open to reason. However, I would appreciate it if someone else undertook that job .

With Love,
Chris"

I remained another eight days in Washington. Wallgren requested I make a map with statistics pertaining to the changes we had made in the bill. He was trying to arrange a conference with the President within the next few days.

My expenses were about $12 per day which included hotel, meals, taxi hire, shave, shoe shine, telegrams, and some entertaining. If you wanted service you had to pay for it and everyone had their hand out for tips. I had to wire for more money and Tom Aldwell came through with $100 from the Chamber of Commerce.

In the final hours of my stay in Washington, D.C., I wrote a personal letter that was delivered to President Roosevelt appealing for a park not over 780,000 acres, giving him all the reasons why locking up any more area than that would deny the people of the Peninsula their future livelihood.

Letter: Chris to President Roosevelt, March 1, 1938 (hand delivered)

"Dear President Roosevelt,

The total area as now proposed for a National Park includes land lying east of the range line between Ranges 10 and 11 and totals approximately 780,000 acres. This area includes much of the most outstanding forest on the Olympic Peninsula. Many trees of all native species are found, some with a diameter of from 6 to 14 feet and a height of 300 feet and many of them are 1000 years old. An understory of broad-leafed maples and others with trailing moss draped from their grotesque trunks and limbs, give part of these forests a tropical appearance. These forests are located on the lower mountain slopes in the upper river valleys. There would be little objection of creating on these 780,000 acres a well balanced park.

Fully 99% of the people of the State of Washington together with all Peninsular industries and settlers object to the proposed inclusion of any land lying west of the range line between Ranges 10 and 11 for the following reasons:---

The area includes mostly privately owned land.

The timber of this area consists of about 80% pulp species, 12% shingle cedar and 8% Douglas fir. The four rayon and pulp and paper mills are located on the north side of the Peninsula and these mills own much of this forest from which they are dependent on a continuous supply of pulpwood.

These mills worked continuously at fair pay employing 3000 men throughout the entire depression. All of these men are home owners or in the process of acquiring homes.

Within this proposed inclusion are located forty little farms. Most of these families are pioneers of over forty years and these farms are all they have. They do not wish to sell out and go.

There are also within this area nine cabin resorts with store and gas stations. These businessmen are serving the traveling public.

County Commissioners are objecting to this inclusion because of loss of tax revenue if the federal government acquires title. Most of this land has paid taxes for over thirty-five years.

The State and Counties have constructed and maintained more than sixty-five miles of highway and roads at a cost of many millions of dollars. Would the government maintain these roads?

Oil companies have leased several thousand acres of land on this proposed inclusion. Three of them are now drilling with encouraging showings.

Many years ago the Washington State Legislature set aside for public use all of the Ocean Beach as a public highway and playground between Cape Flattery and Grays Harbor.

Many small school districts have consolidated and have built modern schools with modern equipment, such as at Forks and Clearwater. They have issued bonds against the taxable property within their respective districts. What will happen to these bonds when the government condemns and takes over this property?

It is for these reasons and others that the people of the Peninsula and the entire state enter protest of this western inclusion.

It is now generally conceded that a well balanced park, such as outlined in the first part of this letter, is needed and will have the support of the people of the State of Washington. If, however, these Bogachiel and Hoh River extensions, as proposed, are included, it would take away another 120,000 acres of mostly taxable property, withdrawing 5,200,000,000 board feet of timber. This would then bring the entire timber withdrawal to a total of 14,950,000,000 board feet. This would necessarily stop all *further development and expansion of the pulp industry on the Peninsula.*

Sincerely,
Chris Morgenroth"

Telegram: Chris to Thomas T. Aldwell, President Port Angeles C. of C.

"Mr. Thos. T. Aldwell---Conference this morning set hearing with President, have no assurance I will be included in hearing. I stand "pat" on excluding western extension. Have made map and letter giving reasons for our objections to be presented at Executive hearing. Cards seem stacked against us by President's wishes, Park and Forest Service. Will stay until I learn result of conference with President."

Chris continues:

As a result of this final appeal, the President ordered a private hearing for Congressman Wallgren and myself with National Park, U.S. Forest Service, Geodetic and Wildlife Service officials. Congressman Wallgren backed up my arguments and we won out. As a result H.R. 10024 would be re-written providing for the establishment of a park of 643,000 acres.

Letter: T.T. Aldwell, President Port Angeles Chamber of Commerce, to Chris in Washington, D.C., March 1, 1938

"Associated Press says the two arms have been eliminated. You and Mon Wallgren have really won the fight for us. You both have done our community a splendid service, and you might please thank him for the good work which he has done. I am confident the details will be worked out satisfactory to all.

Sincerely, Tom"

Newspaper Article: Port Angeles Evening News, March 1, 1938
"SCHMITT IS HOME, SAYS PARK IN BAG"

"I am certain that the Mt. Olympus National Park, as presently boundaried, will be passed by the present session of Congress," declared Mike Schmitt, who returned last night from Washington D.C., where he and Chris Morgenroth went by airplane 2 weeks ago to secure elimination of the Hoh and Bogachiel Corridors from the Wallgren bill.

"We also were assured that the wilderness clause would be eliminated and that the National Park people have in contemplation completion of the mountain highways between Deer Park and

Obstruction Point and the Olympic and Sol Duc Hot Springs. Also considerable development of the Deer Park Area for winter sports which already has been rapidly developed by the forest service."

Schmitt had high praise for Congressman Wallgren and went on to say "Officials at Washington were deeply impressed at the experience and knowledge and fight of Chris Morgenroth. Used to the slicker type of lobbyist they found Chris as a man who knew the entire country involved in the park, and they listened to him as a real authority. Although one of the park's greatest advocates, Chris charged right into the national park headquarters and asked Director Arno Cammerer in forceful language why it was necessary to include so much land and cause so much unnecessary hardship."

Letter: Chris to his family, March 3, 1938

"In checking new Park map, I found two places where the Park Service had made mistakes and had included a little more land than had been agreed on in accordance with our final conference on March 1. I pointed these errors out to Wallgren to have them corrected before forming the new bill. He will take it up with the Park Service tomorrow. We succeeded in doing what seemed impossible when we first came here, and while we did not get everything we asked for, we got more than anyone here wanted to concede to us. So I am not ashamed to come back home and face our people. The suggestions in our last Port Angeles meeting, of doing this work by letters would have gotten us nowhere.

I am buying my return ticket over Pennsylvania R.R. to Chicago, thence by Great Northern to Seattle, Pullman fare is $108.67. Hope you are O.K.

With Love, Chris"

Chris continues:

I left Washington, D.C. satisfied that if the boundaries settled on were finally enacted into law at this session of Congress, the Olympic Peninsula would have an outstanding park that would contain all scenic areas of national park calibre and more than enough would be withheld for our present pulp mills with plenty left for their expansion.

On June 28, 1938, H.R. 10024 was signed into law by Franklin D. Roosevelt. A clause was added giving the President the power to increase the size of the park to a maximum of 899,292 acres within the next eight months.

I did not like the clause giving F.D.R. power to add more land than what had been agreed upon. The Olympic Park Committee and all of the

North Olympic Peninsula likewise did not like the clause. It was the North Olympic Peninsula people who, after years of dedicated effort, staggering obstacles and reverses, and compromising their future economic benifits, should be given the most credit for the establishment of Olympic National Park. The affirmative arguments presented to Congress for preserving the great stands of timber falling to the logger's saw were counterbalanced by the other side of the coin---that recreation and scenery could be sold over and over again and it would still be there to pass on to future generations.

With other conservationists I had worked long and diligently for a National Park and it will perhaps be my last job of pioneering.

Thomas T. Aldwell, President of Port Angeles Chamber of Commerce wishing good luck to Chris and Mike J. Schmitt, delegates to the Congressional Hearings in Washington, D.C., regarding creation of Olympic National Park. April 20, 1936.

Chris in Washington, D.C. for hearings, April 1938.

Part VIII

"Conclusion, 1939-1941"

Chris suffered a heart attack in the summer on 1939. As he lay ill he received much correspondence including a particularly poignant letter from Bianca Butler, his neighbor for over 25 years.

Letter: Bianca Butler to Chris, August 14, 1939
Bonnie Brae Resort, Lake Crescent

"Dear Chris,

Here is a little note of good wishes for your health. Sorry to hear that you had to go to bed again, but patience is a great virtue, so you will just have to grin and bear this being housed up.

Wherever I look around the countryside, there are tokens of your love of the beautiful in nature. Early in the season there was a glory of the Scotch Broom, then the Foxglove, the California Poppy, Daisy and those lovely yellow flowers that I know not the name of, and others. I think of your hands reaching in your pocket for some seeds and giving them to Mother Earth to do her best, then a little rain, a bright smile from our friend the sun and we have a monument to the love Chris Morgenroth had for these wonderful mountains. Thousands of tourists exclaim when they see a bright flower peeping out of the wilderness. Have your ears been ringing?---for it is often that I talk of you to people stopping here and it would do your heart good to hear of their appreciation of one that thought not of himself but of others, that walked many long weary miles as a pioneer to open these mountains to people from far and wide, that they may have that thrill that you had when weary and discouraged you came on some lovely view of the valleys and mountains.

How about your robins, did they nest a second time? Mine came back and I thought of you, wonder if another family was started under your eaves.

Yes, Chris, I realize what you have done for not only the people of this part of the country but for people that come from all over. You are the Great Man of the Northwest.

Well, here I was just going to write a little note, but it seemed I was talking with you and so it is an epistle.

Now cheer up Chris, just know as the sailor on watch calls out when the night is dark, that 'All is Well' .

Sincerely,
Bianca M. Butler"

Chris died on August 24, 1939.

EULOGY
By M.J. (Mike) Schmitt, Given August 26, 1939

"Last evening I sat by the radio and listened to a travelogue on the Olympic Peninsula, based on the experience of the man in whose honor we are gathered here this evening.

As we had done before, we wandered slowly up the Elwha through the fragrant forests, enjoying Mother Nature, over the Divide, and at dusk arrived at Enchanted Valley where all cares and sorrows cease.

Chris Morgenroth's entire life was spent in service to others and he, more than anyone else deserves credit for the development of this area and the setting aside of the mountains he loved so well as a National Park, to be enjoyed by all the people and generations to come.

I well remember standing with him on Bogachiel Peak, overlooking the Seven Lakes Basin on one side and the mile deep Hoh Valley and mighty Mount Olympus on the other side, when he turned to me and said, "Mike, when I die, I want my ashes scattered from here." I agreed with his wishes for I felt that this was a fitting resting place for a man who had fought consistently for the preservation of its natural beauty and for the trails and roads that had been built to make it accessible to the public.

Again I remember a Congressional hearing in Washington, D.C. where Congressmen listened with rapt attention to his story and a year later a conference with the heads of the National Park Service in the Department of the Interior, where he stated in no uncertain terms that the inclusion of timber necessary for the preservation of existing industries was wrong, and with his own hand drew the line which now marks the present western boundary of the Park.

During the quarter of a century he spent with Olympic National Forest he was responsible for the building of most of the existing roads and trails. Volumes could be written about his work in the Forest Service.

Chris's working years were spent in closest contact with nature which he loved so well and God in his infinite wisdom permitted him to see the accomplishment of his life's ambition, the creation of a National Park for all the world to enjoy.

I love to think of him, looking down from High Olympus, and happy in the knowledge that his life has been well spent in the service of his fellowmen."

Letter: Rudo L. Fromme, Supervisor Olympic National Forest, 1912 to 1928.
Written Sept. 21, 1939

"Dear Mrs. Morgenroth,

Somehow or other I had carried the impression that the Chris, whom I had tramped and camped with on so many enjoyable, if not somewhat strenuous occasions, was destined to carry on almost as long as the Olympic Mountains, which he so dearly loved. I feel sure that his memory, the many memories of his effective life there, will virtually live forever. I am truly thankful that I learned to know him so well, especially during my most active years.

Your friend,
Rudo Fromme"

Letter: Arno B. Cammerer, Director National Park Service
Written Nov. 1, 1939

"Dear Mike Schmitt,

I have just learned that our beloved friend Chris Morgenroth had taken the long trail from which there is no returning. I had looked forward to seeing him and you on a trip into the Olympic country that had been planned for next summer.

When one thinks of a fellow like Chris passing one is mute for words adequate to express one's sorrow, a hand clasp would be better to tell the feelings in our hearts. He was the type whom people respected and admired from the moment they met him, whether they agreed with his views or not. He and I saw eye to eye on many subjects, on others we had divergent views, but they only brought us closer to knowing and liking each other by the opportunities for discussion which they gave. I know that not only I, but all of those in the Park Service who had the privilege of meeting and knowing him are going to miss him in our contact work around the Olympic National Park area. I felt impelled to address you since you two were such close friends.

Sincerely yours,
Arno B. Cammerer"

Letter: Lovejoy to Mrs. Morgenroth, Jan 5, 1940

".After putting it off and off . . . I want to tell you that for Chris to be "gone" somehow hurt a lot.

I was close to Chris even tho' I'd been so far from him all those years. My years in the Olympics were full and good years and Chris was built into and an integral part of them. One of the few people I've ever known or worked with who at the time and always afterward, seemed to have been Right and full-up with his job and always 'Doing His Stuff', dependable and well. But words don't help much so I shall not try, beyond saying this: I'm glad I had a chance to know and work with him in his mountains.

P.S. Lovejoy"

Newspaper Column: "The Wandering Scribe," by Jack Henson Port Angeles Evening News, August, 1941.

Some years ago Chris Morgenroth led a party including me on a hike to Bogachiel Peak. We stood on the peak at night and saw the silvery full moon shining on the blue ice of Mt. Olympus glacier to create a weird and beautiful spectacle.

On another occasion we walked through sunny fields of alpine flowers along the crest of High Divide. At one side we looked at mighty Mount Olympus, with its crags and glaciers. Below was the Hoh River, starting its march to the ocean. On the other side was the Seven Lakes Basin, with its scores of gemlike lakes whose shores were studded with mountain flowers and picture-book alpine trees.

One of these lakes, perhaps the most beautiful of all, we promptly named Morgenroth Lake, in honor of the man who was our guide on the trips. It was Chris Morgenroth on each of these trips, who stood entranced at the changing scenes of beauty and who was eloquent as he expressed his love for the area.

From high Bogachiel Peak, in the heart of the Olympic National Park, you can see the birth of three great rivers and trace their winding way to the Pacific Ocean. The rivers are the Hoh, Bogachiel and Soleduck, all beautiful streams dear to the hearts of old timers.

Two years ago Chris Morgenroth died. He said before he died that he wanted to go back to the High Divide and that he wished his ashes could be scattered there to be carried down through the pleasant waters of these rivers to the ocean. Last week Chris Morgenroth's ashes were carried to the High Divide by his son John. They were scattered to the winds to reach the three rivers.

Always in his heart was that particular shrine -- that high country where the three rivers are born, and through the ages his spirit will walk the shores of his lake, stand on Bogachiel Peak to see the varied scenes of beauty, wander through the alpine flowers of the High Divide to watch the births of the rivers and to hear the rumble of the glacier ice as it tumbles from Mount Olympus.

Seven Lakes, Basin, Lake Morgenroth

"EPILOGUE"

Chris made a decision at the age of fifteen to leave home and make a new life for himself in a new world 5,000 miles away. Three years later at the age of eighteen he was 3,000 miles farther from home and more determined than ever to get to a new frontier and help be a part of its development. Implanted in him was a strong sense of love and honor of God and his adopted country, and a responsibility to do something worthwhile for his fellow man.

In writing about his adventures and experiences he had unknowingly turned a camera on his inner self, showing his growing sensitivity to the world around him. All these experiences and adventures added perspective and meaning to what he wanted for future generations. He came to understand the dual role the forest played in man's life -- to nurture his soul on the one hand and to provide for his needs on the other. His twenty-three years in the Forest Service were filled with an endeavor to accomplish this balance.

During Chris's career in the Forest Service he developed an ability to reconcile anyone and was often called upon to publicly speak or write his views on subjects relating to the forest. When after retirement creation of a national park seemed to be the ultimate solution to permanent protection of the Olympic Wonderland, Chris gladly gave his time and physical strength to pursue that goal. He probably did more than any other person to appease the many differences that arose during the formation of Olympic National Park. Many have said 'he knew the Olympic woods better than any man of his time.' . . . Editor

Chris rescuing Elk calf.

Sources Consulted

Published Works

Adams, Clarence. "Historical Notes". U.S. Forester, January, 1926.

Adams, Clarence. Historical Data. Olympia: Olympic National Forest Office, April 15, 1946.

Craig, Gordon A. Germany 1866 to 1945. London: Oxford University Press, 1978.

Dodwell, Arthur and Rixon, Theodore F. Olympic Forest Reserve, Washington State. Washington, D.C.: Government Printing Office, 1900.

Gilman, S.C. "The Olympic Country". Washington, D.C.: National Geographic Magazine. April 1896, 133-140.

Kirk, Ruth. Exploring the Olympic Peninsula. Seattle: University of Washington Press, 1978.

Lloyd's Register of British and Foreign Shipping, 1886 to 1887. London: Lloyd's Insurance Company, 1886.

Port Angeles Chamber of Commerce, Forestry Committee. Forest Research of Clallam County. Port Angeles Chamber of Commerce, June, 1930.

Schmitz, Henry. The Long Road Traveled. Seattle: Arboretum Foundation, 1978.

Treasury Department, Commission on Fish and Fisheries. Reports on Conditions of Seal Life in the Rookeries of the Pribilof Islands, 1893 to 1895. Washington D.C.: Government Printing Office, 1896.

Treasury Department, Bureau of Navigation. List of Merchant Vessels of the United States, 1896. Washington, D.C.: Government Printing Office, 1896.

U.S. Congress, House. Committee on Public Lands. A Bill to Establish Olympic National Park in the State of Washington and for Other Purposes, H.R. 7086; Hearing Before the Committee on Public Lands. Washington D.C.: Government Printing Office, 1936.

U.S. Congress, House. Committee on Public Lands. A Bill to Establish Olympic National Park, H.R. 10024; Hearings Before the Committee on Public Lands. Washington, D.C.: Government Printing Office, 1938.

Unpublished Sources

Clallam County Courthouse. Miscellaneous records. Port Angeles, Washington.

Downing, Lois Chapman. Miscellaneous correspondence with the editor, and pictures of Fairholme.

Fletcher, Lena Huelsdonk. Miscellaneous personal interviews and correspondence, 1972 to 1980.

Fromme, Rudo L. Fromme's Olympic Memoirs. University of Washington Archives, Seattle, Washington.

Howser, Margery. Personal interview with editor.

Jefferson County Historical Museum and Maritime Library. Port Townsend, Washington. Miscellaneous navigation records about the "Bering Sea'.

Jefferson County Recorder of Deeds. Jefferson County Courthouse, Port Townsend, Washington.

Johnson, Olive Laufeld. Personal interview with the editor, and miscellaneous correspondence.

Kirkpatrick, Gertrude Rixon. Personal correspondence and interviews with editor.

Larsen, Lars, Captain. Logbook, "Bering Sea". National Archives and Records Service, Seattle, Washington.

Laufeld, Lucia. Personal interview, miscellaneous correspondence and pictures.

Lovejoy, Parish J. Memo for Fromme. Washington State Department of Forestry Library, 1912.

National Archives and Records Service. Miscellaneous U.S. Forest Service Records Concerning Olympic National Forest, Seattle, Washington, and Washington, D.C.

Tuttle, F., Captain. Logbooks, U.S. Revenue Cutter "Bear", Commencing April, 1896 at San Francisco and Ending November 4, 1896 at Port Townsend. Located in the Oakland History Room of the Oakland, California Public Library.

University of Washington Library Special Collection. Belt Line Railway. Seattle. (Researched by Richard Engeman, Librarian.)

Index

COLOPHON

The Chris Morgenroth, *FOOTPRINTS IN THE OLYMPICS, AN AUTOBIOGRAPHY*, as edited by his daughter, Katherine Morgenroth Flaherty, was printed in the workshop of Glen Adams, which is located in the quiet country village of Fairfield, southern Spokane County in Washington state. The Morgenroth family supplied camera ready pages except for the title page and the colophon page. A limited amount of typesetting was done by Pat Nigh using a Compugraphic Ediwriter 7300. Camera/darkroom work was done by Susan Paulson and Vern Stevens, using a 20x24 inch DS (Japanese) camera and a 25 inch LogE automatic film developing machine. The film was stripped by Pat Nigh and Susan Paulson. Printing plates were done by Susan Paulson. The sheets were printed by Vern Stevens using a 28 inch Heidelberg press model KORS. The sheets were folded by Garry Adams using a three stage Baum Dial-O-Matic folding machine. Assembly was by the Ye Galleon crew. The paper stock is seventy pound Island Offset, a Canadian sheet. Hard case binding was done by Willem Bosch of Oakesdale, Washington. The books were sewn by Heidi Doneen using a National book sewing machine. Paper copies were bound by Glen Adams and Garry Adams using a Sulby adhesive binding machine. This was a fun project. We had no special difficulty with the work.

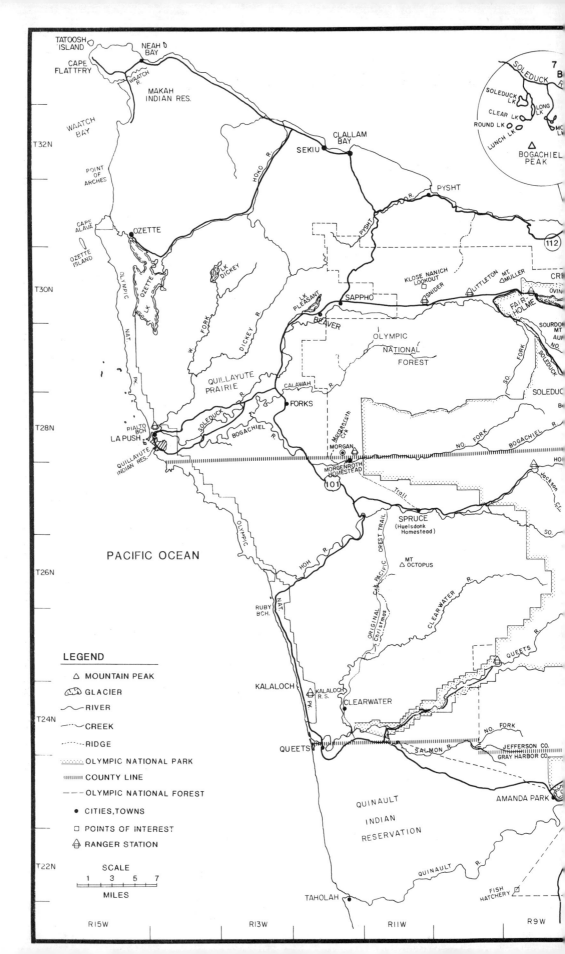

OLYMPIC NATIONAL PARK

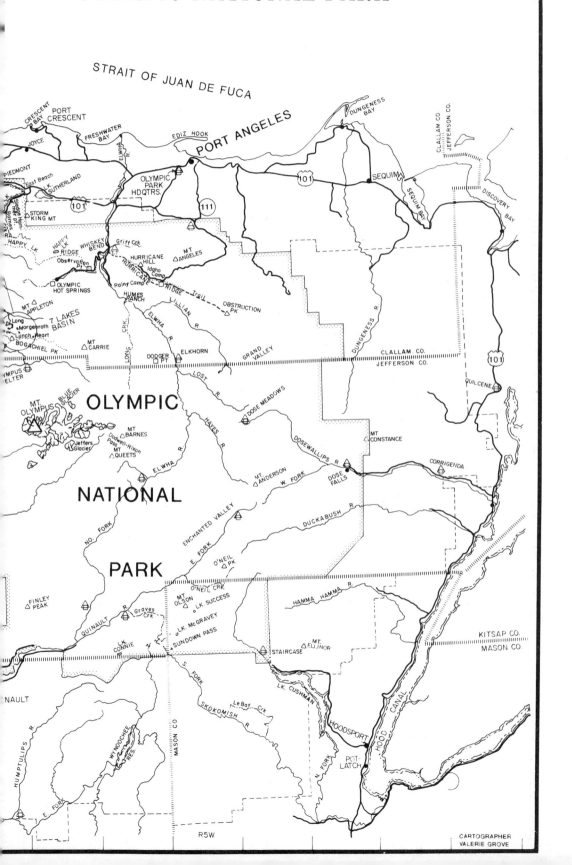

STRAIT OF JUAN DE FUCA

CRESCENT BAY
PORT CRESCENT
JOYCE
FRESHWATER BAY
EDIZ HOOK
PORT ANGELES
DUNGENESS BAY
CLALLAM CO.
JEFFERSON CO.
PIEDMONT
East Beach
LK. SUTHERLAND
ELWHA R.
OLYMPIC PARK HDQTRS.
SEQUIM
DISCOVERY BAY
101
STORM KING MT
SHADE PT.
Barnes
RA
HAPPY
HAPPY LK.
HAPPY LK. RIDGE
Observation
WHISKEY BEND
Griff Crk.
HURRICANE HILL
HURRICANE
Idaho Camp
RIDGE Trail
111
MT ANGELES
SEQUIM BAY
101
OLYMPIC HOT SPRINGS
Rainy Camp
HUMES RANCH
OBSTRUCTION PK.
MT APPLETON
7 LAKES BASIN
Long
Morgenroth
Lunch
Heart
ELWHA R.
LONG CRK.
LILLIAN R.
GRAND VALLEY
DUNGENESS R.
CLALLAM CO.
JEFFERSON CO.
101
BOGACHIEL PK.
MT CARRIE
DODGER PT
ELKHORN
LOST R.
OLYMPUS SHELTER
DOSE MEADOWS
QUILCENE
MT OLYMPUS
BLUE GLACIER
OLYMPIC
MT BARNES
Dodwell-Rixon Pass
MT QUEETS
Jeffers Glacier
ELWHA R.
HAYES R.
MT ANDERSON
W. FORK
DOSEWALLIPS R.
MT CONSTANCE
CORRIGENDA
NATIONAL
NO. FORK
ENCHANTED VALLEY
E. FORK
O'NEIL PK.
DOSE FALLS
DUCKABUSH R.
PARK
FINLEY PEAK
QUINAULT R.
Graves Crk.
O'NEIL CRK.
MT OLSON
LK. SUCCESS
LK. McGRAVEY
SUNDOWN PASS
HAMMA HAMMA R.
KITSAP CO.
MASON CO.
LK. CONNIE
STAIRCASE
MT ELLINOR
NAULT
S. FORK
LK. CUSHMAN
MASON CO.
LeBar Crk.
SKOKOMISH R.
HOODSPORT
HOOD CANAL
HUMPTULIPS R.
WYNOOCHEE RES.
N. FORK
POT-LATCH
E. FORK
R5W

CARTOGRAPHER
VALERIE GROVE